A

LIST

Hard Core Logo

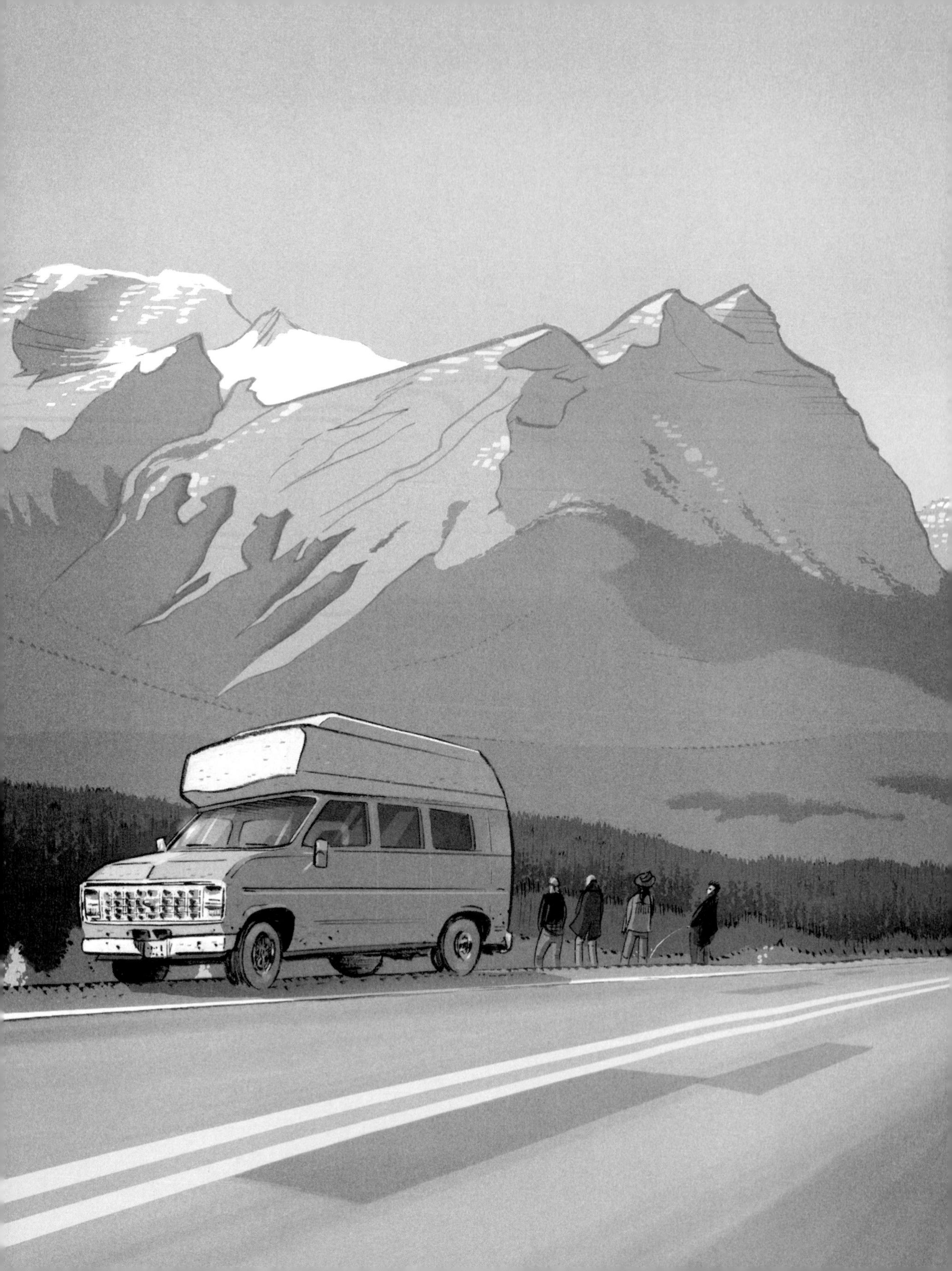

Hard Core Logo

Portrait of a Thousand Punks

BASED ON THE FEATURE FILM BY BRUCE McDONALD
AND THE NOVEL BY MICHAEL TURNER

NICK CRAINE

A LIST

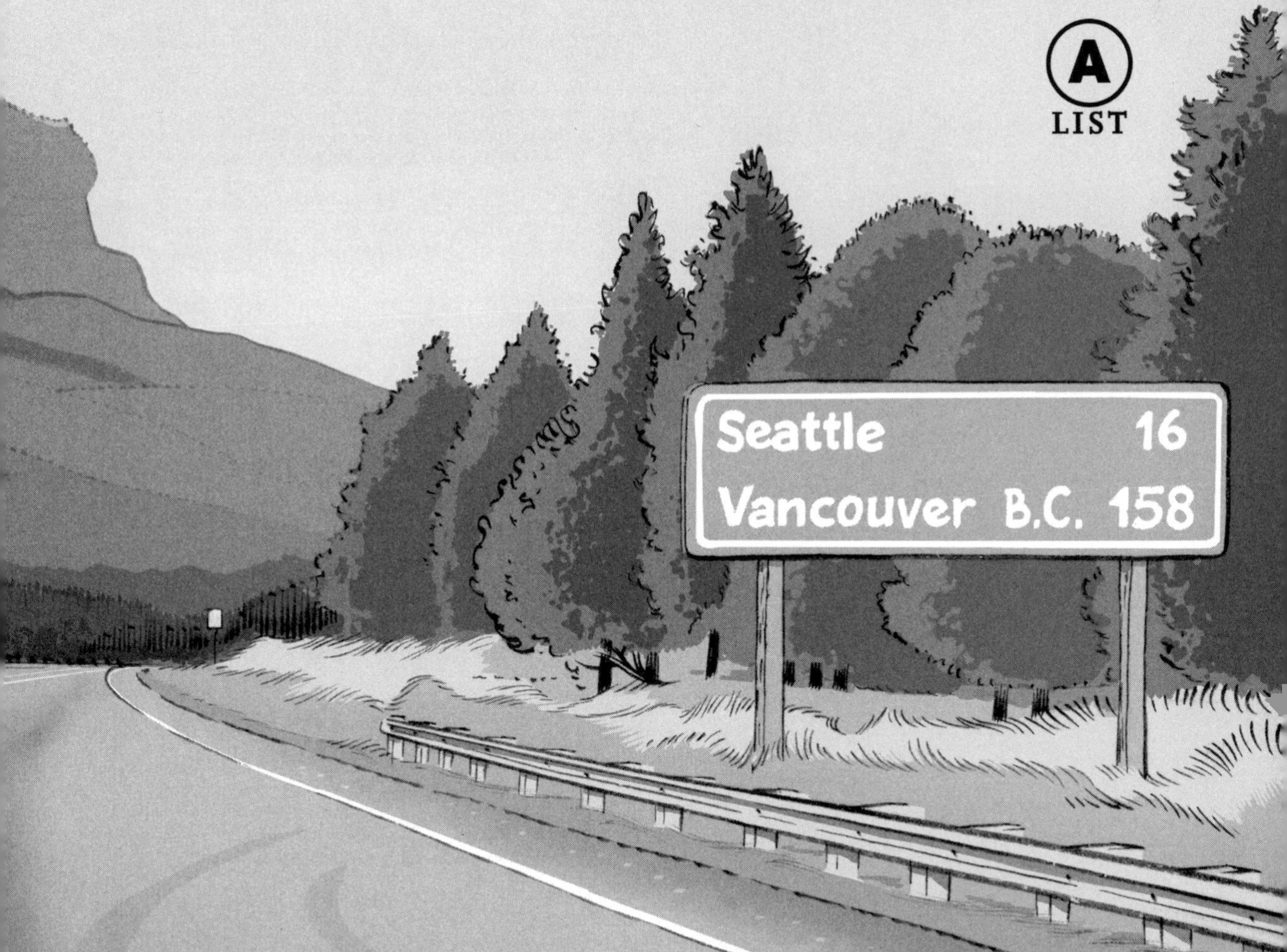
Seattle 16
Vancouver B.C. 158

INTRODUCTION BY Lynn Crosbie
FOREWORD BY Michael Timmins

First published in 1997 by House of Anansi Press Inc. under the title
Portrait of a Thousand Punks: Hard Core Logo
This edition published in Canada in 2017 and the USA in 2017
by House of Anansi Press Inc.
www.houseofanansi.com

House of Anansi Press is committed to protecting our natural environment. As part of our efforts, the interior of this book is printed on paper that contains 100% post-consumer recycled fibres, is acid-free, and is processed chlorine-free.

20 19 18 17 16 1 2 3 4 5

Library and Archives Canada Cataloguing in Publication

Craine, Nick, 1971–
[Portrait of a thousand punks]
Hard Core Logo : portrait of a thousand punks / Nick Craine.

Previously published under title: Portrait of a thousand punks, Hard Core Logo. Published by: Concord, Ont. : House of Anansi Press, 1997.
Graphic novelization of the 1993 novel of the same name written by Michael Turner, and of the 1996 motion picture of the same name directed by Bruce McDonald.
Issued in print and electronic formats.
ISBN 978-1-4870-0192-6 (softcover).—ISBN 978-1-4870-0193-3 (epub).—
ISBN 978-1-4870-0194-0 (Kindle)

1. Graphic novels. 2. Adaptations. I. McDonald, Bruce, 1959–
II. Turner, Michael, 1962– . Hard Core Logo. III. Title. IV. Title:
Portrait of a thousand punks.

PN6733.C75H37 2017 741.5'971 C2016-906852-8
C2017-901123-5

Library of Congress Control Number: 2016962170

Interior photography by Trina Koster
Opening sequence line-up penciled by Scott Mooney
"Super Excess Man" created by Sam Cino
Post-production design/layout by Sara Soskolne @ Silo

Series design by Brian Morgan
Cover illustration by Nick Craine

Canada Council for the Arts / Conseil des Arts du Canada
ONTARIO ARTS COUNCIL / CONSEIL DES ARTS DE L'ONTARIO
an Ontario government agency / un organisme du gouvernement de l'Ontario

We acknowledge for their financial support of our publishing program the Canada Council for the Arts, the Ontario Arts Council, and the Government of Canada through the Canada Book Fund.

Page 113 constitutes a continuation of this copyright page.

Printed and bound in Canada

FSC www.fsc.org
MIX
Paper from responsible sources
FSC® C004071

INTRODUCTION
by Lynn Crosbie

Nick Craine's graphic novel is subtitled "Portrait of a Thousand Punks" for any number of reasons, one being the sameness of punk/hardcore bands, the music and followers, in spite of the movement having been predicated on garish individuality not—*pure laine* punk John Lydon would come to observe—a gathering of "coat hangers," as in "just put a leather jacket on over the hanger and stand there."

Or, Craine's is a sly reference to the thousand or so punks minimum involved in the many spinoffs of Michael Turner's 1993 collection of poems, *Hard Core Logo*, full stop.

It's hard to imagine a lithe volume of avant-garde Canadian work-poetry exploding into an entire devotional industry, like the Jackson 5 during their tenure at Motown.

But Turner's 1993's *Hard Core Logo* did just that.

The book is a series of interconnected, bare-bones poems about the eponymous punk band, shuffled in with faxes, road receipts, guitar tablature, transcripts, posters, and photographs of well-groomed and strategically headless men holding cans of beer and acoustic guitars—not the iconic 1978 punk scene by any means, but the band, in its first inception, is not at all hardcore and in fact too timid to sing "fuck." (The deeply silly "Who the Hell Do You Think You Are?" is a Genie Award–winning title.)

Almost twenty-five years after its publication, one can still find a wealth of critical essays, fan pages, and HCL merch online: largely T-shirts, but one is certain that tiny, hand-sewn fetish dolls appear on Etsy periodically.

A brief three years after its publication, the harder-core film adaptation, directed by Canada's *enfant terrible* Bruce McDonald, appeared to rave reviews — "It's so authentic that it practically gives off feedback," one acolyte gushed.

In 1996, an unofficial soundtrack was released, entitled *A Tribute to* Hard Core Logo, featuring various Canadian musicians covering the songs from the book and film. Noel Baker's *Hard Core Roadshow: A Screenwriter's Diary* appeared in 1997: it is a remarkably unaffected, candidly nerdulent diary that announces his and the director's early plan to make "the definitive (and "the coolest") Canadian rock 'n' roll movie."

The variations would stagger Bach: in 2011, a "punk-ass piece of music theatre" or live adaptation of the book showed up, alongside an intelligent if denatured critical study by Paul McEwen, called *Bruce McDonald's* Hard Core Logo — more evidence of the original text's place among the undead.

In 2013, Celine Dion had leopard spots shaved into her skull and performed "Edmonton Block Heater" on the corner of Yonge and Dundas, causing a harmless, invigorating riot.*

And, circling back, we have this graphic novel, the best and most logical heir to the Turner–McDonald industry.

Arriving in 1997, this unusual, compelling artifact by visual

---

*   One of these HCL tributes/events has been fabricated. If you think you know the answer, write it on a scenic postcard and send it to House of Anansi, c/o HARD CORE LOGO CONTEST. The first five correct answers will win a copy of Craine's new book. Good luck!

artist Nick Craine is a hybrid, a close retelling of the book and the film, with a decided emphasis on the second.

As such, it would appear to appeal only to intellectual collectors and devotees of the original book and the film; i.e., *Hard Core Logo with a Vengeance*.

It is true that Craine's book may be, happily, read as a version of the (unofficial) Turner–McDonald collaboration, but only in the sense that, say, John Dryden's *All for Love* is a *version* of Shakespeare's *Antony and Cleopatra*. That is, there are certain stories — say, the filthy Canadian road trip and the rise and fall, in this case, of a lousy Canadian band — that, like the story of Rome and Egypt, transcend their source text(s), given their enormous familiarity.

A better lens for the graphic novel is T. S. Eliot's essay, "Tradition and the Individual Talent," which asserts that "…no artist of any art, has his complete meaning alone. His significance, his appreciation is the appreciation of his relation to…the poets and artists [preceding him]."

What is this relation?

And how does Craine make this story new?

The artist is scrupulously respectful of the story of Hard Core Logo, the defunct band, crossing the coast from show to show towards reestablishing themselves — he does not deviate from the narrative any more than Christopher Nolan swerved from *The Killing Joke* in his reinvention of Batman's most tragic antagonist.

New, however, is the physical appearance of the band mates. If the poetry-turned-novel offered us no faces, the film — beautifully cast — served up characters too striking, too charismatic, to forget.

Assailing this predicament, Craine gives us a Joe Dick (the Steve Goof–lookalike Hugh Dillon in the film) with the same mohawk and almost vestal long, sweeping black coat, but a very different, very malleable face.

This Joe Dick (such a perfectly Vancouver punk name, re: The Skulls'/D.O.A.'s Joey Shithead) looks, at turns, sunken, heroic, vacant, feminine, cinematically handsome, rotund, and corpse-like: in other words, he is a screen against which the character's entire life is projected, with remarkable acuity.

The bricolage in the comic is more extensive than Turner's or McDonald's play with this tactic, which is exceedingly pleasing to look at, to read. And, by tearing up all the rules, Craine only enforces them: the teleology of tragedy is something like an unstoppable force meeting an immovable object.

Or—spoiler alert—a bullet zooming through the skull of a heartbroken punk.

Screenwriter Noel Baker offered us a brilliant revision of the necessarily flat, static ending of Turner's books: more existentialist than nihilist, Turner's work is often scored with a cat-calm sense of life's absurdity.

Craine downplays the worst or most hectic of the film (the ritualized, grotesque drug-gathering on a Winnipeg farm) and gathers up what is best, adding a stunning flourish to Baker's and McDonald's shocking finale with an image that not only anticipates the gynocentric 2010 film sequel, but makes a devastating comment about the consumerism assailing Joe Dick (if not the near-perfect marriage of highly individuated poetry and cinema that is *Hard Core Logo*, the book and movie.)

Poetry in Canada is, in the main, "fat and ugly," to quote the mythic band, and Craine draws out here what is starkly lovely about Turner's poems *and* what is big and bold and unrepentantly awesome about McDonald's reverent vision.

"And in the end it's love," chants the unmedicated bassist John Oxenburger as the story unfolds, explodes, and lies suspended.

The book's epigraph cites "The Revelation to John" cleverly, oh so cleverly, intimating what Craine will cherry-pick as the film's instance of sheer majesty, and how *he* will render this dreadful, gorgeous scene.

He does so with punk daring: in the end, there's nothing but blackness, then the long, staggered crawl.

LYNN CROSBIE is a cultural critic, writer, and poet. She is the author of *Life Is About Losing Everything*; the Trillium Book Award–nominated novel *Where Did You Sleep Last Night*; and, most recently, a book of poetry called *The Corpses of the Future*. A Ph.D. in English literature with a background in visual studies, she teaches at the University of Toronto and the Art Gallery of Ontario.

For Sandy Atanasoff and Michael Craine

Foreword

* * *

Who was Joe Dick? Was he a punk?
First off, I guess you'd have to figure out what punk is.

Punk is: Buddy Bolden high-stepping through the French quarter, blowing maniacally; Robert Johnson returning from the crossroads; Hank Williams with his voice and pen spilling tears and blood; Charlie Parker cutting all comers on 58th Street; Elvis Presley launching into "That's All Right"; John Lennon shredding his vocal chords on "Twist and Shout"; Ornette Coleman weaving his plastic alto through smaller and smaller concentric circles; and Patti Smith firing her opening salvo with the line "Jesus died for somebody's sins but not mine."

Punk is standing up and declaring "Fuck this and Fuck that . . . I'll do it my way."

It is taking on convention and
deliberately
forcefully
and most importantly
gleefully
tearing convention down.

It is action and commitment.

It is not hair colour, clothing, accents, age, record sales,
recording contracts, press clippings, poses, T-shirts, badges,
body fluids, videos, or tattoos.

It is energy.
An energy complex and mysterious enough to destroy and create at the same time.
Not possible to harness.
Not possible to bottle.
Not possible to recreate once dissipated.
Of the eight punks listed earlier six died
prematurely.

An energy that burns too hot to be contained by mere skin.

It is a form of expression that hits you
so hard and
so deep and
so meaningfully   it
grabs you by the stomach
picks you up out of your chair
drags you across the floor
and knocks you so silly that by the time it's through with you
you are seeing the world
your life
in a completely new light.

So, who was Joe Dick? Was Joe a punk? Did Hard Core Logo play
punk music?   Maybe.   I don't know.

Did they attract, night after night, some 18-year-old kid who
sat stage-side in front of the PA stack,   ears bleeding,   skin
bursting with absorbed energy,   his life twisted and turned
inside out until all became clear, until he knew what he had
to do for the rest of his life?

If they did that then I know. If they did that, Joe was a punk.

So, who was Joe Dick? Was he a punk? A person who by force of
expression touched and changed the lives of
one
two
ten
one hundred
one thousand   or more people.
A person who burned with such a passionate intensity that it
finally consumed everything in him worth consuming. A person who gave it all away because
he had no choice. Or was he just another asshole with a melon-sized ego, ripening in
the spotlight, pointing fingers, bellowing,

"LOOK AT ME! LOOK AT ME!"

I don't know. You figure it out.

* * *

Michael Timmins AUGUST 1996

"Fear not; I am the first and the last: I am he that liveth, and was dead; and, behold, I am alive for evermore, Amen; and have the keys of hell and death."

THE REVELATION TO JOHN 1:17-18

"The future to us is a dare"

THURSTON MOORE

Hard Core Logo

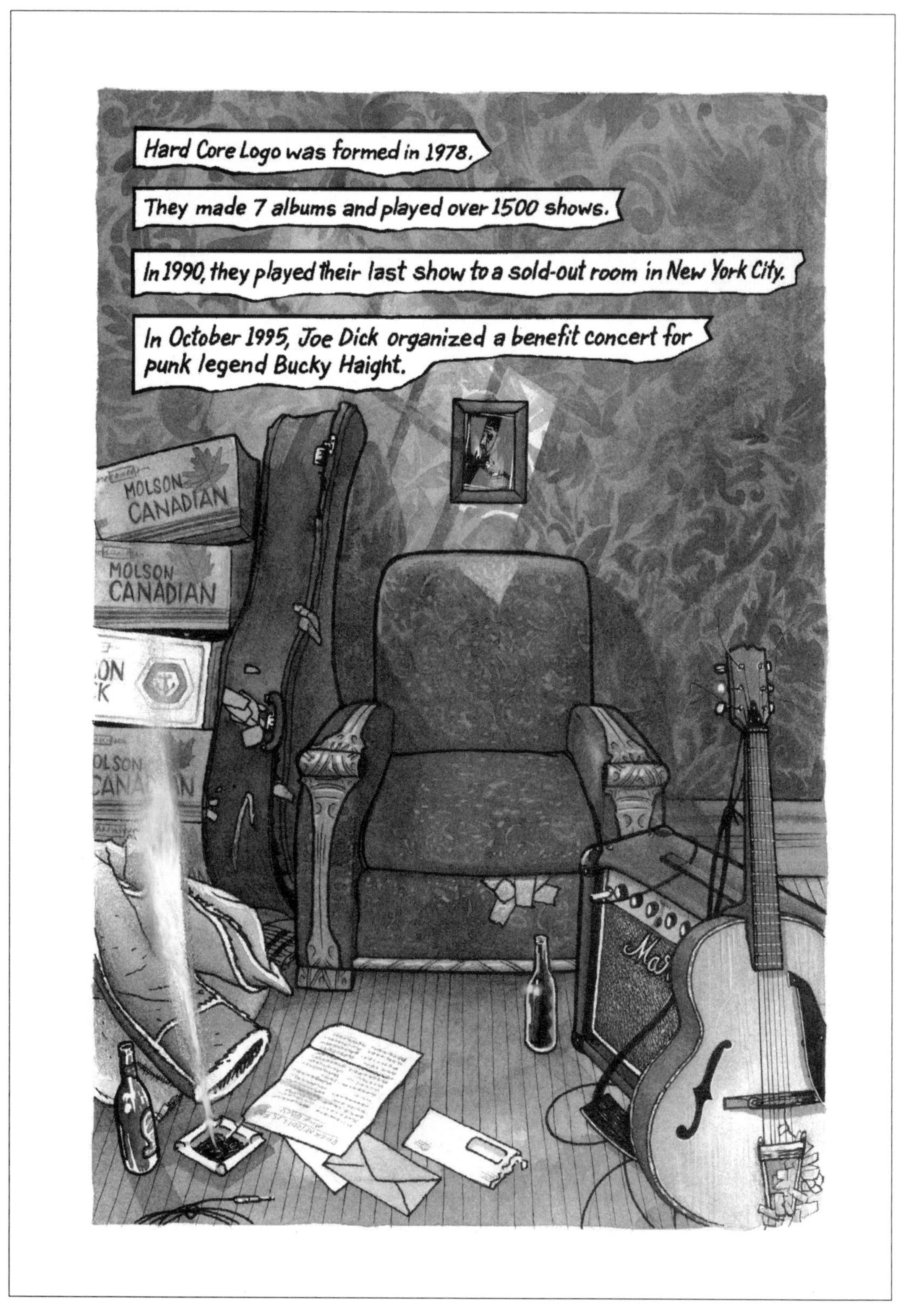

Hard Core Logo was formed in 1978.
They made 7 albums and played over 1500 shows.
In 1990, they played their last show to a sold-out room in New York City.
In October 1995, Joe Dick organized a benefit concert for punk legend Bucky Haight.
MOLSON CANADIAN
MOLSON CANADIAN

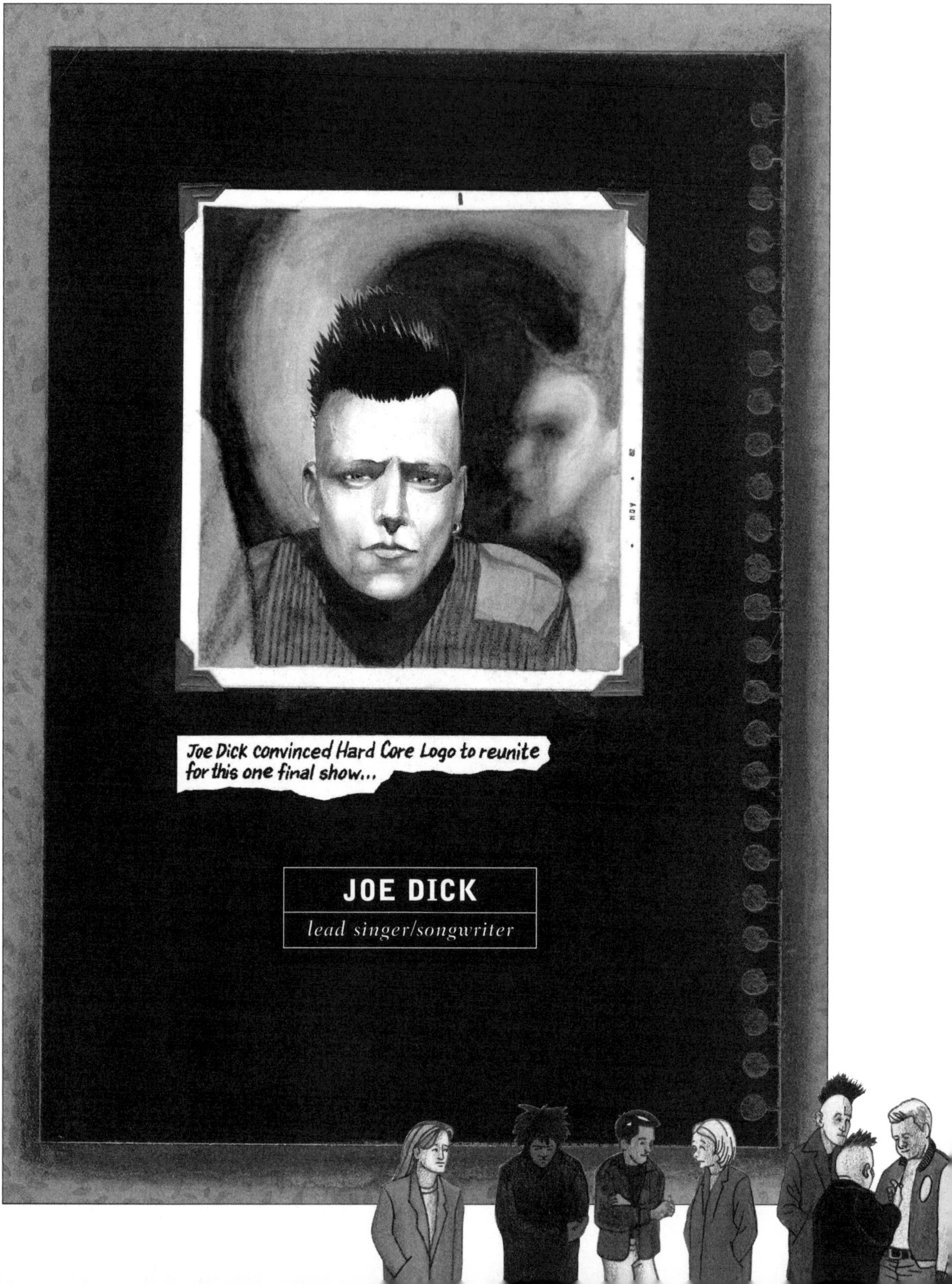

Joe Dick convinced Hard Core Logo to reunite for this one final show...
JOE DICK
lead singer/songwriter

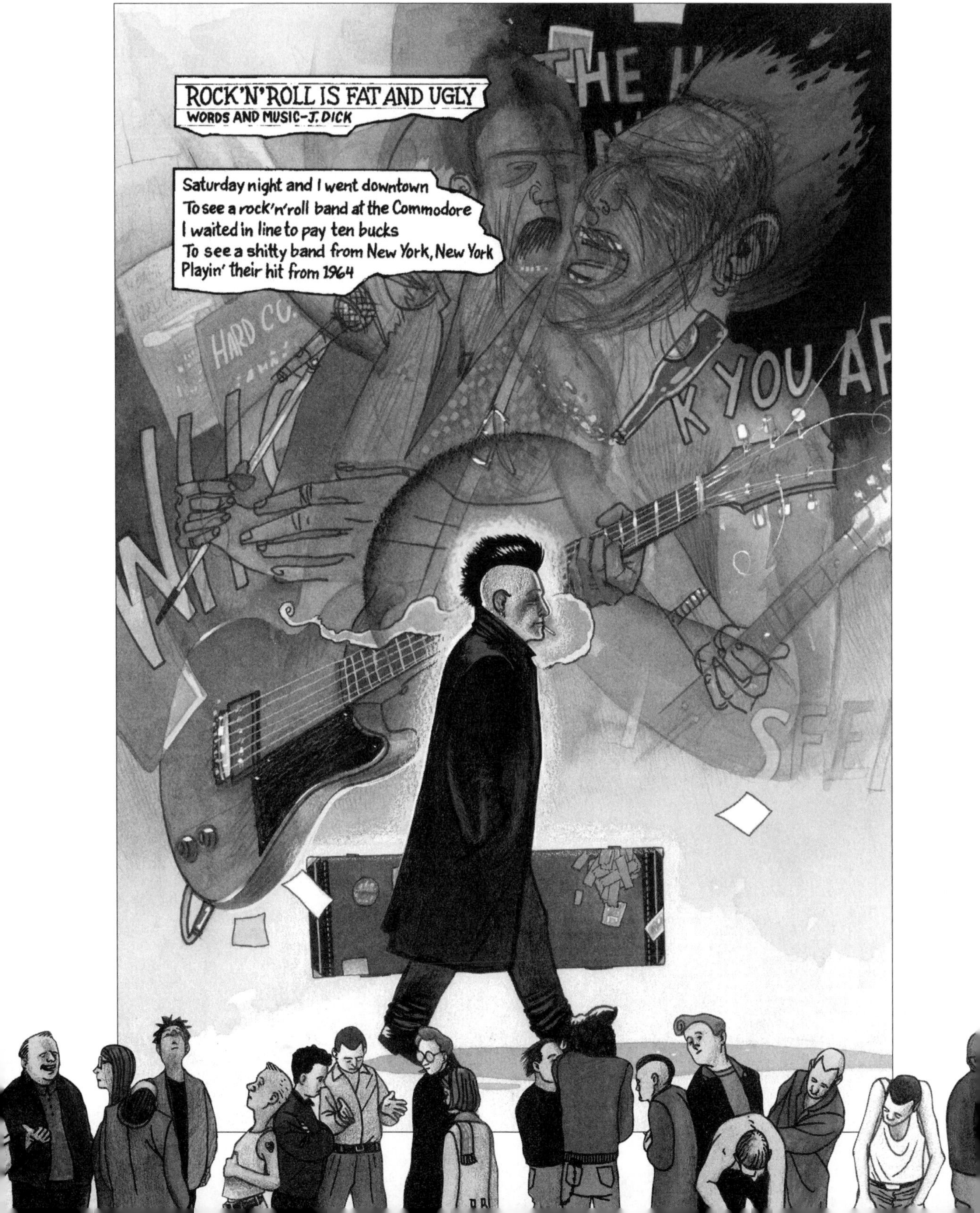
ROCK'N'ROLL IS FAT AND UGLY
WORDS AND MUSIC–J. DICK
Saturday night and I went downtown
To see a rock'n'roll band at the Commodore
I waited in line to pay ten bucks
To see a shitty band from New York, New York
Playin' their hit from 1964
HARD CO
K YOU AR

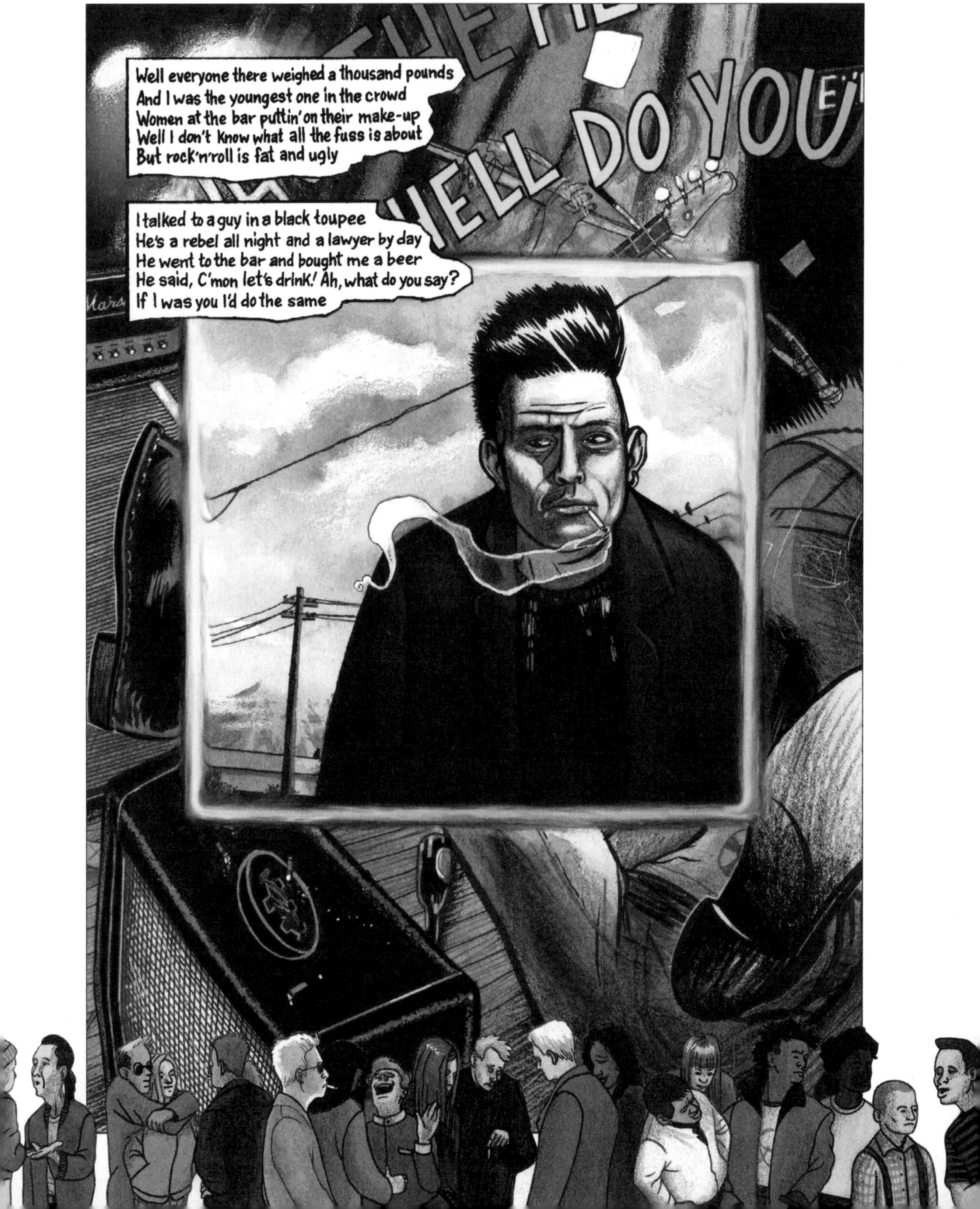

Well everyone there weighed a thousand pounds
And I was the youngest one in the crowd
Women at the bar puttin' on their make-up
Well I don't know what all the fuss is about
But rock'n'roll is fat and ugly
I talked to a guy in a black toupee
He's a rebel all night and a lawyer by day
He went to the bar and bought me a beer
He said, C'mon let's drink! Ah, what do you say?
If I was you I'd do the same
HELL DO YOU

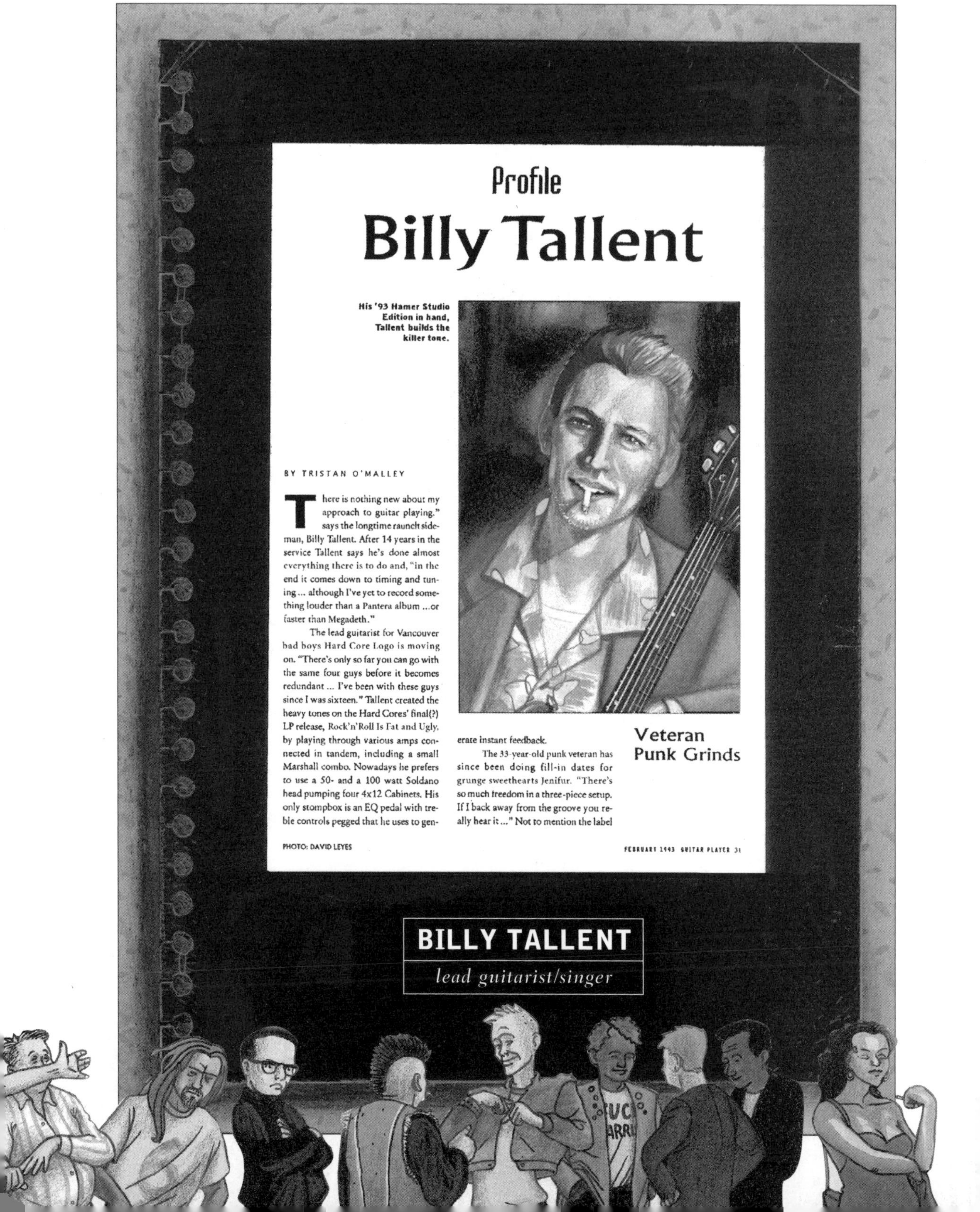

Profile

Billy Tallent

His '93 Hamer Studio Edition in hand, Tallent builds the killer tone.

BY TRISTAN O'MALLEY

There is nothing new about my approach to guitar playing." says the longtime raunch sideman, Billy Tallent. After 14 years in the service Tallent says he's done almost everything there is to do and, "in the end it comes down to timing and tuning ... although I've yet to record something louder than a Pantera album ...or faster than Megadeth."

The lead guitarist for Vancouver bad boys Hard Core Logo is moving on. "There's only so far you can go with the same four guys before it becomes redundant ... I've been with these guys since I was sixteen." Tallent created the heavy tones on the Hard Cores' final(?) LP release, Rock'n'Roll Is Fat and Ugly, by playing through various amps connected in tandem, including a small Marshall combo. Nowadays he prefers to use a 50- and a 100 watt Soldano head pumping four 4x12 Cabinets. His only stompbox is an EQ pedal with treble controls pegged that he uses to generate instant feedback.

The 33-year-old punk veteran has since been doing fill-in dates for grunge sweethearts Jenifur. "There's so much freedom in a three-piece setup. If I back away from the groove you really hear it ..." Not to mention the label

Veteran Punk Grinds

PHOTO: DAVID LEYES

FEBRUARY 1993 GUITAR PLAYER 31

BILLY TALLENT
lead guitarist/singer

And I talked to a woman from Florida
She was married to the guy playing lead guitar
She drove up north for her alimony
And she brought her kids; they were out in the car
Ah rock'n'roll is sad and lonely

Hey little boy
Hey little girl
Do you wanna grow up
In a world where rock'n'roll's
Misunderstanding?

Well I couldn't bear just another song
Yah I tried to dance but the beat was wrong
I took a walk to the other side of town
And I ended up at an orphanage

STORE LOGO: John Oxenburger (left), Joe Dick, Pipefitter and Billy Tallent at

BY STEPHEN DEMOREST

DURING THE ten days be- tween February 7 and 17/79 ...ran toppled the ...n ambassador ...inated in Afganistan ...t Carter was ...r Primandal...

phychedelic menu that looks like an old Filmore poster.
"It's too friendly," mumbles Joe Dick before downing another slug of Heineken. "Got a smoke? ... gimme a smoke." The Hard Core lead singer is wearing black—All the band dress like leather boys offstage; strayp... up against ...Sa... cisco but Joe ...ld Sa... br... ...tter voic...

one of the good things -ed is you have time read. At school they stupid way of doing books for life. It, you started g... ...ring a...

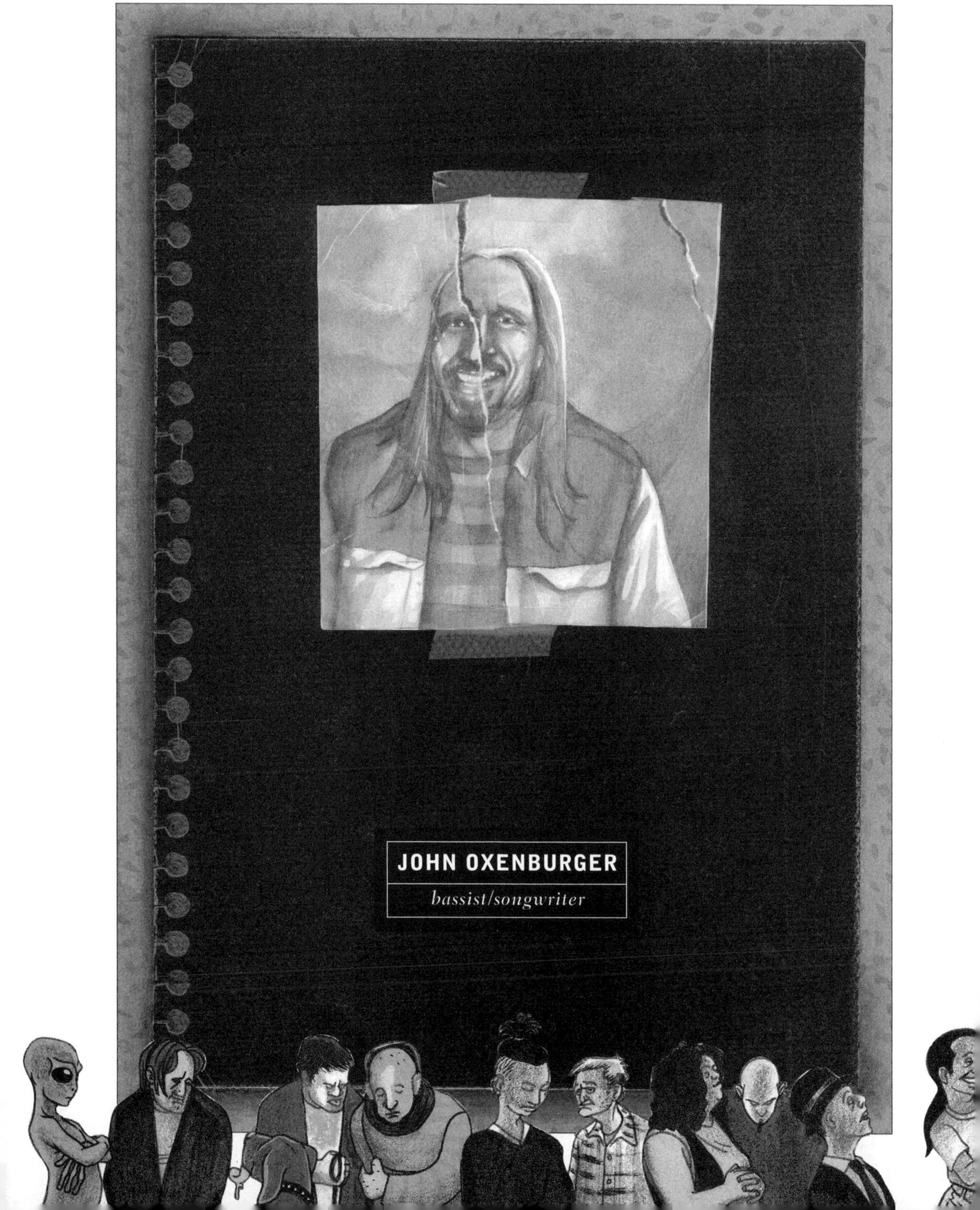
JOHN OXENBURGER
bassist/songwriter

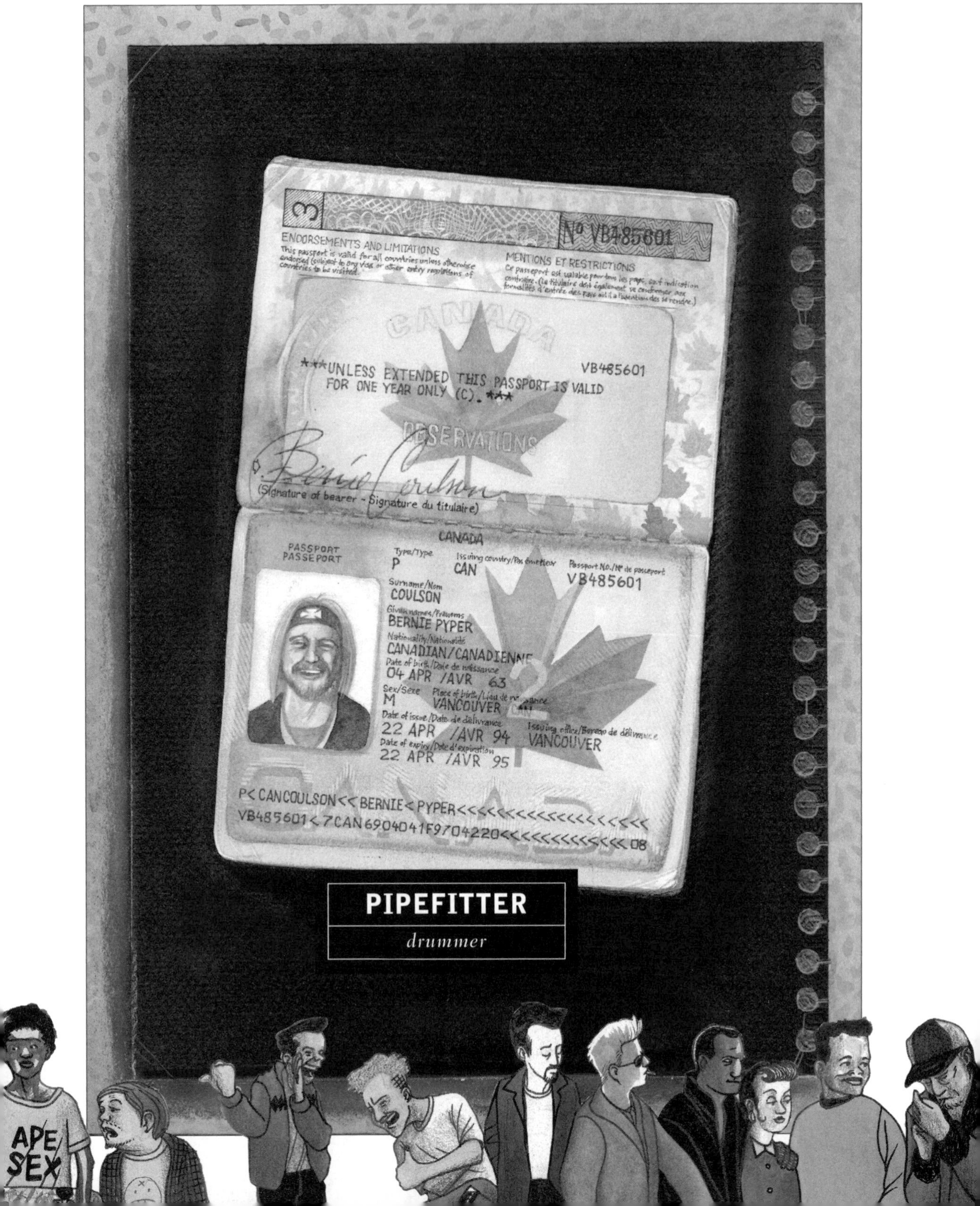
3
Nº VB485601
ENDORSEMENTS AND LIMITATIONS
MENTIONS ET RESTRICTIONS
CANADA
UNLESS EXTENDED THIS PASSPORT IS VALID FOR ONE YEAR ONLY (C).
VB485601
OBSERVATIONS
(Signature of bearer - Signature du titulaire)
CANADA
PASSPORT
PASSEPORT
Type/Type
P
Issuing country/Pays émetteur
CAN
Passport No./Nº de passeport
VB485601
Surname/Nom
COULSON
Given names/Prénoms
BERNIE PYPER
Nationality/Nationalité
CANADIAN/CANADIENNE
Date of birth/Date de naissance
04 APR /AVR 63
Sex/Sexe
M
Place of birth/Lieu de naissance
VANCOUVER
Date of issue/Date de délivrance
22 APR /AVR 94
Issuing office/Bureau de délivrance
VANCOUVER
Date of expiry/Date d'expiration
22 APR /AVR 95
P<CANCOULSON<<BERNIE<PYPER<<<<<<<<<<<<<<<<<<<<<<<
VB485601<7CAN6904041F9704220<<<<<<<<<<<<<<08
APE SEX

PIPEFITTER

drummer

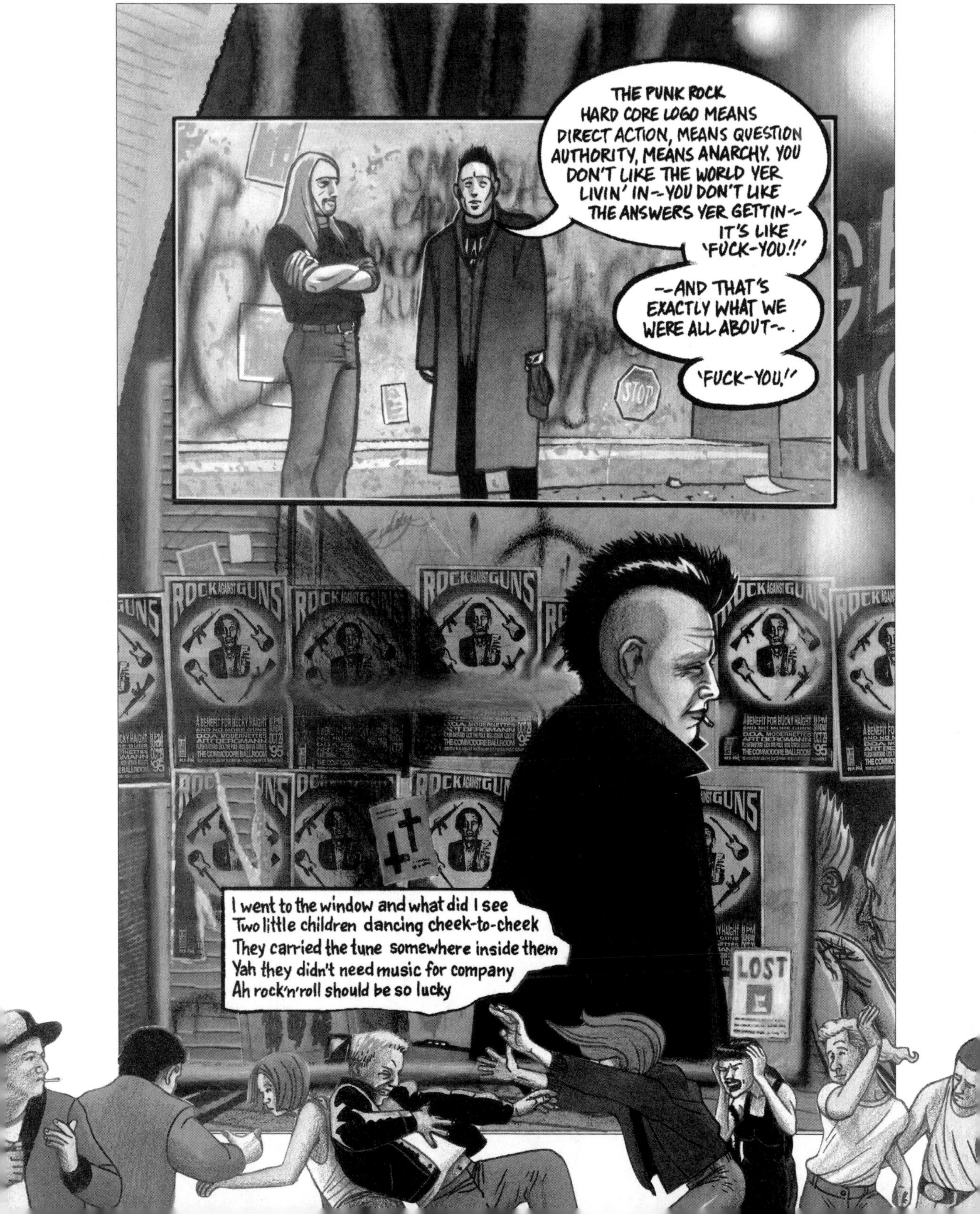
THE PUNK ROCK HARD CORE LOGO MEANS DIRECT ACTION, MEANS QUESTION AUTHORITY, MEANS ANARCHY. YOU DON'T LIKE THE WORLD YER LIVIN' IN--YOU DON'T LIKE THE ANSWERS YER GETTIN-- IT'S LIKE 'FUCK-YOU!!'
--AND THAT'S EXACTLY WHAT WE WERE ALL ABOUT--.
'FUCK-YOU!'
STOP
ROCK AGAINST GUNS
A BENEFIT FOR BUCKY HAIGHT
THE COMMODORE BALLROOM
LOST
I went to the window and what did I see
Two little children dancing cheek-to-cheek
They carried the tune somewhere inside them
Yah they didn't need music for company
Ah rock'n'roll should be so lucky

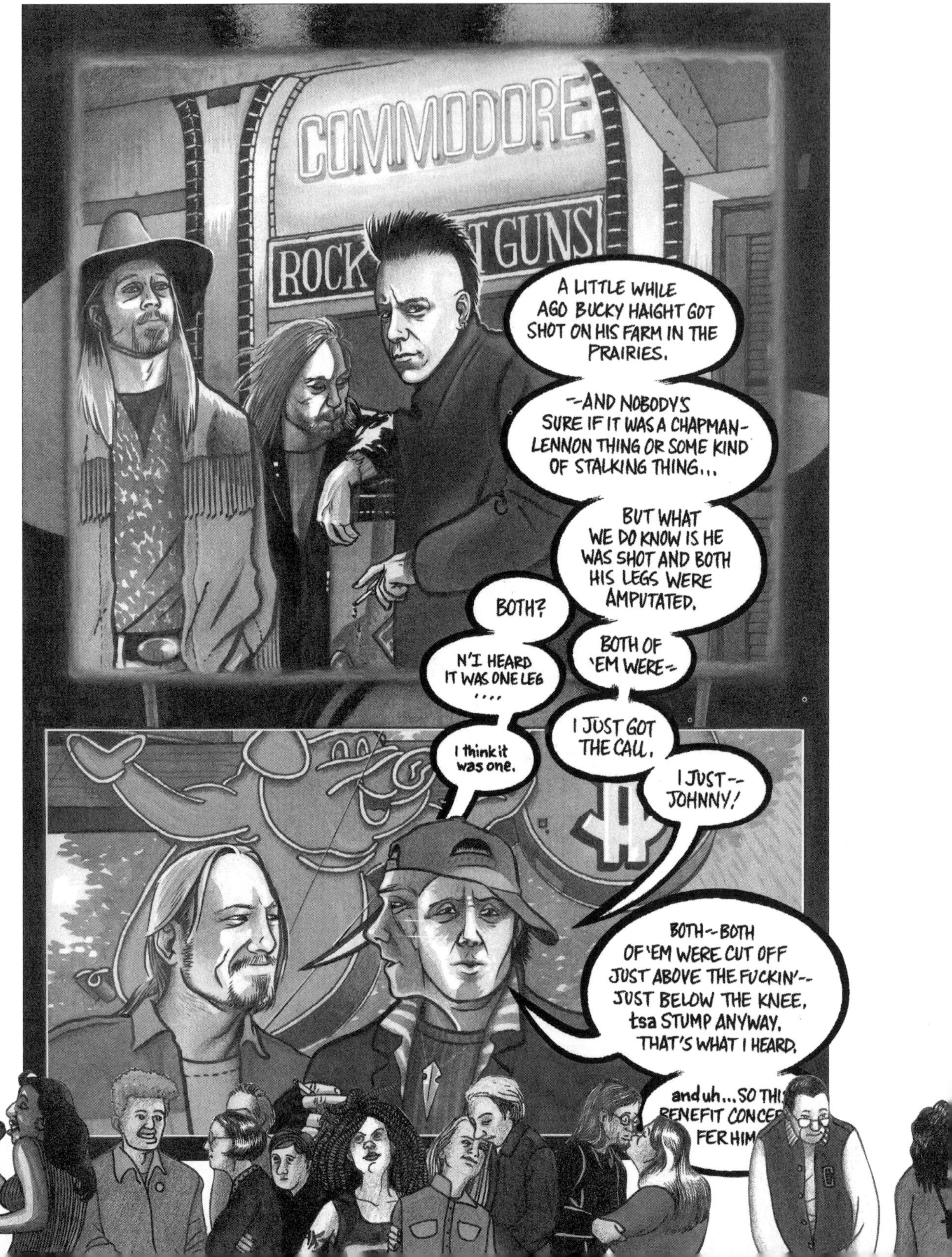
COMMODORE
ROCK
GUNS
A LITTLE WHILE AGO BUCKY HAIGHT GOT SHOT ON HIS FARM IN THE PRAIRIES.
--AND NOBODY'S SURE IF IT WAS A CHAPMAN-LENNON THING OR SOME KIND OF STALKING THING...
BUT WHAT WE DO KNOW IS HE WAS SHOT AND BOTH HIS LEGS WERE AMPUTATED.
BOTH?
N'I HEARD IT WAS ONE LEG ....
BOTH OF 'EM WERE--
I think it was one.
I JUST GOT THE CALL.
I JUST-- JOHNNY!
BOTH--BOTH OF 'EM WERE CUT OFF JUST ABOVE THE FUCKIN'-- JUST BELOW THE KNEE, tsa STUMP ANYWAY. THAT'S WHAT I HEARD.
and uh... SO THI BENEFIT CONCE FER HIM

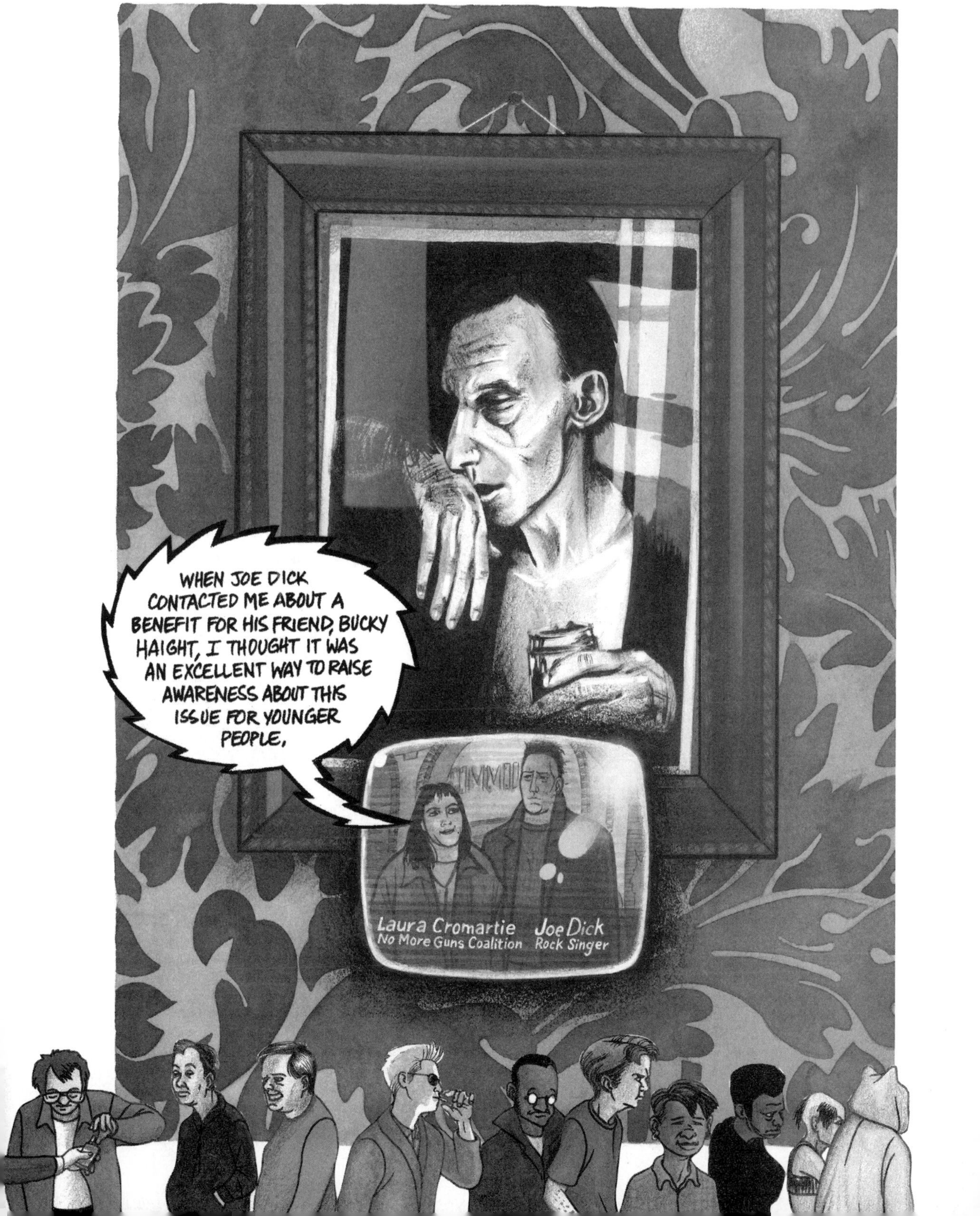
WHEN JOE DICK CONTACTED ME ABOUT A BENEFIT FOR HIS FRIEND, BUCKY HAIGHT, I THOUGHT IT WAS AN EXCELLENT WAY TO RAISE AWARENESS ABOUT THIS ISSUE FOR YOUNGER PEOPLE.
Laura Cromartie
No More Guns Coalition
Joe Dick
Rock Singer

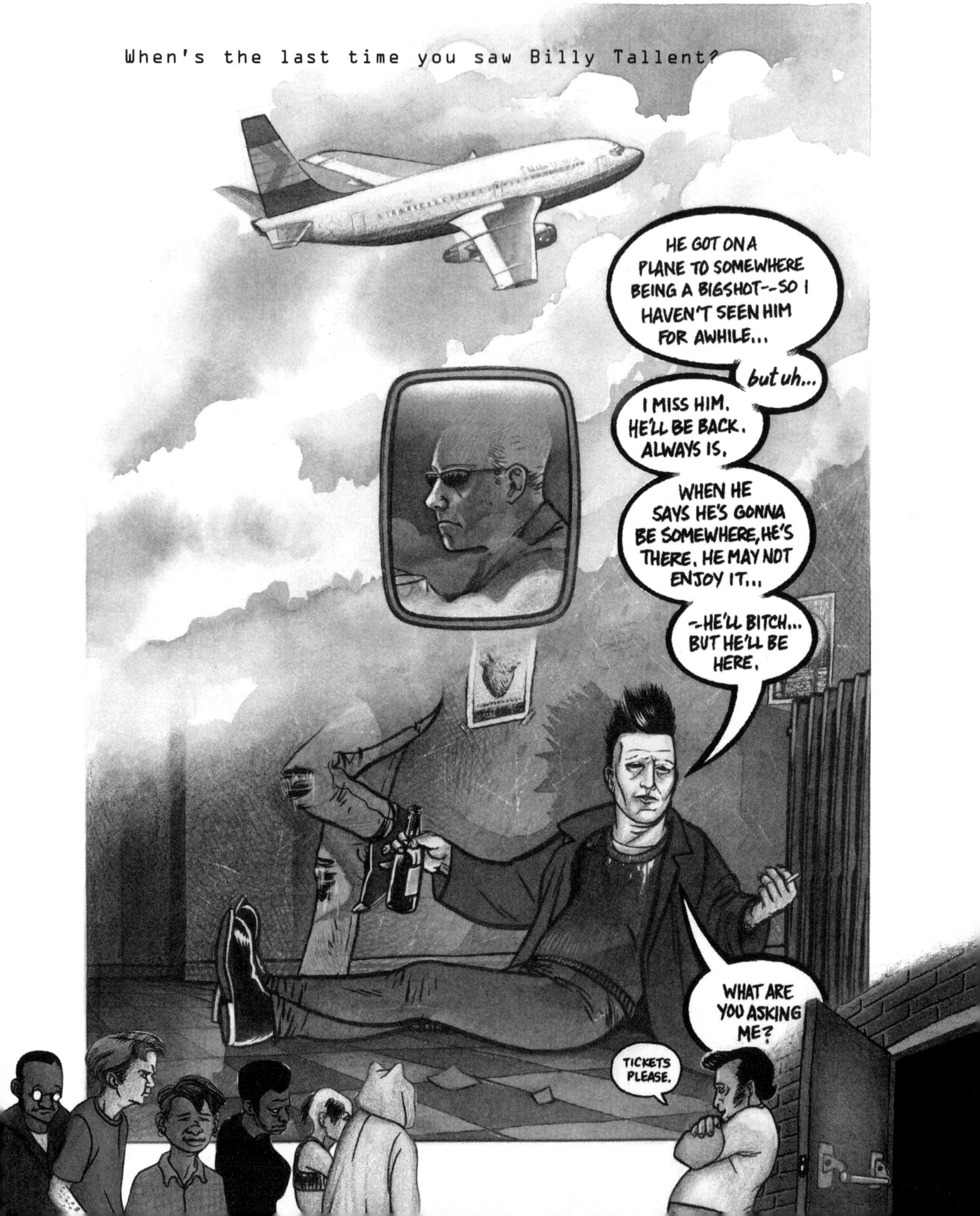

When's the last time you saw Billy Tallent?
HE GOT ON A PLANE TO SOMEWHERE BEING A BIGSHOT--SO I HAVEN'T SEEN HIM FOR AWHILE...
but uh...
I MISS HIM. HE'LL BE BACK. ALWAYS IS.
WHEN HE SAYS HE'S GONNA BE SOMEWHERE, HE'S THERE. HE MAY NOT ENJOY IT...
--HE'LL BITCH... BUT HE'LL BE HERE.
WHAT ARE YOU ASKING ME?
TICKETS PLEASE.

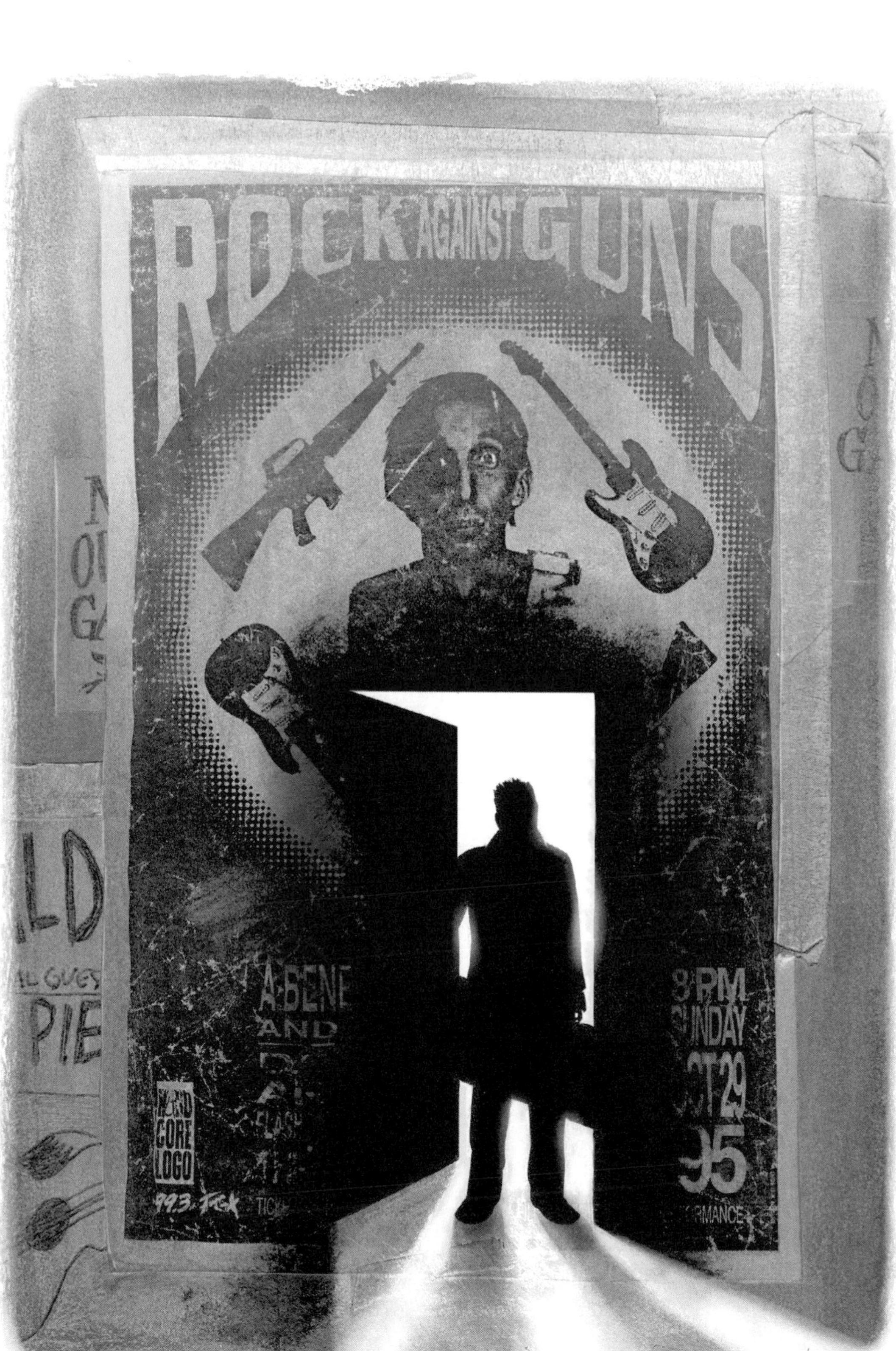
ROCK AGAINST GUNS
8 PM
AND

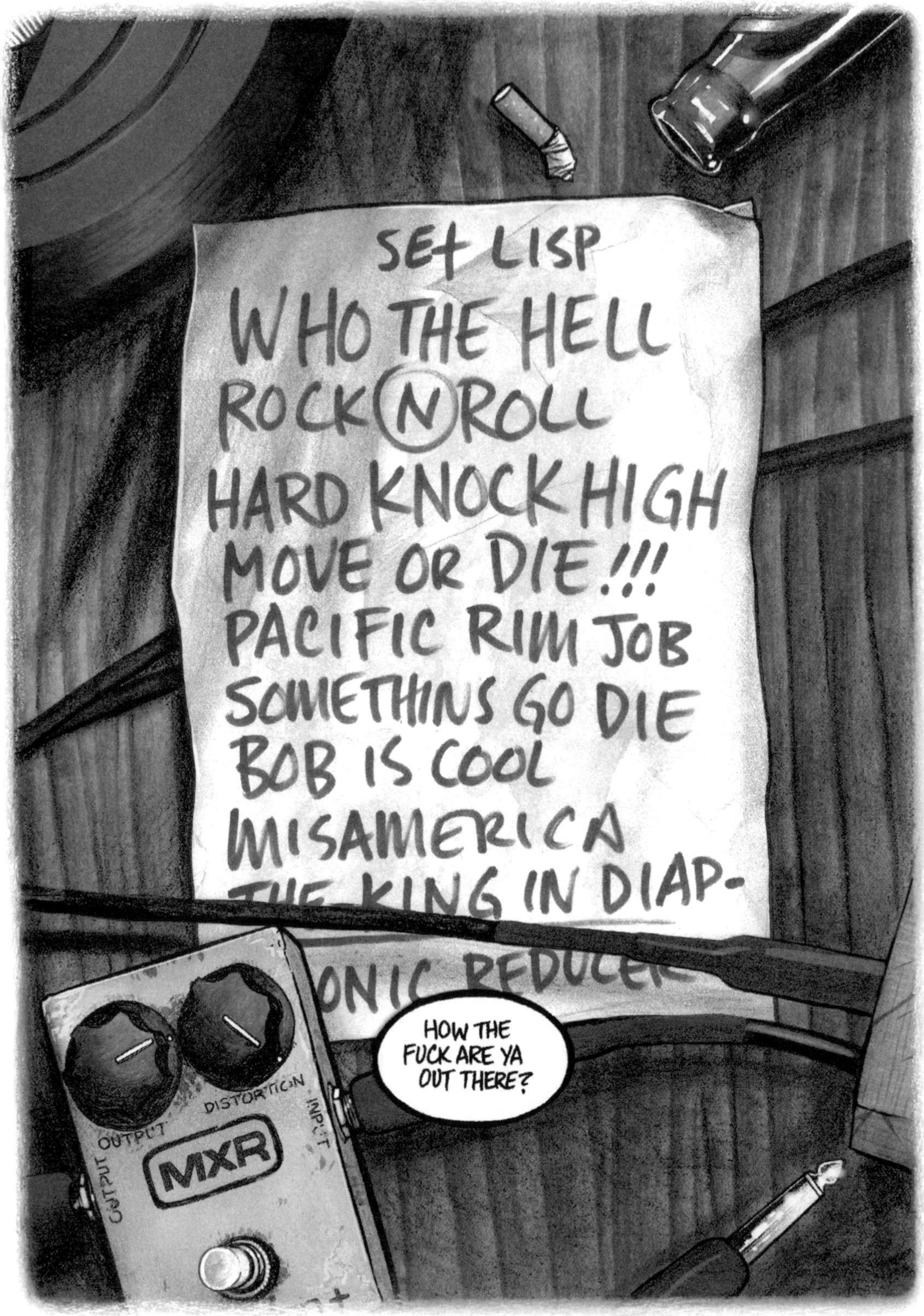
SET LISP
WHO THE HELL
ROCK N ROLL
HARD KNOCK HIGH
MOVE OR DIE!!!
PACIFIC RIM JOB
SOMETHINS GO DIE
BOB IS COOL
MISAMERICA
THE KING IN DIAP-
HOW THE FUCK ARE YA OUT THERE?
DISTORTION
OUTPUT
OUTPUT
INPUT
MXR

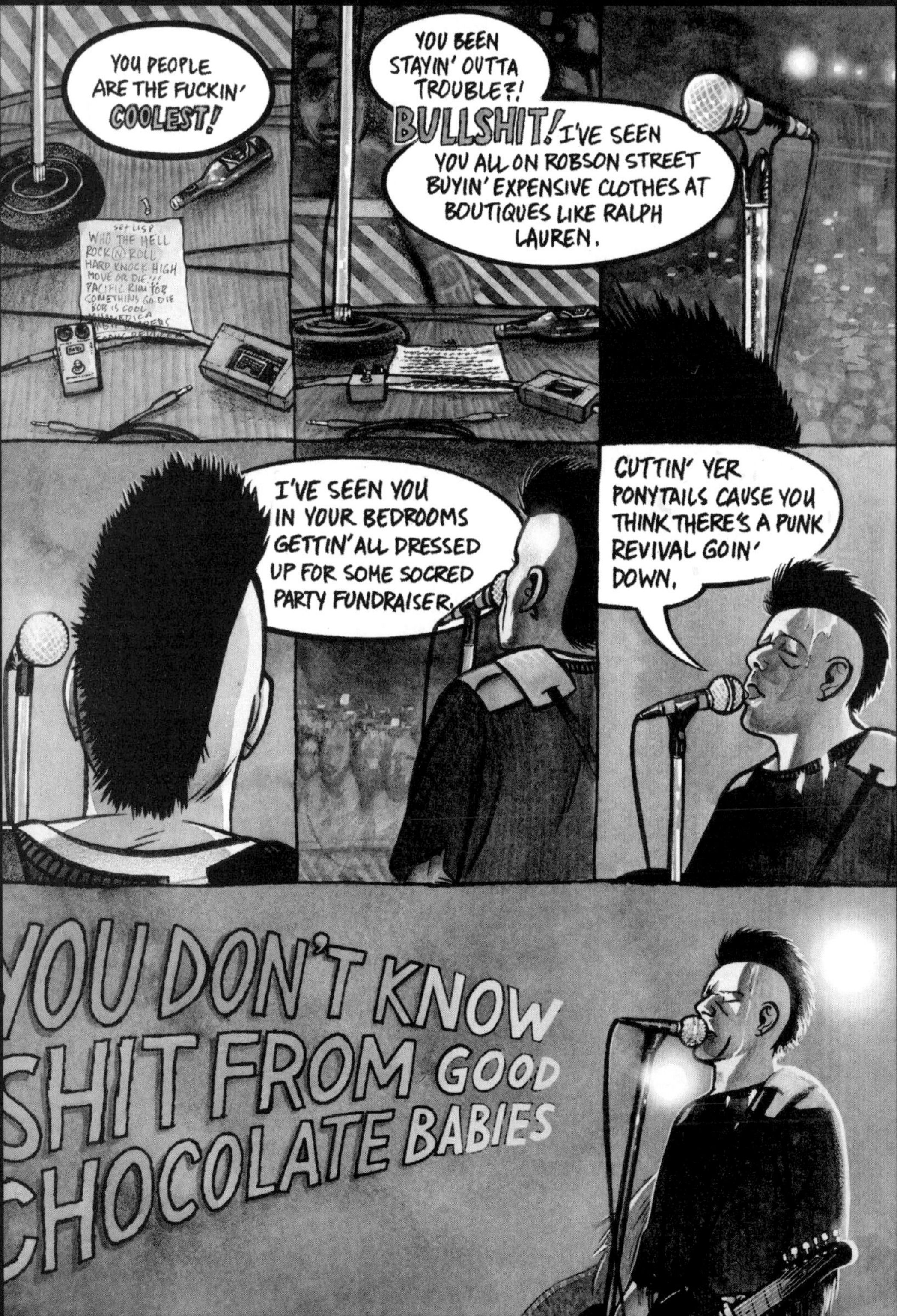
YOU PEOPLE ARE THE FUCKIN' COOLEST!
SET LIST
WHO THE HELL
ROCK N ROLL
HARD KNOCK HIGH
MOVE OR DIE!!!
PACIFIC RIM FOR
SOMETHING GO DIE
BOB IS COOL
YOU BEEN STAYIN' OUTTA TROUBLE?! BULLSHIT! I'VE SEEN YOU ALL ON ROBSON STREET BUYIN' EXPENSIVE CLOTHES AT BOUTIQUES LIKE RALPH LAUREN.
I'VE SEEN YOU IN YOUR BEDROOMS GETTIN' ALL DRESSED UP FOR SOME SOCRED PARTY FUNDRAISER.
CUTTIN' YER PONYTAILS CAUSE YOU THINK THERE'S A PUNK REVIVAL GOIN' DOWN.
YOU DON'T KNOW SHIT FROM GOOD CHOCOLATE BABIES

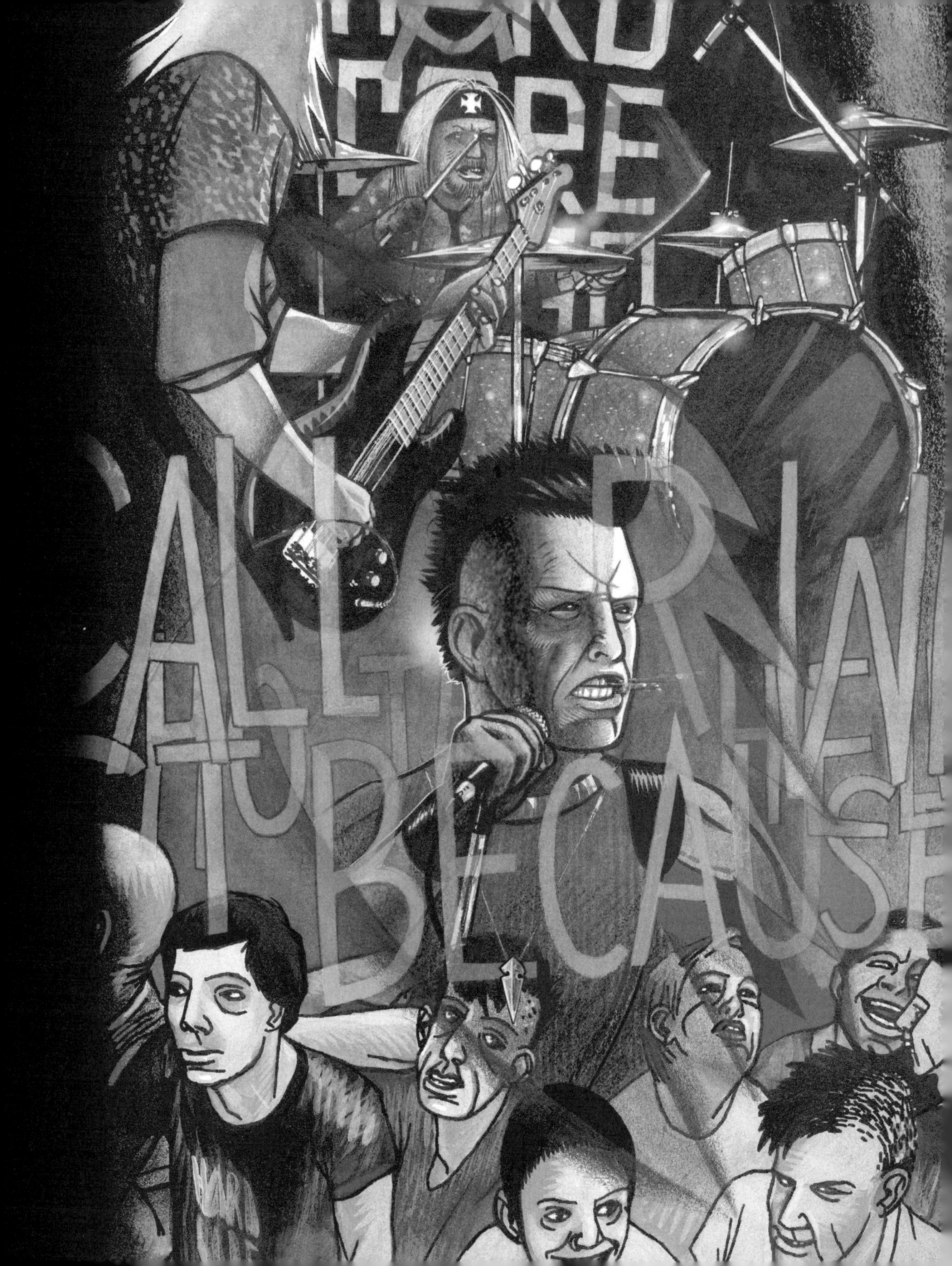
BECAUSE

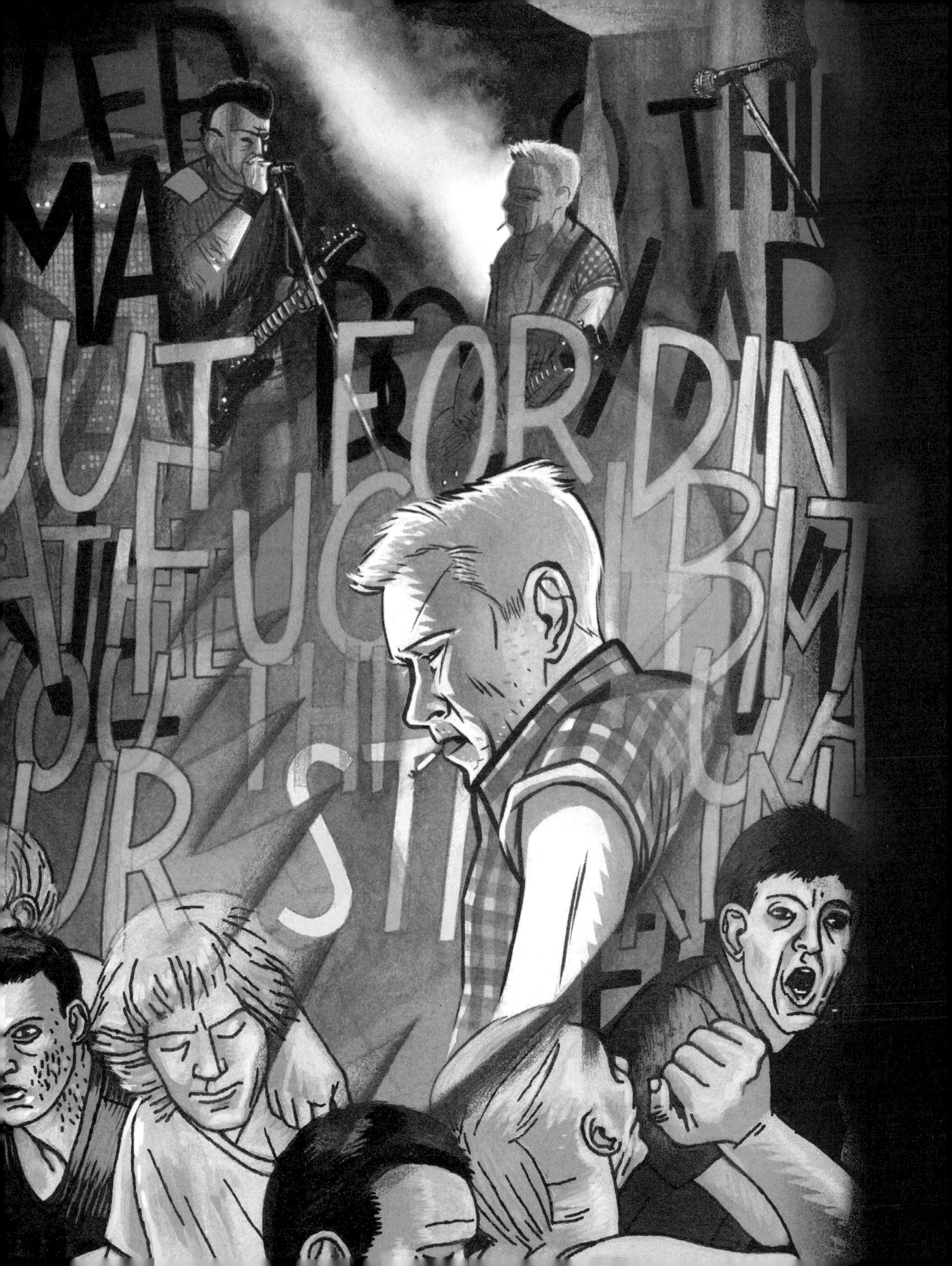

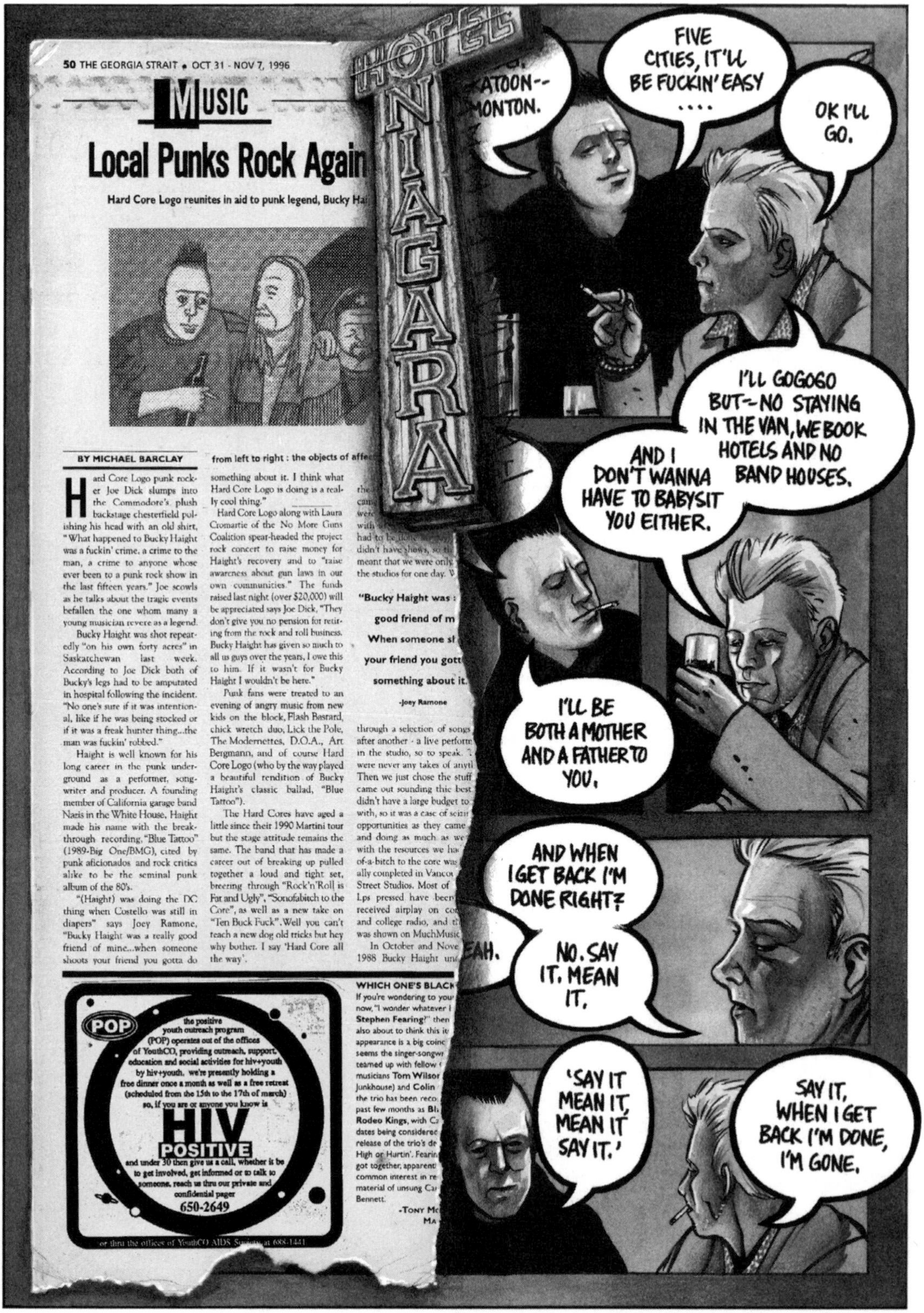
50 THE GEORGIA STRAIT • OCT 31 - NOV 7, 1996
MUSIC
Local Punks Rock Again
Hard Core Logo reunites in aid to punk legend, Bucky Ha
BY MICHAEL BARCLAY
from left to right : the objects of affe
Hard Core Logo punk rocker Joe Dick slumps into the Commodore's plush backstage chesterfield polishing his head with an old shirt, "What happened to Bucky Haight was a fuckin' crime, a crime to the man, a crime to anyone whose ever been to a punk rock show in the last fifteen years." Joe scowls as he talks about the tragic events befallen the one whom many a young musician revere as a legend.
Bucky Haight was shot repeatedly "on his own forty acres" in Saskatchewan last week. According to Joe Dick both of Bucky's legs had to be amputated in hospital following the incident. "No one's sure if it was intentional, like if he was being stocked or if it was a freak hunter thing...the man was fuckin' robbed."
Haight is well known for his long career in the punk underground as a performer, songwriter and producer. A founding member of California garage band Nazis in the White House, Haight made his name with the breakthrough recording, "Blue Tattoo" (1989-Big One/BMG), cited by punk aficionados and rock critics alike to be the seminal punk album of the 80's.
"(Haight) was doing the DC thing when Costello was still in diapers" says Joey Ramone, "Bucky Haight was a really good friend of mine...when someone shoots your friend you gotta do something about it. I think what Hard Core Logo is doing is a really cool thing."
Hard Core Logo along with Laura Cromartie of the No More Guns Coalition spear-headed the project rock concert to raise money for Haight's recovery and to "raise awareness about gun laws in our own communities." The funds raised last night (over $20,000) will be appreciated says Joe Dick, "They don't give you no pension for retiring from the rock and roll business. Bucky Haight has given so much to all us guys over the years, I owe this to him. If it wasn't for Bucky Haight I wouldn't be here."
Punk fans were treated to an evening of angry music from new kids on the block, Flash Bastard, chick wretch duo, Lick the Pole, The Modernettes, D.O.A., Art Bergmann, and of course Hard Core Logo (who by the way played a beautiful rendition of Bucky Haight's classic ballad, "Blue Tattoo").
The Hard Cores have aged a little since their 1990 Martini tour but the stage attitude remains the same. The band that has made a career out of breaking up pulled together a loud and tight set, breezing through "Rock'n'Roll is Fat and Ugly", "Sonofabitch to the Core", as well as a new take on "Ten Buck Fuck". Well you can't teach a new dog old tricks but hey why bother. I say 'Hard Core all the way'.
the
can
were
with
had to be done
didn't have shows, so th
meant that we were only
the studios for one day. V
"Bucky Haight was
good friend of m
When someone sl
your friend you gott
something about it.
-Joey Ramone
through a selection of songs
after another - a live perform
in the studio, so to speak.
were never any takes of anyt
Then we just chose the stuff
came out sounding thic best
didn't have a large budget to
with, so it was a case of seizi
opportunities as they came
and doing as much as we
with the resources we ha
of-a-bitch to the core was
ally completed in Vanco
Street Studios. Most of
Lps pressed have been
received airplay on co
and college radio, and t
was shown on MuchMusic
In October and Nove
1988 Bucky Haight un
POP
the positive youth outreach program (POP) operates out of the offices of YouthCO, providing outreach, support, education and social activities for hiv+youth by hiv+youth. we're presently holding a free dinner once a month as well as a free retreat (scheduled from the 15th to the 17th of march) so, if you are or anyone you know is
HIV POSITIVE
and under 30 then give us a call, whether it be to get involved, get informed or to talk to someone. reach us thru our private and confidential pager
650-2649
WHICH ONE'S BLACK
If you're wondering to you
now, "I wonder whatever I
Stephen Fearing?" then
also about to think this i
appearance is a big coinc
seems the singer-songwr
teamed up with fellow
musicians Tom Wilso
Junkhouse) and Colin
the trio has been reco
past few months as Bl
Rodeo Kings, with C
dates being considere
release of the trio's de
High or Hurtin'. Fearin
got together, apparent
common interest in re
material of unsung Ca
Bennett.
-TONY M
MA
HOTEL
NIAGARA
ATOON--
MONTON.
FIVE CITIES, IT'LL BE FUCKIN' EASY ....
OK I'LL GO.
I'LL GOGOGO BUT--NO STAYING IN THE VAN, WE BOOK HOTELS AND NO BAND HOUSES.
AND I DON'T WANNA HAVE TO BABYSIT YOU EITHER.
I'LL BE BOTH A MOTHER AND A FATHER TO YOU.
AND WHEN I GET BACK I'M DONE RIGHT?
EAH.
NO. SAY IT. MEAN IT.
'SAY IT MEAN IT, MEAN IT SAY IT.'
SAY IT, WHEN I GET BACK I'M DONE, I'M GONE.

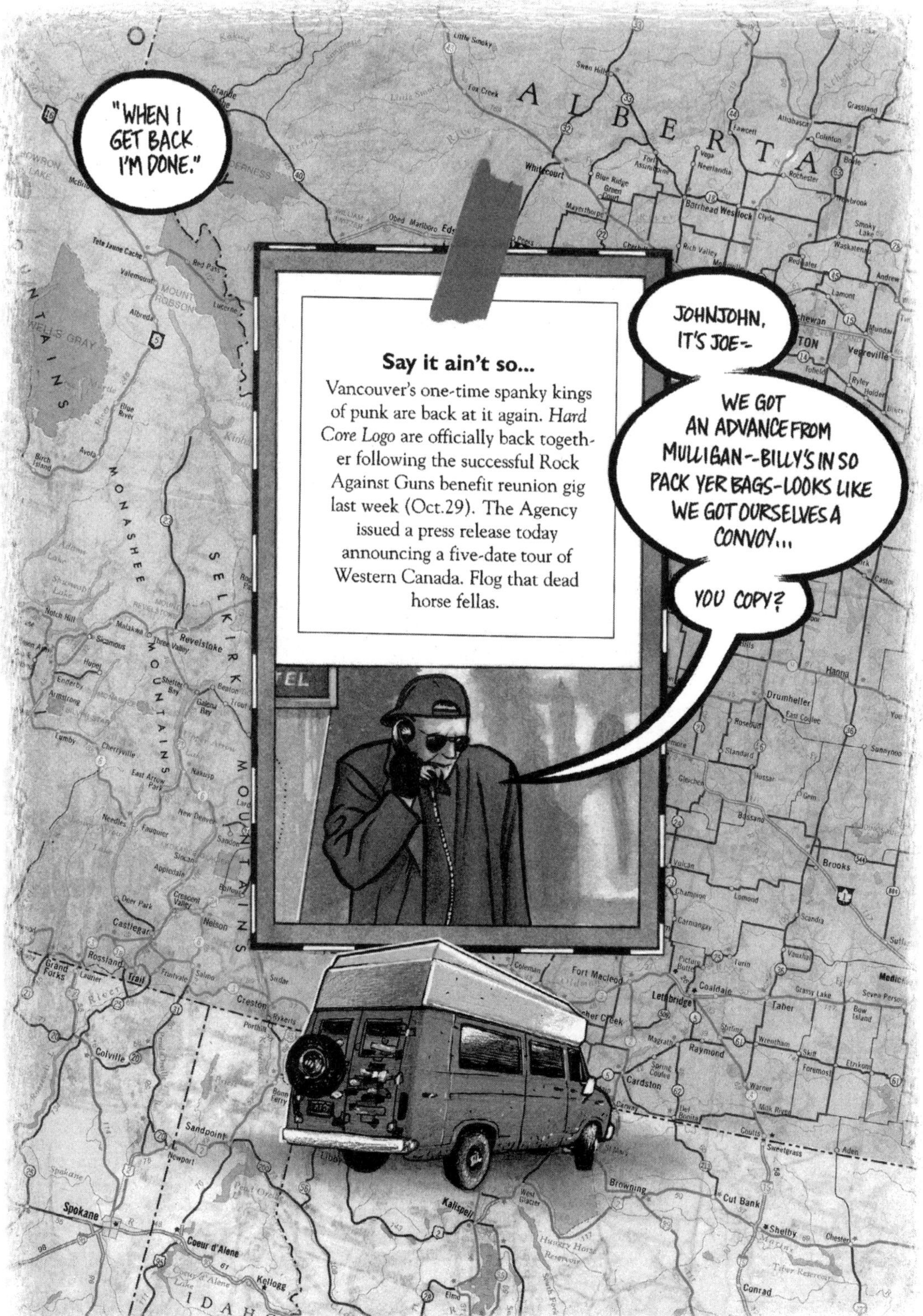
"WHEN I GET BACK I'M DONE."
Say it ain't so...
Vancouver's one-time spanky kings of punk are back at it again. *Hard Core Logo* are officially back together following the successful Rock Against Guns benefit reunion gig last week (Oct.29). The Agency issued a press release today announcing a five-date tour of Western Canada. Flog that dead horse fellas.
JOHNJOHN, IT'S JOE--
WE GOT AN ADVANCE FROM MULLIGAN--BILLY'S IN SO PACK YER BAGS-LOOKS LIKE WE GOT OURSELVES A CONVOY...
YOU COPY?
ALBERTA
MONASHEE MOUNTAINS
SELKIRK MOUNTAINS
IDAHO

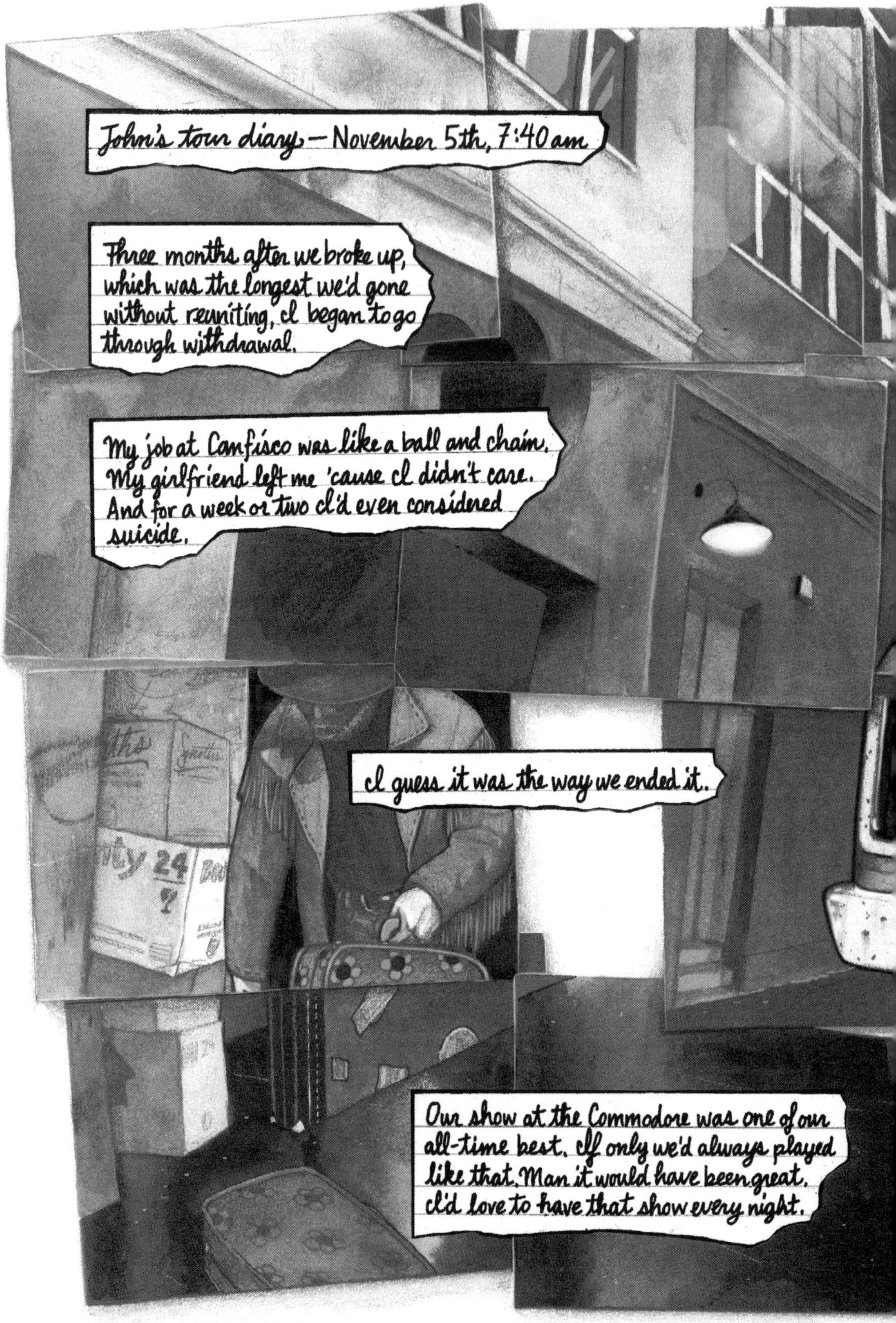
John's tour diary — November 5th, 7:40 am
Three months after we broke up, which was the longest we'd gone without reuniting, I began to go through withdrawal.
My job at Canfisco was like a ball and chain. My girlfriend left me 'cause I didn't care. And for a week or two I'd even considered suicide.
I guess it was the way we ended it.
Our show at the Commodore was one of our all-time best. If only we'd always played like that. Man it would have been great. I'd love to have that show every night.

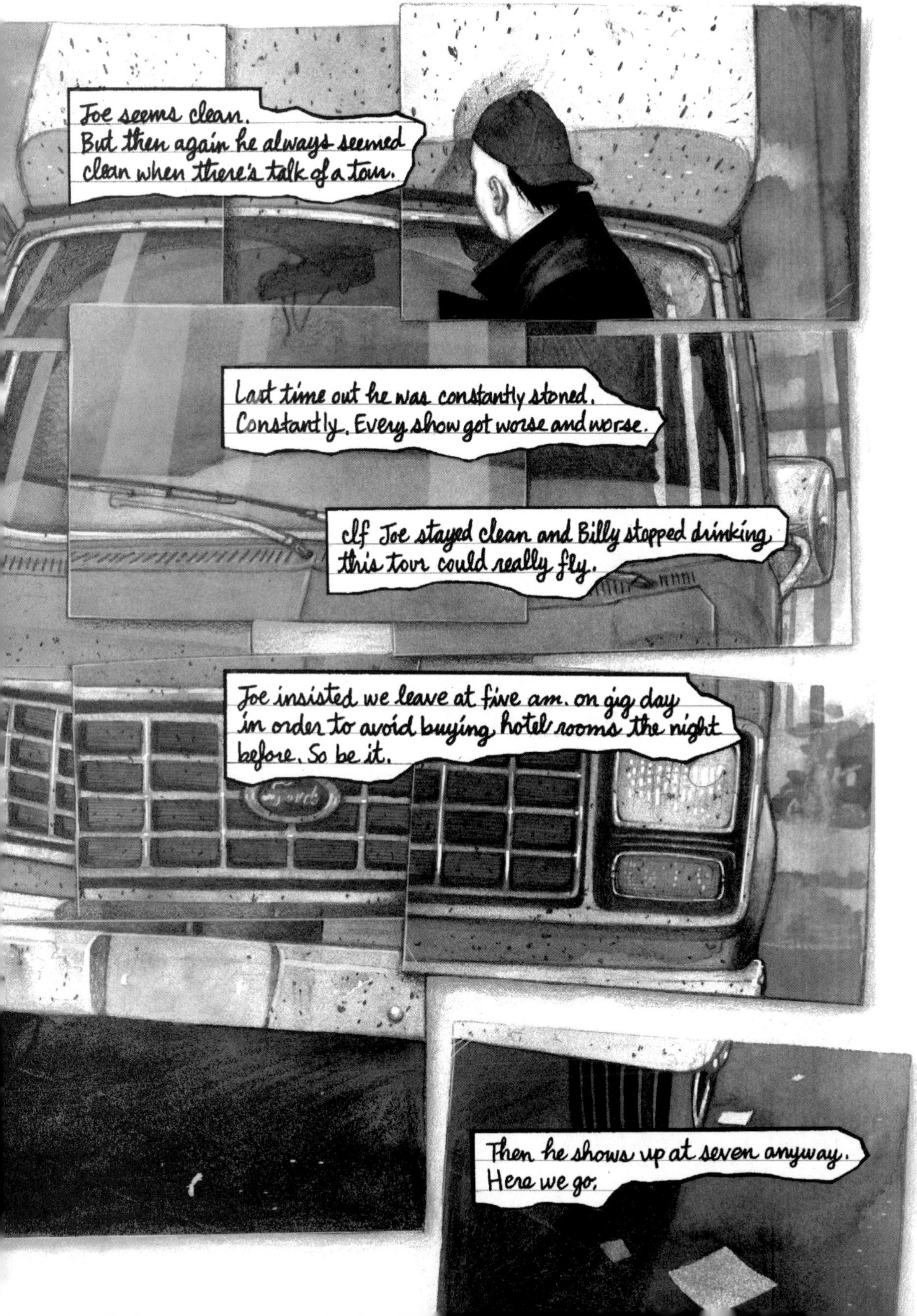
Joe seems clean. But then again he always seemed clean when there's talk of a tour.
Last time out he was constantly stoned. Constantly. Every show got worse and worse.
If Joe stayed clean and Billy stopped drinking this tour could really fly.
Joe insisted we leave at five am. on gig day in order to avoid buying hotel rooms the night before. So be it.
Then he shows up at seven anyway. Here we go.

John's tour diary – November 5th. am

We stopped at Herbies for breakfast. Pipe, who had fallen asleep with his mouth open, remained in the van, Billy sat by himself at the coffee bar reading True Detective, fliting with the waitresses. Joe and I occupied a booth by the window, watching the tourists gawk at Pipe's gaping mouth. Jeanne C. Riley was being featured on a radio program.

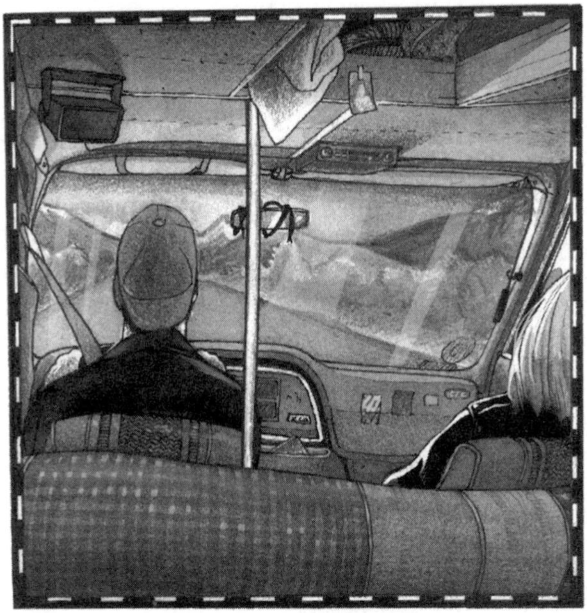

Joe was convinced that the cassette we were selling, entitled Herd it through the Bovine, was the best thing we've done in five years — even though it was recorded live on a Sony at the Commodore gig. I told him I hadn't even heard it yet. He produced a copy from his coat pocket. The cover was hand drawn and child-like. (There was a sad looking cow in the middle, taking a dump.) It looked like a bootleg.

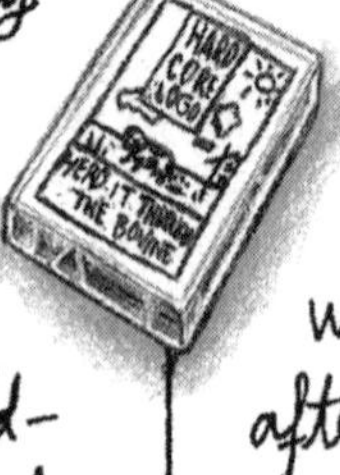
HARD CORE LOGO
HERD IT THRU THE BOVINE

Pipe woke up five minutes out of Hope, complaining of an intense hunger. Joe refused to stop until we needed gas again. Pipe then threatened to piss all over the van unless we did. Billy started siding with Pipe, and the two of them began to ride Joe. Pipe had his prick out, screaming, "It's gonna blow! It's gonna blow!" Just then Pipe's foot went through the floor of the van and he started flippin' out — We pulled him out expecting to see a mangled bloody stump, but instead his foot remained unscathed. In the meantime he had pissed all over his own self. (Nice van Joe!) Everybody calmed down and we drove in silence. Five minutes after that Joe pulled over at a fruit stand. Pipe stood, whining, in his underwear and leather jacket. I called home just to hear her voice.

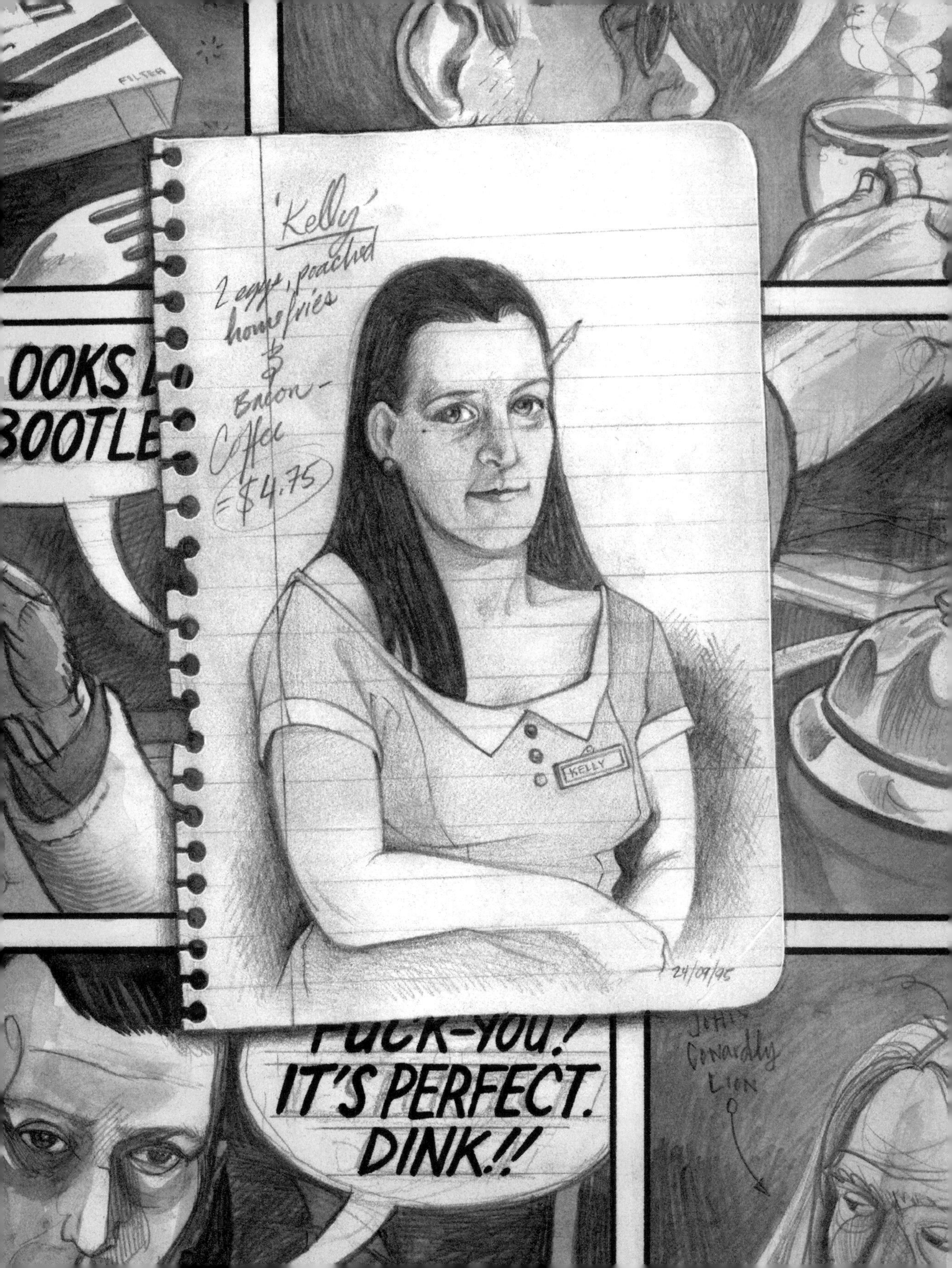
'Kelly'
2 eggs, poached
home fries
&
Bacon -
Coffee
= $4.75
KELLY
24/09/95
IT'S PERFECT.
DINK.!!

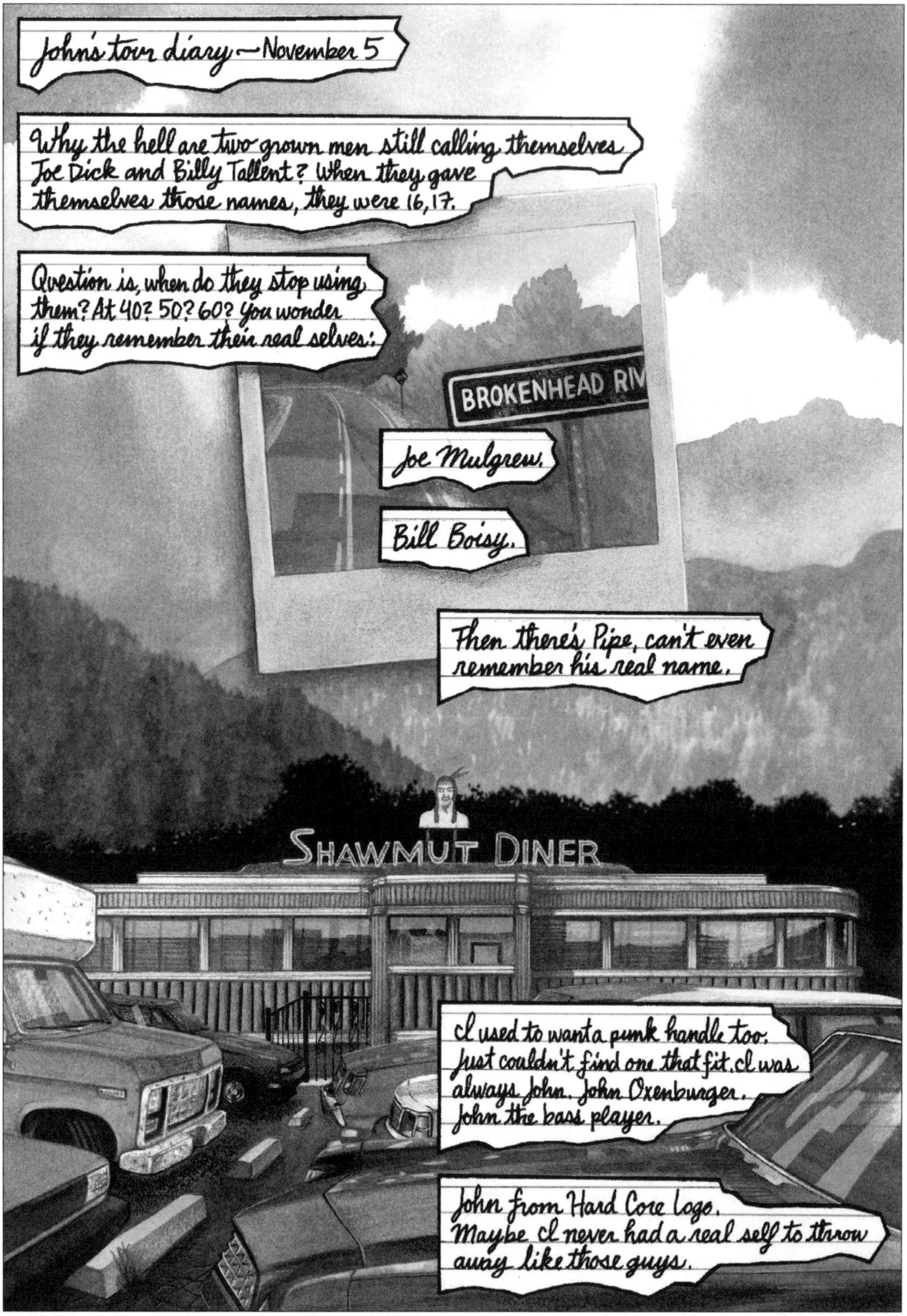
John's tour diary — November 5
Why the hell are two grown men still calling themselves Joe Dick and Billy Tallent? When they gave themselves those names, they were 16, 17.
Question is, when do they stop using them? At 40? 50? 60? You wonder if they remember their real selves:
BROKENHEAD RIV
Joe Mulgrew.
Bill Boisy.
Then there's Pipe, can't even remember his real name.
SHAWMUT DINER
I used to want a punk handle too. Just couldn't find one that fit. I was always John. John Oxenburger. John the bass player.
John from Hard Core Logo. Maybe I never had a real self to throw away like those guys.

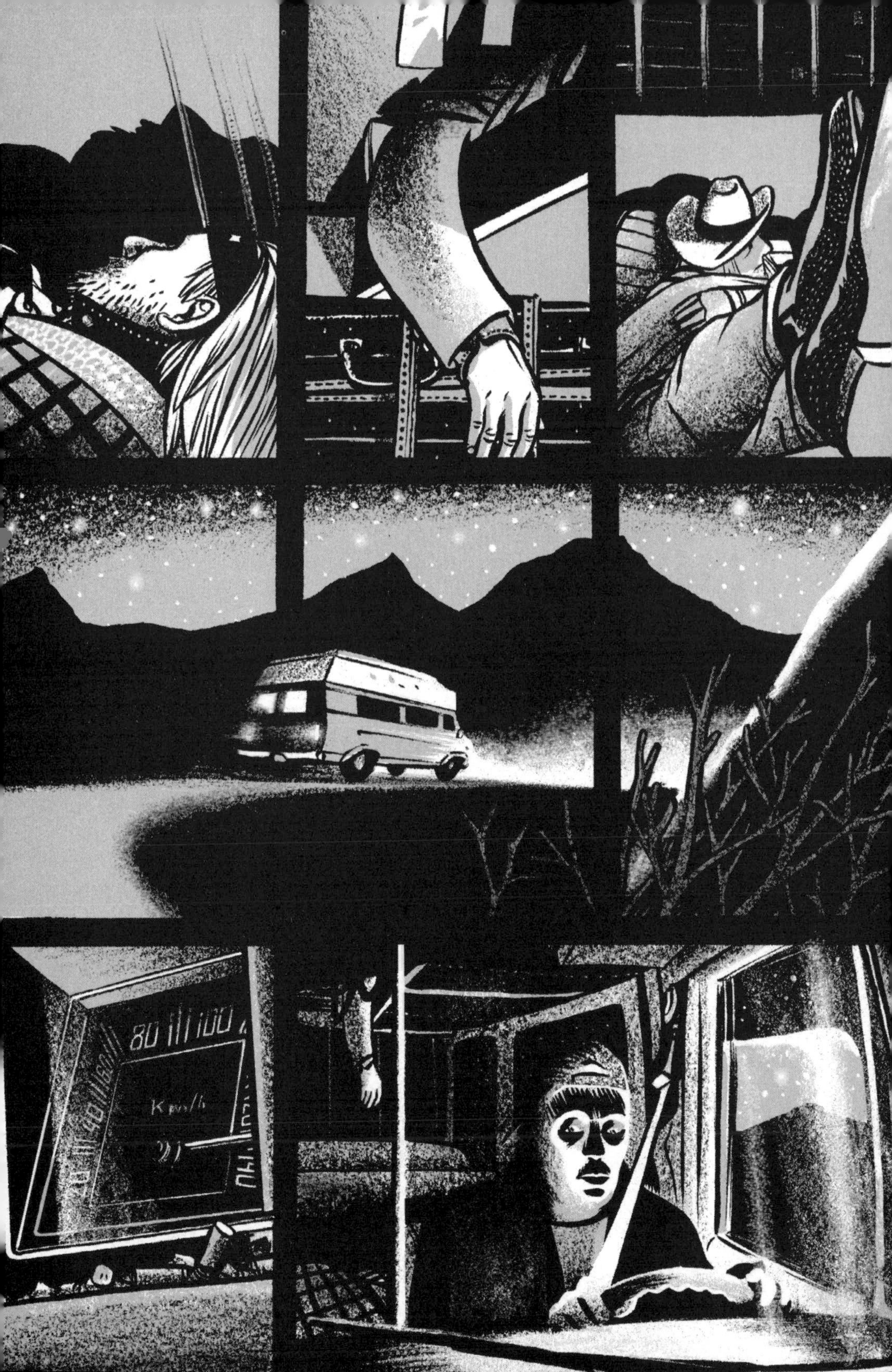
Km/h

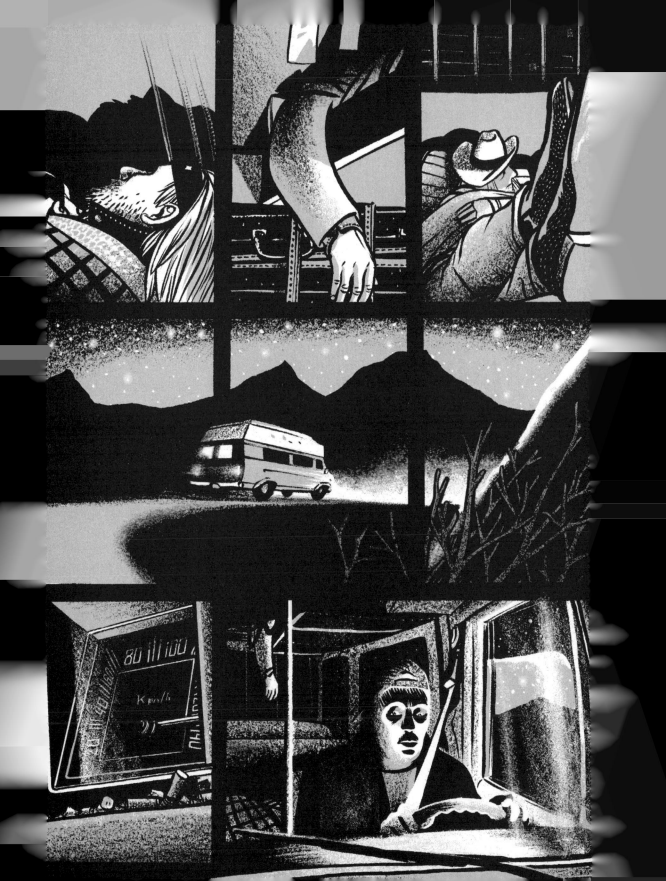

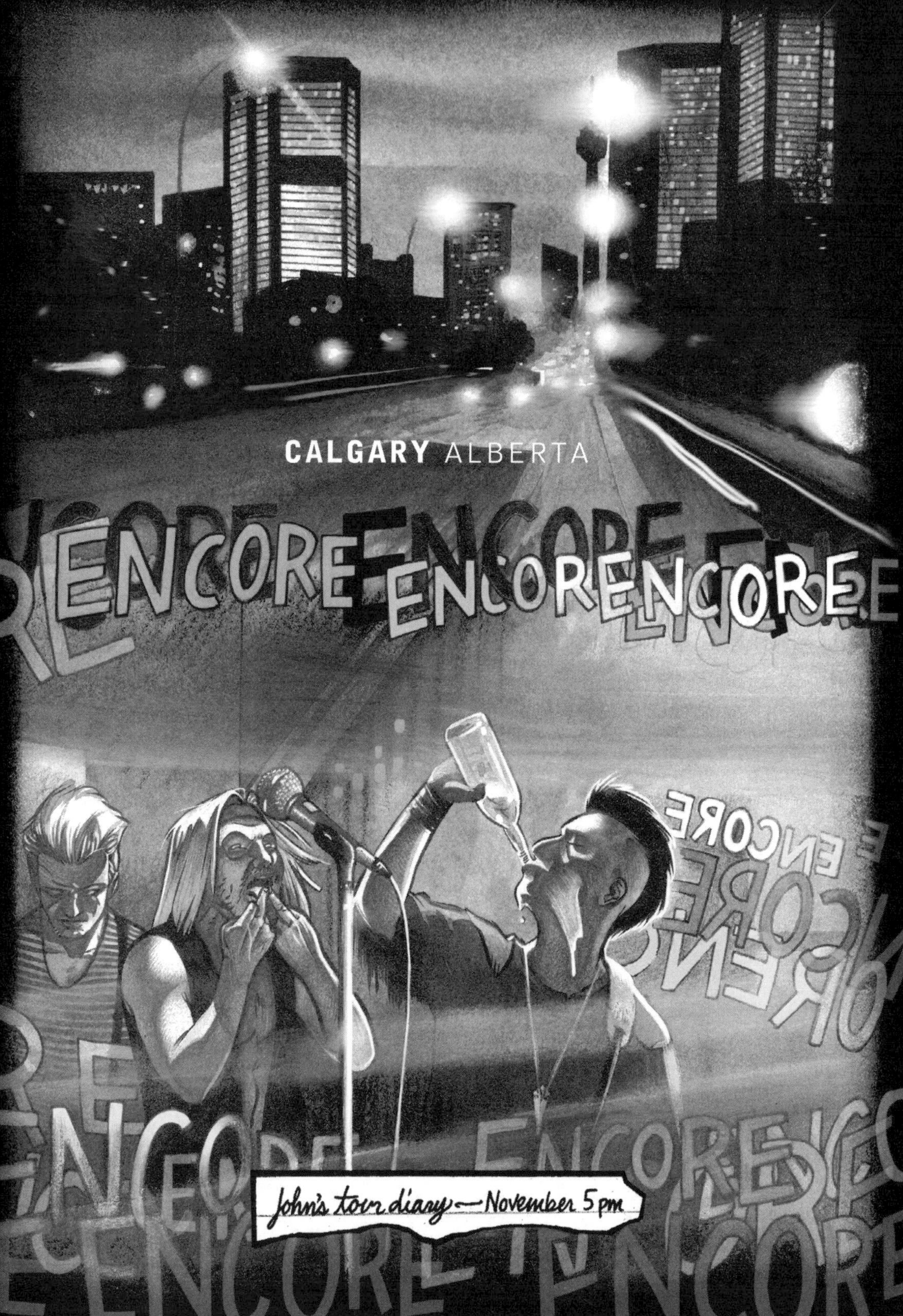
CALGARY ALBERTA
ENCORE ENCORE ENCORE
ENCORE
ENCORE ENCORE
ENCORE ENCORE
John's tour diary — November 5 pm

CHUNK
ONETWOTHREEFOUR!
CHUNK
Calgary's the same as ever: big friendly smiling beef eating faces. Good faces here.
Better than L.A. with its go-for-it stoner faces, or Toronto with its smug little rat race faces, or Montreal with its separatist chain smoker faces.

I always felt welcome here. These are non-judgmental faces. They do what they're told.
HARD CORE LOGO
BLACKOUT
NEW YORK
JULY

ly, why did Hard Co ogo break up

Billy Tallent: Because we didn't get along any more--musically speaking.

Billy Tallent: Yah.
Skid: So, all music aside, why are you back together touring Western Canada after all these years?
BT: We did a benefit in Vancouver on the 29th of October for Bucky Haight and I guess Joe felt we still had a few more shows left in us. I don't know, It's Joe's band . . . It's good to see him scowl again.
S: Bucky Haight. I heard there was an attempt made on Bucky's life . . .
BT: He was shot on his farm in Saskatchewan. I think it was like a . . . a hunter thought he was a moose or something, something crazy in the woods. Who knows why, Joe says that he's just fucked. I don't know. But yeah it was a great show . . . D.O.A. Art Bergmann, Modernettes, it was great to see all those guys again. I think they pulled in something like 20 grand. So the anti-gun people are getting a nice chunk and Bucky's getting a nice chunk so it worked out well for everybody. Everybody's happy happy. Except Bucky's got no legs.
S: Bucky lost his legs?
BT: Had to amputate. Shotgun blast.
S: Ooowww.
BT: Yeah.

S: So how did the whole thing with Jenifur come about?
BT: When I first got down to L.A. I was jamming with Trevor and then Earl got sick and I filled in on a couple of Lollapallooza dates and I guess now he's out for good.
S: Ok ok so the Jenifur thing . . . done deal? Officially you're part of the band?
BT: Just waiting for papers, waiting for papers. Green card. Then I'm gone. I'll be making real money for the first fuckin' time.
S: Doesn't Ed Festus manage Jenifur?
BT: Yeah.
S: Hard Core Logo's ex-manager.
BT: Anything that happened between Hard Core Logo and Ed Festus is ancient history. I have no bones with the man. It's a whole other lifetime.
S: I read an interview with Ed Festus where he calls you one of the top five thrash guitarists of all time.
BT: Really.
S: He also went on to say that you and Joe fought like

"some tanked up white trash married couple in a trailer park . . . "
BT: Water under the bridge.
S: According to Ed Festus you flushed something of Joe's down the toilet and this is why Hard Core Logo broke up.
BT: Like I said, the differences were musical . . . musical differences are good for a band.

S: There are a lot of people who read the magazine I'm submitting this interview to who are too young to emember when Hard Core Logo was just another band from Vancouver. Could you describe your beginnings? Maybe your first gig or something.
BT: Our first gig? . . . Our first gig as Hard Core Logo was at the Old American Hotel on Main Street. That was . . . 1977. The place was full of bikers and transsexuals and drug addicts . . . and then we walk in with crew cuts, army boots, ripped t-shirts (laughter). We got the gig through a guy named Mace. His real name was something like Jerry Macy, but he adopted 'Mace' cause it made him sound tough even though he wasn't. Anyway Mace was a friend of Joe's older brother, and he offered us a hundred bucks to open for one of his Steppenwolf-like cover bands. So there we were, hangin' by the backstage door cause we were under-aged and scared shitless. There was this huge biker sitting front-and-centre starin' at us, punching his fist into his open hand like this. Looking back I think he was hired by Mace to flip us out (laughter). We had twelve songs on our set list and we figured it would cover the forty-five minutes we were supposed to be playing. Anyway we burned through the set without pause, figuring that if we stopped they'd have a chance to beat us up.
We played so fast we finished the set in thirty minutes. Everyone was speechless. It was the first punk rock gig in Vancouver. Mace was standing by the side of the stage waving his arms, going, keep playing, keep playing.

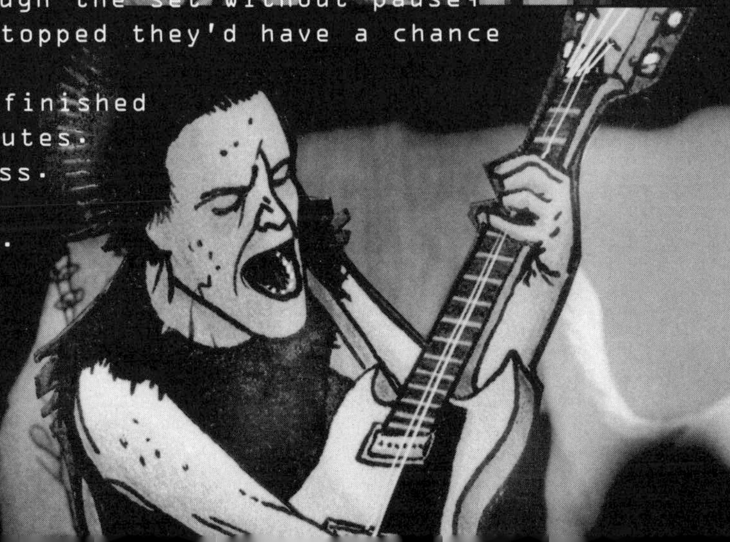

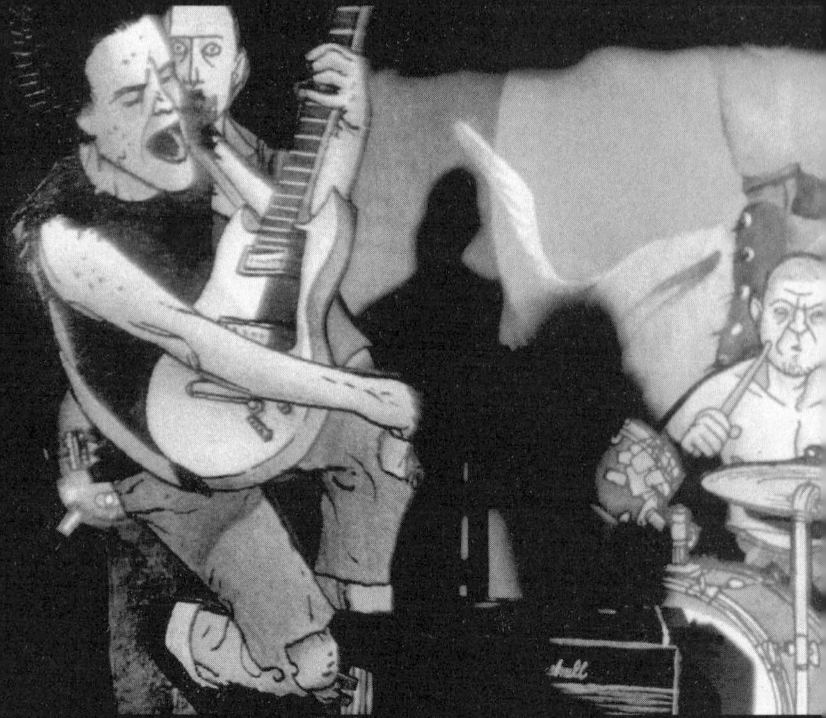

But we didn't have any more songs.

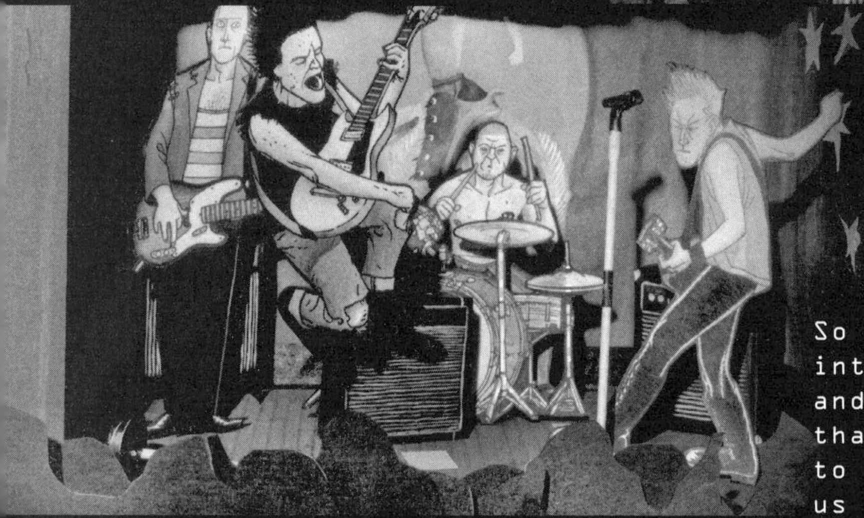

So Joe started into "Proud Mary" and we jammed on that 'til Mace had to literally drag us from the stage.

The crowd was going nuts. They loved it. And that biker from the front table! Man! He came backstage with amyl nitrates for everybody (laughter).

S: Nice. So what's next for Hard Core Logo?

BT: Well that's up to Joe.

S: What do you mean by that?

BT: I don't know yet.

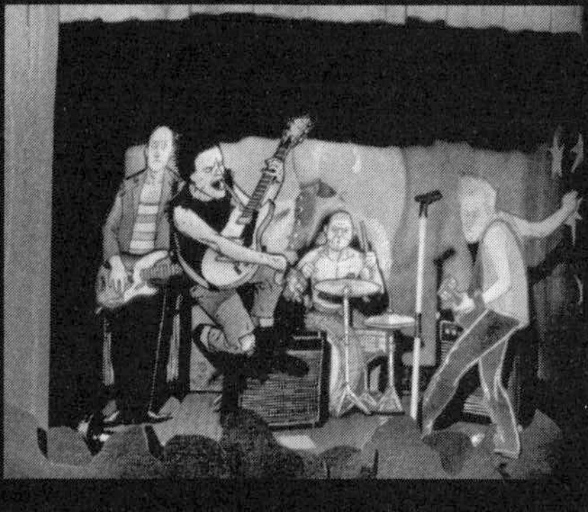

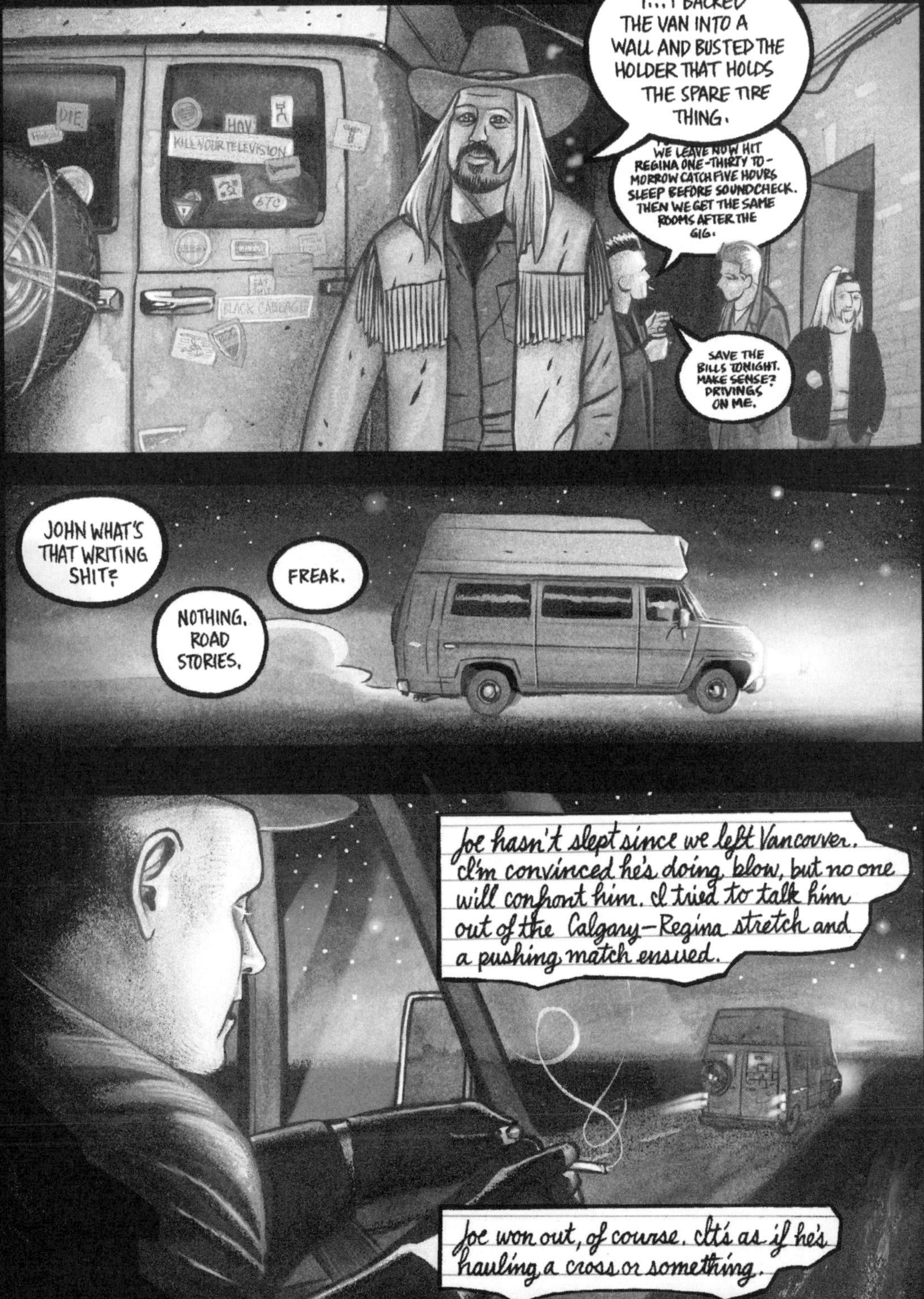
I... I BACKED THE VAN INTO A WALL AND BUSTED THE HOLDER THAT HOLDS THE SPARE TIRE THING.
WE LEAVE NOW HIT REGINA ONE-THIRTY TO-MORROW CATCH FIVE HOURS SLEEP BEFORE SOUNDCHECK. THEN WE GET THE SAME ROOMS AFTER THE GIG.
SAVE THE BILLS TONIGHT. MAKE SENSE? DRIVINGS ON ME.
JOHN WHAT'S THAT WRITING SHIT?
NOTHING. ROAD STORIES.
FREAK.
Joe hasn't slept since we left Vancouver. I'm convinced he's doing blow, but no one will confront him. I tried to talk him out of the Calgary–Regina stretch and a pushing match ensued.
Joe won out, of course. It's as if he's hauling a cross or something.

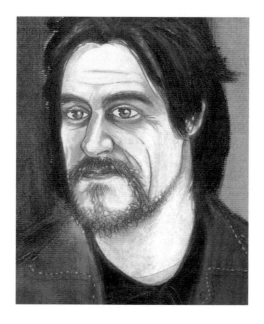

PETER HENDERSON

HARD CORE LOGO ROADIE,
1985-86 CANADIAN TOURS

---

*"They were a great band to work for.
I remember Pipe had a thing for the strippers.
Every time we played anywhere around
Saskatoon we'd go to this one peeler bar . . .
The King Eddie I think it was. Anyway,
they all knew Pipe cause his mom used to
be in the business over in Calgary, was half-
famous for this thing she'd do with reptiles . . .
we'd get free hotel rooms and dancing girls
and Scotch whisky . . . .*

"Sa great gig.
"The Hard Cores took care of their own."

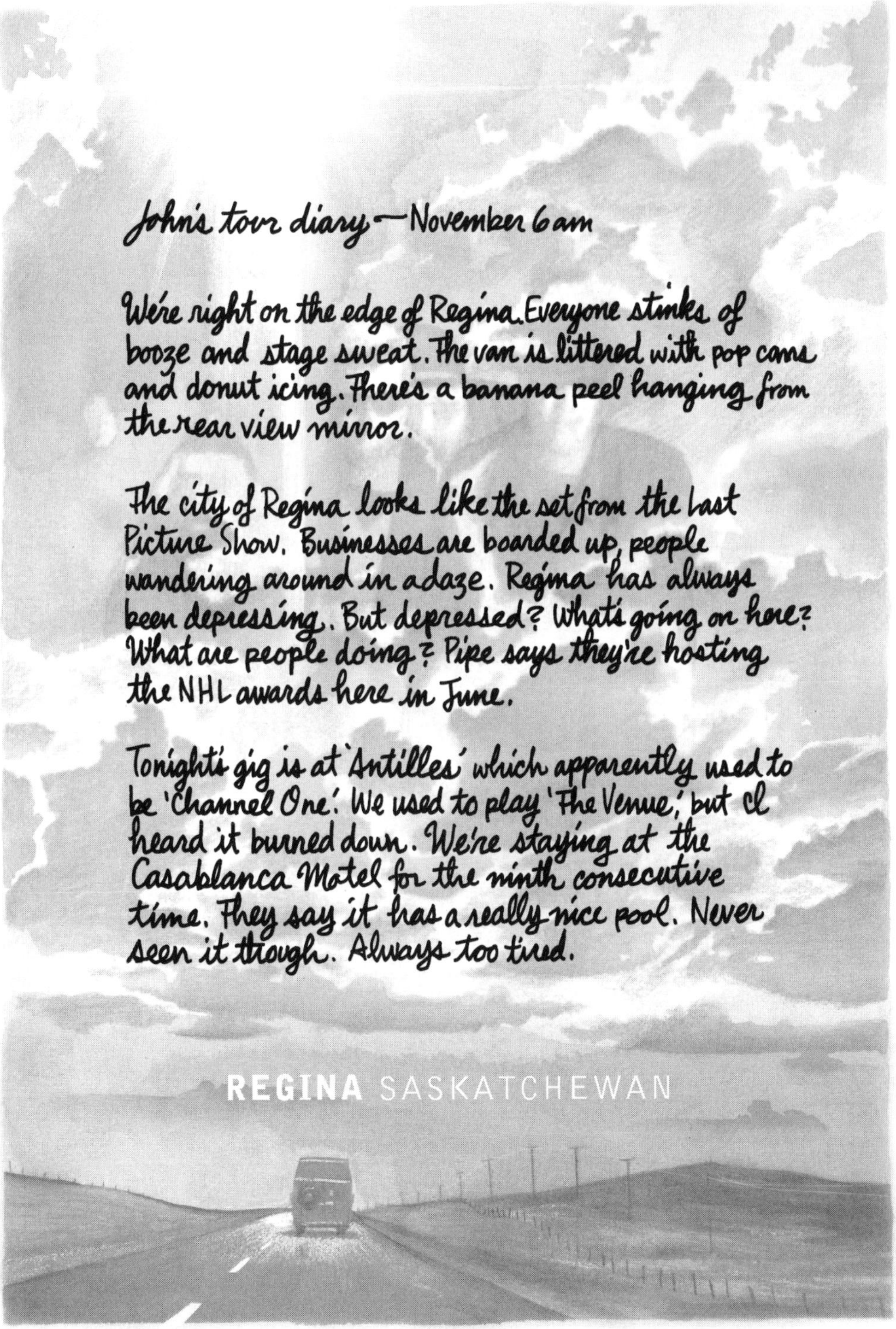
John's tour diary — November 6 am
We're right on the edge of Regina. Everyone stinks of booze and stage sweat. The van is littered with pop cans and donut icing. There's a banana peel hanging from the rear view mirror.
The city of Regina looks like the set from the Last Picture Show. Businesses are boarded up, people wandering around in a daze. Regina has always been depressing. But depressed? What's going on here? What are people doing? Pipe says they're hosting the NHL awards here in June.
Tonight's gig is at 'Antilles' which apparently used to be 'Channel One'. We used to play 'The Venue,' but I heard it burned down. We're staying at the Casablanca Motel for the ninth consecutive time. They say it has a really nice pool. Never seen it through. Always too tired.
REGINA SASKATCHEWAN

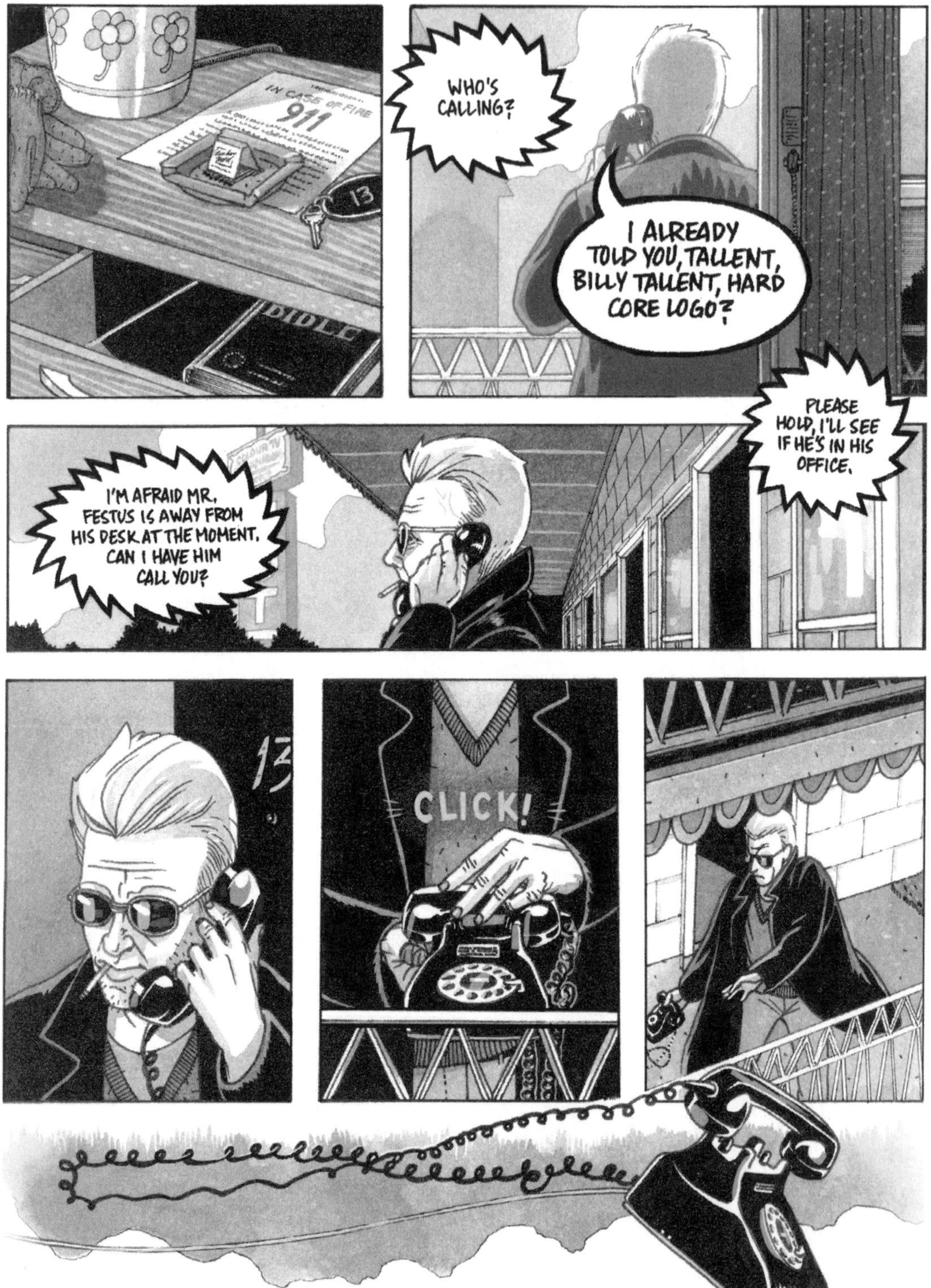
IN CASE OF FIRE
911
WHO'S CALLING?
I ALREADY TOLD YOU, TALLENT, BILLY TALLENT, HARD CORE LOGO?
PLEASE HOLD, I'LL SEE IF HE'S IN HIS OFFICE.
I'M AFRAID MR. FESTUS IS AWAY FROM HIS DESK AT THE MOMENT. CAN I HAVE HIM CALL YOU?
CLICK!

{John's Touring Essentials}
my pills.
cccan't find
mmy prescription
ppills...
Red
Big Red
Sam Shep
Fool For Lo
Other Play

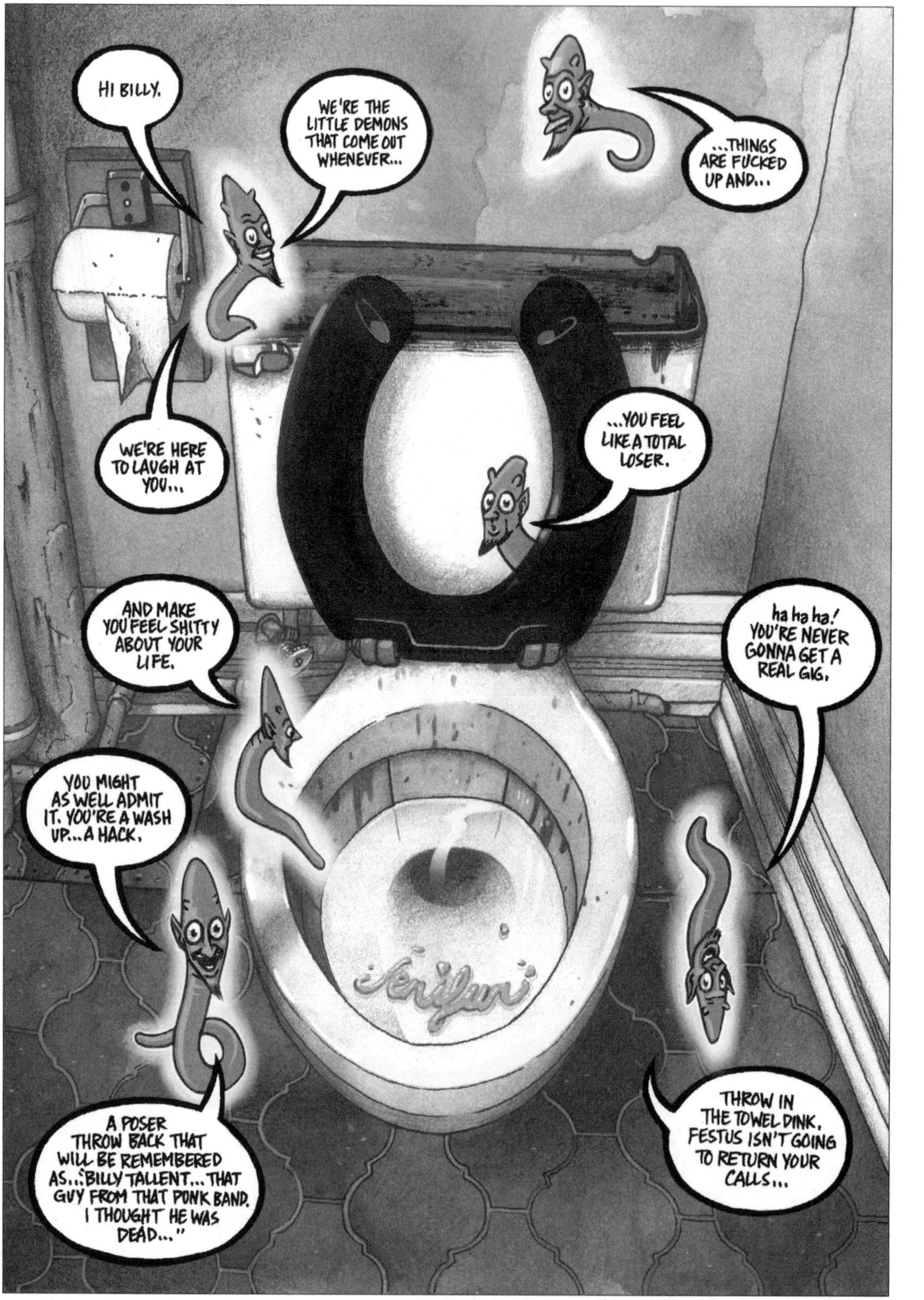
HI BILLY.
WE'RE THE LITTLE DEMONS THAT COME OUT WHENEVER...
...THINGS ARE FUCKED UP AND...
WE'RE HERE TO LAUGH AT YOU...
...YOU FEEL LIKE A TOTAL LOSER.
AND MAKE YOU FEEL SHITTY ABOUT YOUR LIFE.
ha ha ha! YOU'RE NEVER GONNA GET A REAL GIG.
YOU MIGHT AS WELL ADMIT IT. YOU'RE A WASH UP...A HACK.
A POSER THROW BACK THAT WILL BE REMEMBERED AS..."BILLY TALLENT...THAT GUY FROM THAT PUNK BAND. I THOUGHT HE WAS DEAD..."
THROW IN THE TOWEL DINK, FESTUS ISN'T GOING TO RETURN YOUR CALLS...

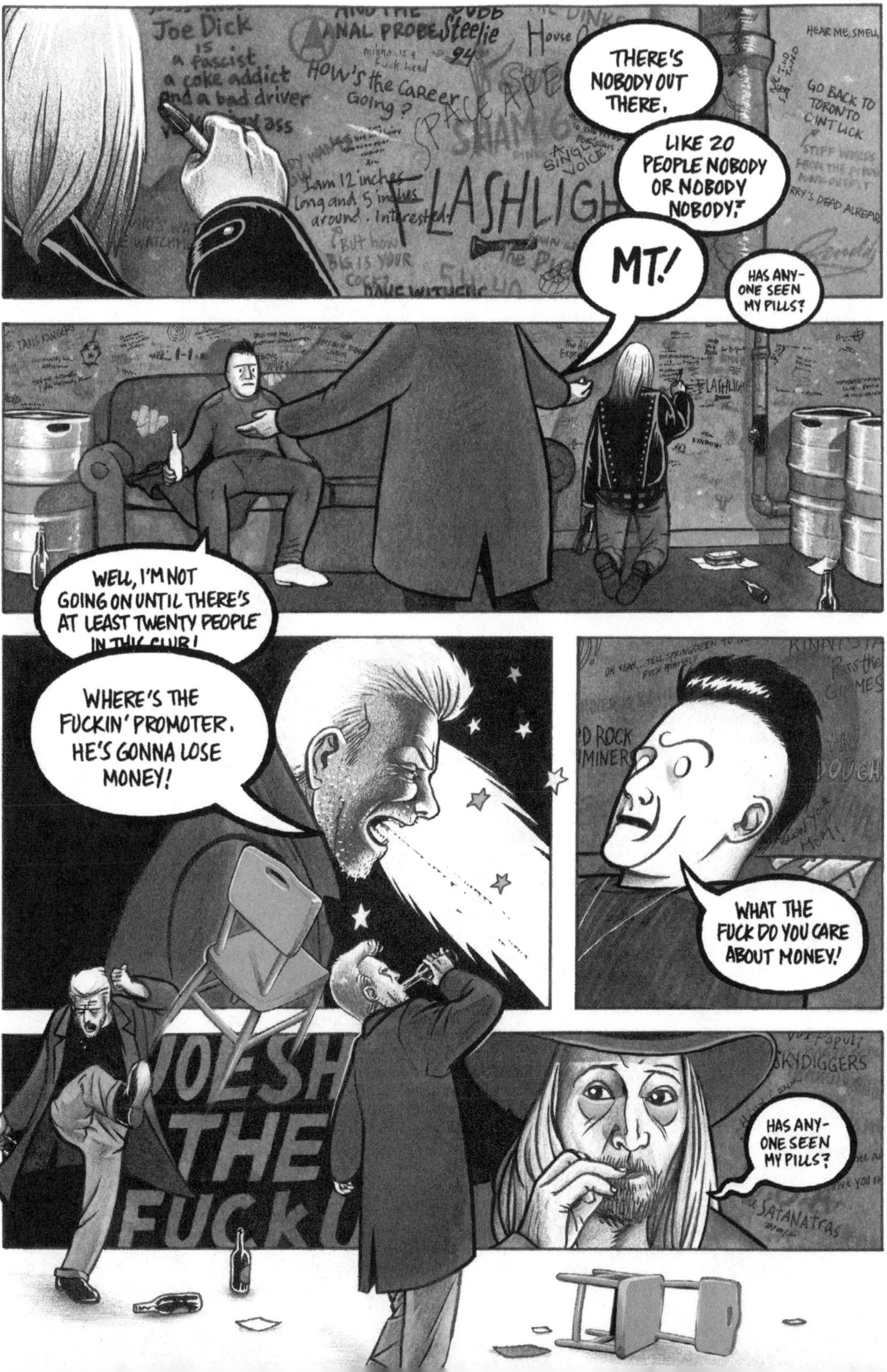
THERE'S NOBODY OUT THERE.
LIKE 20 PEOPLE NOBODY OR NOBODY NOBODY?
MT!
HAS ANY-ONE SEEN MY PILLS?
WELL, I'M NOT GOING ON UNTIL THERE'S AT LEAST TWENTY PEOPLE IN THIS CLUB!
WHERE'S THE FUCKIN' PROMOTER. HE'S GONNA LOSE MONEY!
WHAT THE FUCK DO YOU CARE ABOUT MONEY!
HAS ANY-ONE SEEN MY PILLS?

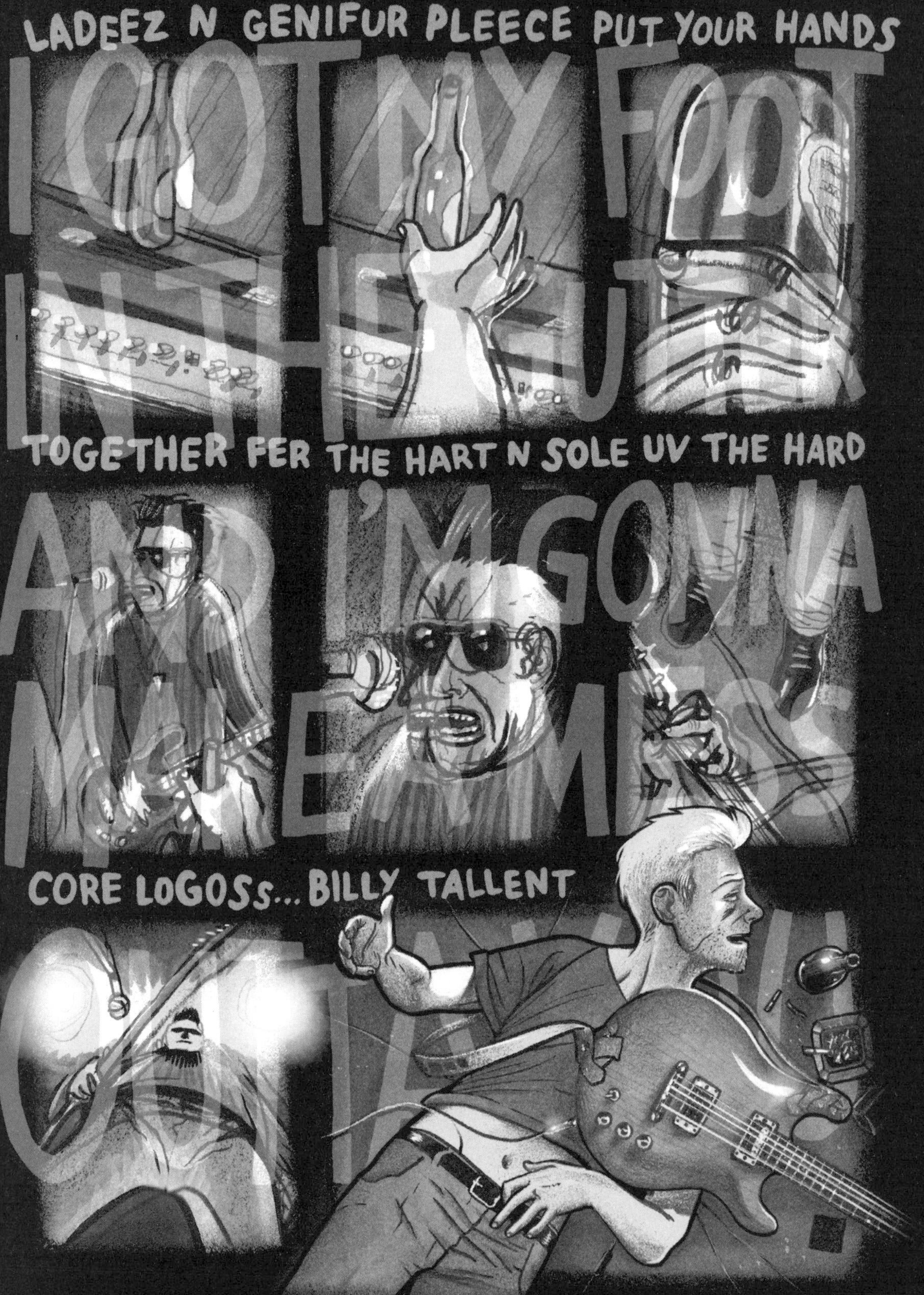
LADEEZ N GENIFUR PLEECE PUT YOUR HANDS
I GOT MY FOOT
TOGETHER FER THE HART N SOLE UV THE HARD
AND I'M GONNA
CORE LOGOSS... BILLY TALLENT

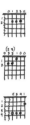

DAVE WITHERS

GUITAR PLAYER/SONGWRITER,
THE MONKEY WRENCH GANG

"I always respected Bill as a guitar player, as a musician. I don't know why he's wasted so much of his career playing in that band . . . I mean don't get me wrong, they were always a great live band, but Joe's just such an asshole.

"I think it's great that Billy's filling in with Jenifur now, I hope he gets the gig. I'd like to see him go all the way. He's paid his dues. As long as he can stay out of detox.

"Twice we opened for them at the Railway and both times he was wasted out of his head. But put a guitar in his hands and he'll play the album note for note. Somehow . . . "

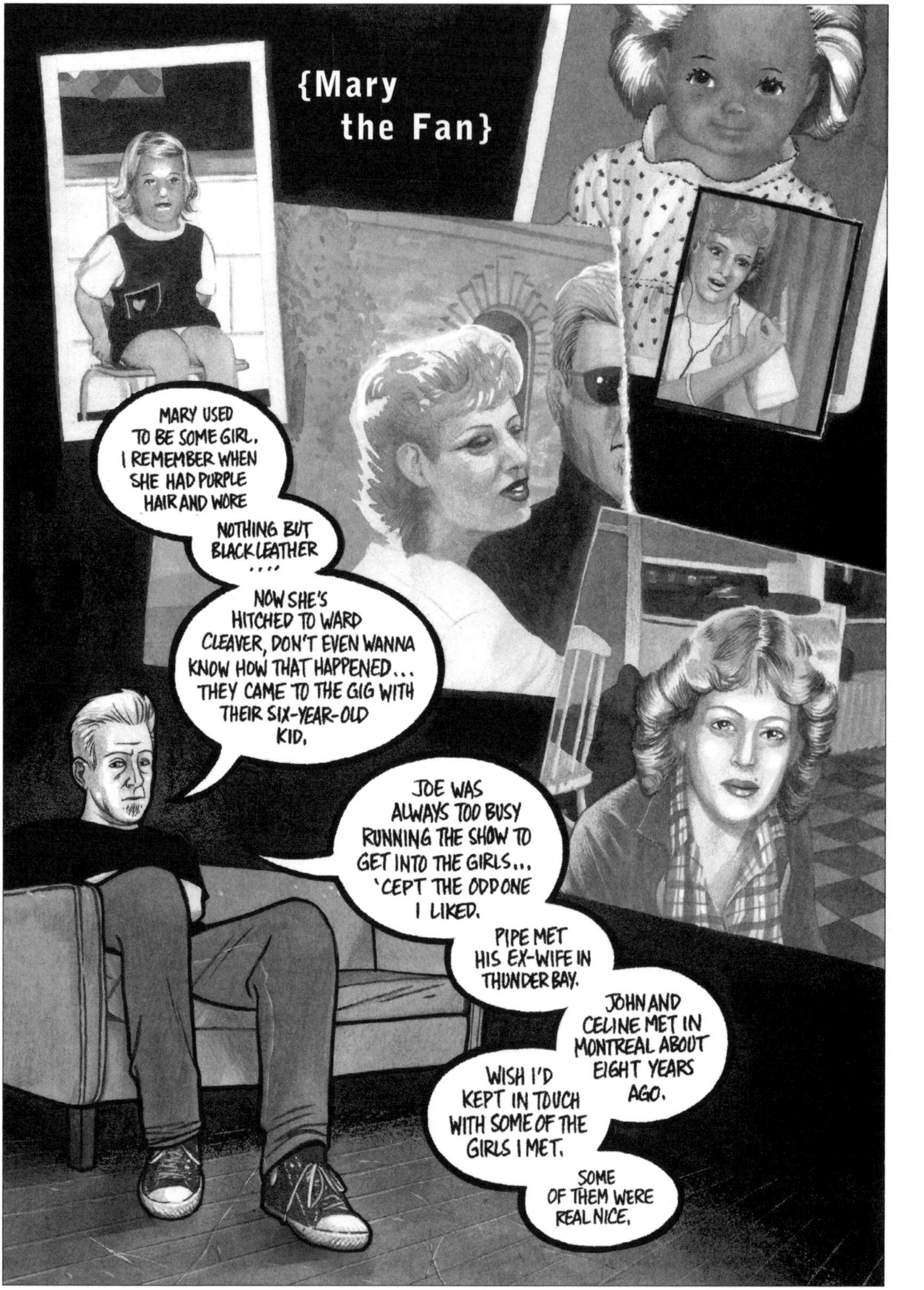
{Mary the Fan}
MARY USED TO BE SOME GIRL. I REMEMBER WHEN SHE HAD PURPLE HAIR AND WORE
NOTHING BUT BLACK LEATHER ....
NOW SHE'S HITCHED TO WARD CLEAVER, DON'T EVEN WANNA KNOW HOW THAT HAPPENED... THEY CAME TO THE GIG WITH THEIR SIX-YEAR-OLD KID.
JOE WAS ALWAYS TOO BUSY RUNNING THE SHOW TO GET INTO THE GIRLS... 'CEPT THE ODD ONE I LIKED.
PIPE MET HIS EX-WIFE IN THUNDER BAY.
JOHN AND CELINE MET IN MONTREAL ABOUT EIGHT YEARS AGO.
WISH I'D KEPT IN TOUCH WITH SOME OF THE GIRLS I MET.
SOME OF THEM WERE REAL NICE.

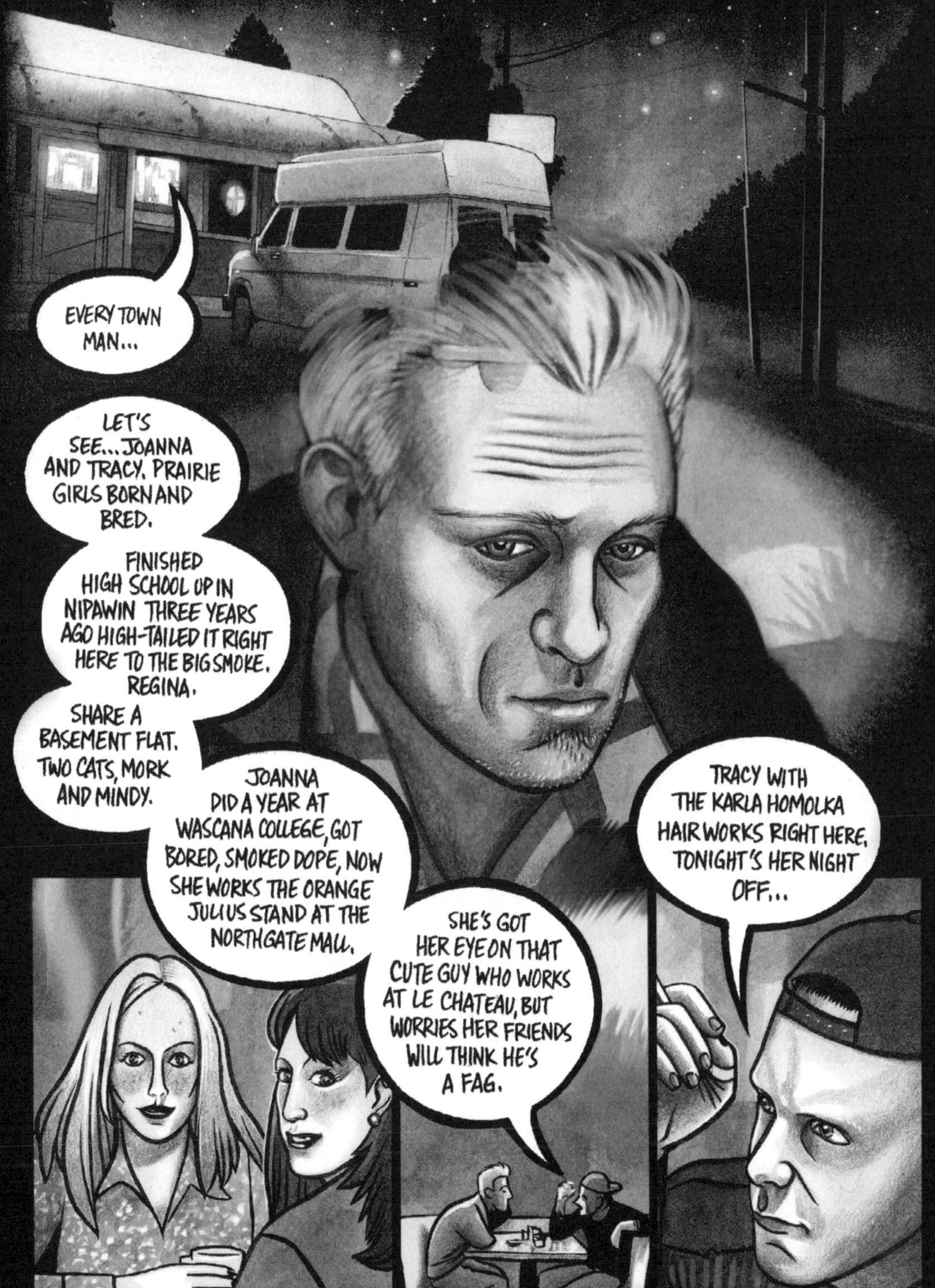
EVERY TOWN MAN...
LET'S SEE... JOANNA AND TRACY. PRAIRIE GIRLS BORN AND BRED.
FINISHED HIGH SCHOOL UP IN NIPAWIN THREE YEARS AGO HIGH-TAILED IT RIGHT HERE TO THE BIG SMOKE. REGINA.
SHARE A BASEMENT FLAT. TWO CATS, MORK AND MINDY.
JOANNA DID A YEAR AT WASCANA COLLEGE, GOT BORED, SMOKED DOPE, NOW SHE WORKS THE ORANGE JULIUS STAND AT THE NORTHGATE MALL.
SHE'S GOT HER EYE ON THAT CUTE GUY WHO WORKS AT LE CHATEAU, BUT WORRIES HER FRIENDS WILL THINK HE'S A FAG.
TRACY WITH THE KARLA HOMOLKA HAIR WORKS RIGHT HERE, TONIGHT'S HER NIGHT OFF...

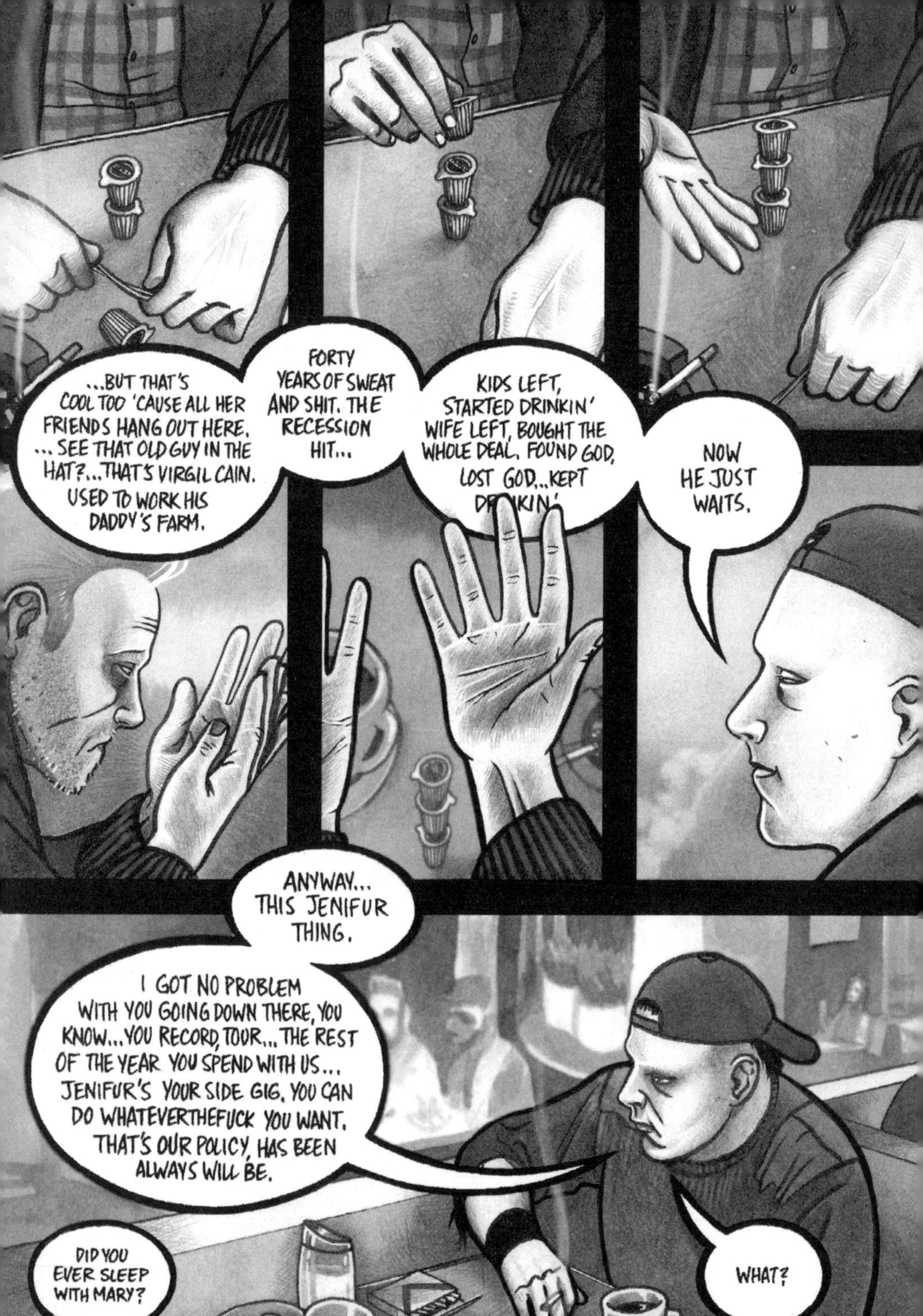
...BUT THAT'S COOL TOO 'CAUSE ALL HER FRIENDS HANG OUT HERE. ... SEE THAT OLD GUY IN THE HAT?...THAT'S VIRGIL CAIN. USED TO WORK HIS DADDY'S FARM.
FORTY YEARS OF SWEAT AND SHIT. THE RECESSION HIT...
KIDS LEFT, STARTED DRINKIN' WIFE LEFT, BOUGHT THE WHOLE DEAL, FOUND GOD, LOST GOD...KEPT DRINKIN'
NOW HE JUST WAITS.
ANYWAY... THIS JENIFUR THING.
I GOT NO PROBLEM WITH YOU GOING DOWN THERE, YOU KNOW...YOU RECORD, TOUR... THE REST OF THE YEAR YOU SPEND WITH US... JENIFUR'S YOUR SIDE GIG. YOU CAN DO WHATEVERTHEFUCK YOU WANT. THAT'S OUR POLICY, HAS BEEN ALWAYS WILL BE.
DID YOU EVER SLEEP WITH MARY?
WHAT?

DID YOU EVER SLEEP WITH MARY?
NO.
BUT I FUCKED HER IN THE BACK OF THE VAN ONCE.
SSBWWA
PFFFARRBPT!
um... ARE YOU GUYS IN A BAND?
YES WE ARE!
AND YOU ARE?...
'WORKING'.
NO.
YES.
NO.
NO.
YES.
YES.
NO.
YES.
NO.
YES.

{Pipe's Latest Brainchild}

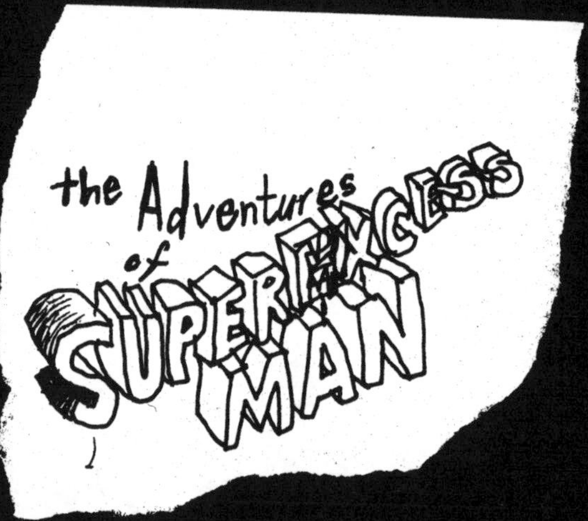
the Adventures of
SUPER EXCESS MAN

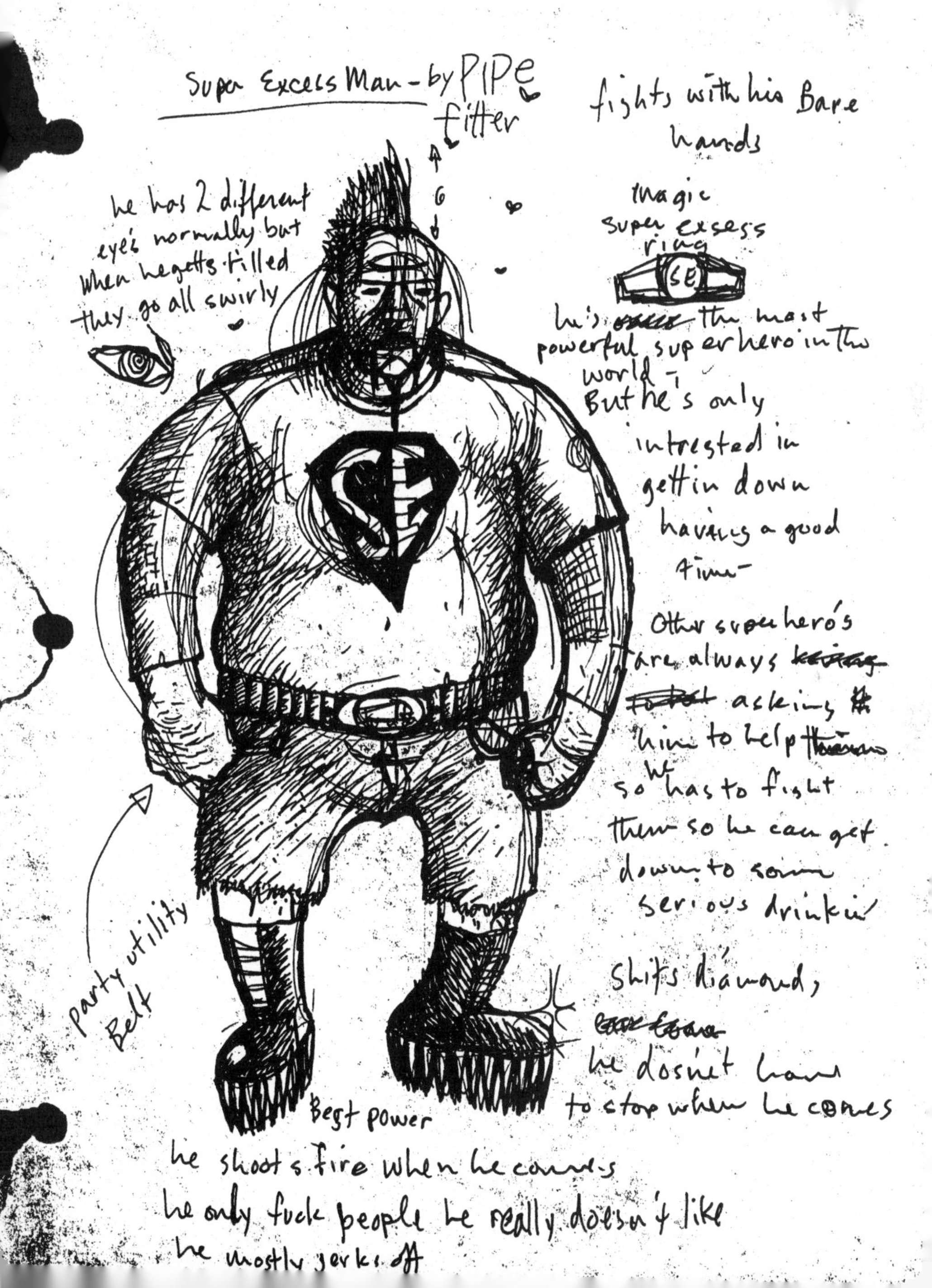
Super Excess Man - by PIPE fitter
fights with his Bare hands
he has 2 different eye's normally but when he getts filled they go all swirly
magic super exsess ring
SE
he's the most powerful superhero in the world - But he's only intrested in gettin down having a good time-
Other superhero's are always asking him to help so he has to fight them so he can get down to some serious drinkin'
Shits diamond,
he dosn't have to stop when he comes
party utility Belt
Best power
he shoots fire when he comes
he only fuck people he really doesn't like
he mostly jerks off

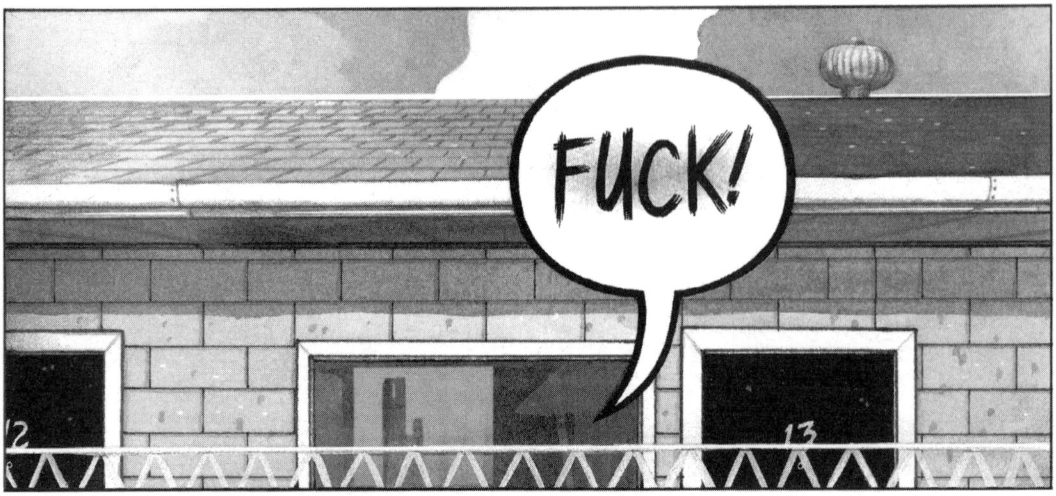
FUCK!
12
13

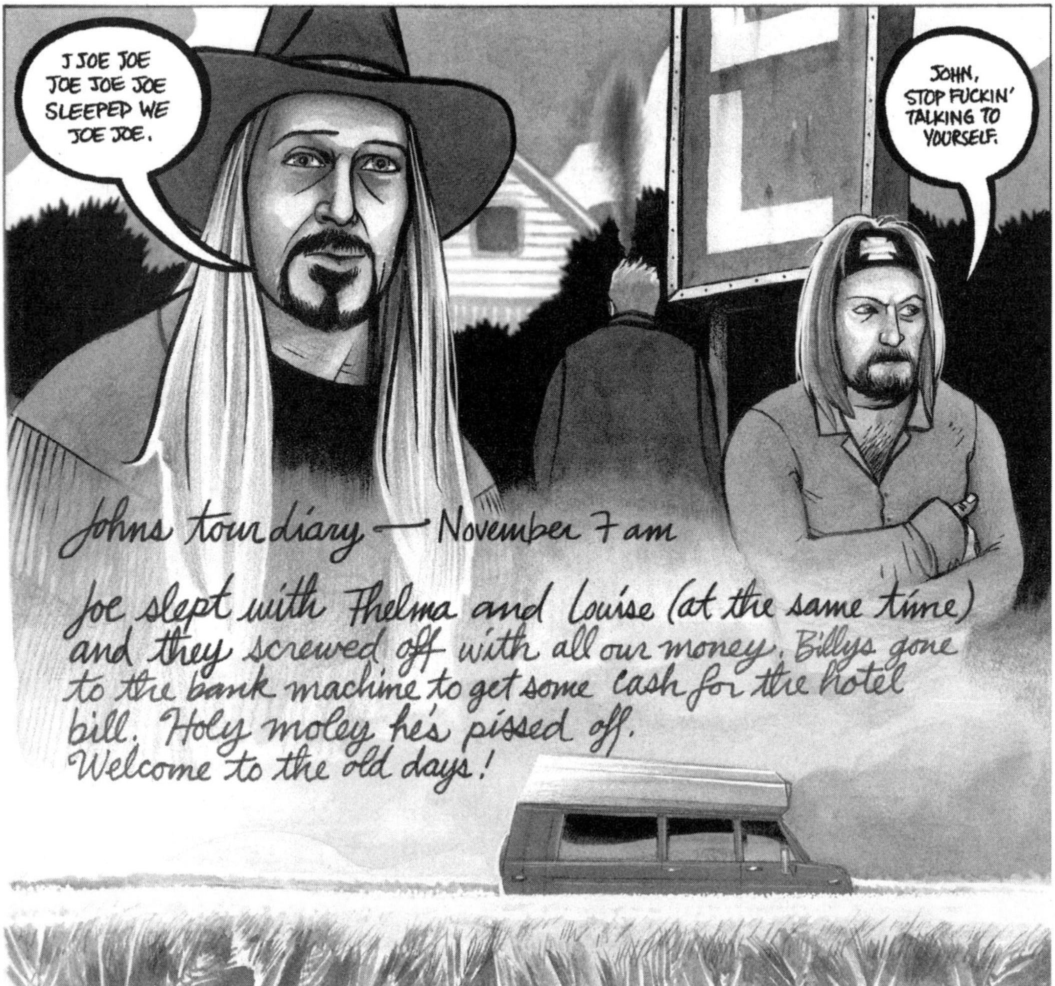
J JOE JOE JOE JOE JOE SLEEPED WE JOE JOE.
JOHN, STOP FUCKIN' TALKING TO YOURSELF.
Johns tour diary — November 7 am
Joe slept with Thelma and Louise (at the same time) and they screwed off with all our money. Billys gone to the bank machine to get some cash for the hotel bill. Holy moley he's pissed off.
Welcome to the old days!

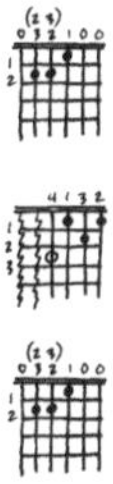

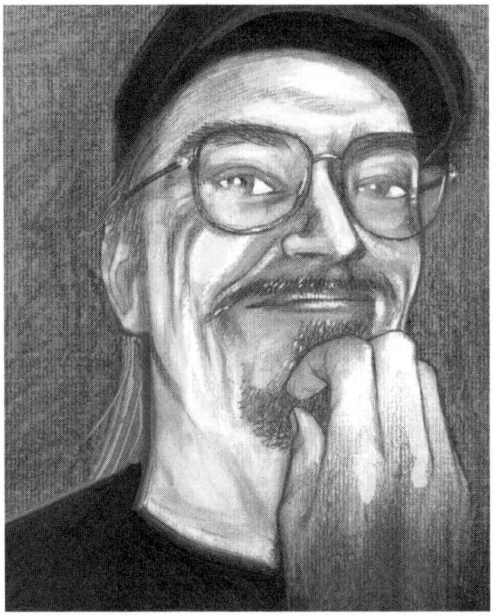

PAT MOONEY

DRUMMER, THE BATTERED WIVES;
SOUNDTECH, 1984-87 CANADIAN TOURS

"The Wives opened for them Stateside and they didn't even hit the stage . . . they did however manage to heckle us our entire set. But that was alright cause we were kind of buddies with them and I think there was like . . . two other people in the room anyways. They tore up the dressing room which was this tiny projection room and started slinging deli meat all over the club. So the cops show up at the tail end of our set and . . . fuck I think they had all done shrooms that night. All I remember is that I was sick as a dog.

"Two years later I was working at Lee's in Toronto, house tech, I get the call from management. They want me to tour with them as soundman on account of Joe likes my "fag haircut" and I was cheap in those days so, long story short . . . fuck were they loud.

"Billy Tallent? I'm amazed he can hear his own name for christsake."

SUZI CHICK

ARTIST/MERCH PERSON, 1984-85 TOURS

"Almost all the musicians I met back then were great. It was the business people in music who were completely fucked.

"I guess you could say I always had a bit of a crush on John. He was always so gentleman-like. He was a gentle lion on the outside but on the inside he was really quite frightened and angry, quite sad I think. He was a man in a constant state of repair. Yeah I always liked him but . . . there was a line there that we never crossed.

"Joe and Billy on the other hand were complete fucking children. In a different life they'd be fucking each other, oh definitely. But in Hard Core Logo they'd lube up the audience. They were like a couple of lions having it out with each other, you know, to see who gets to like, stick the audience with their meaningful lyrics. A real boys' club. Fuck yeah."

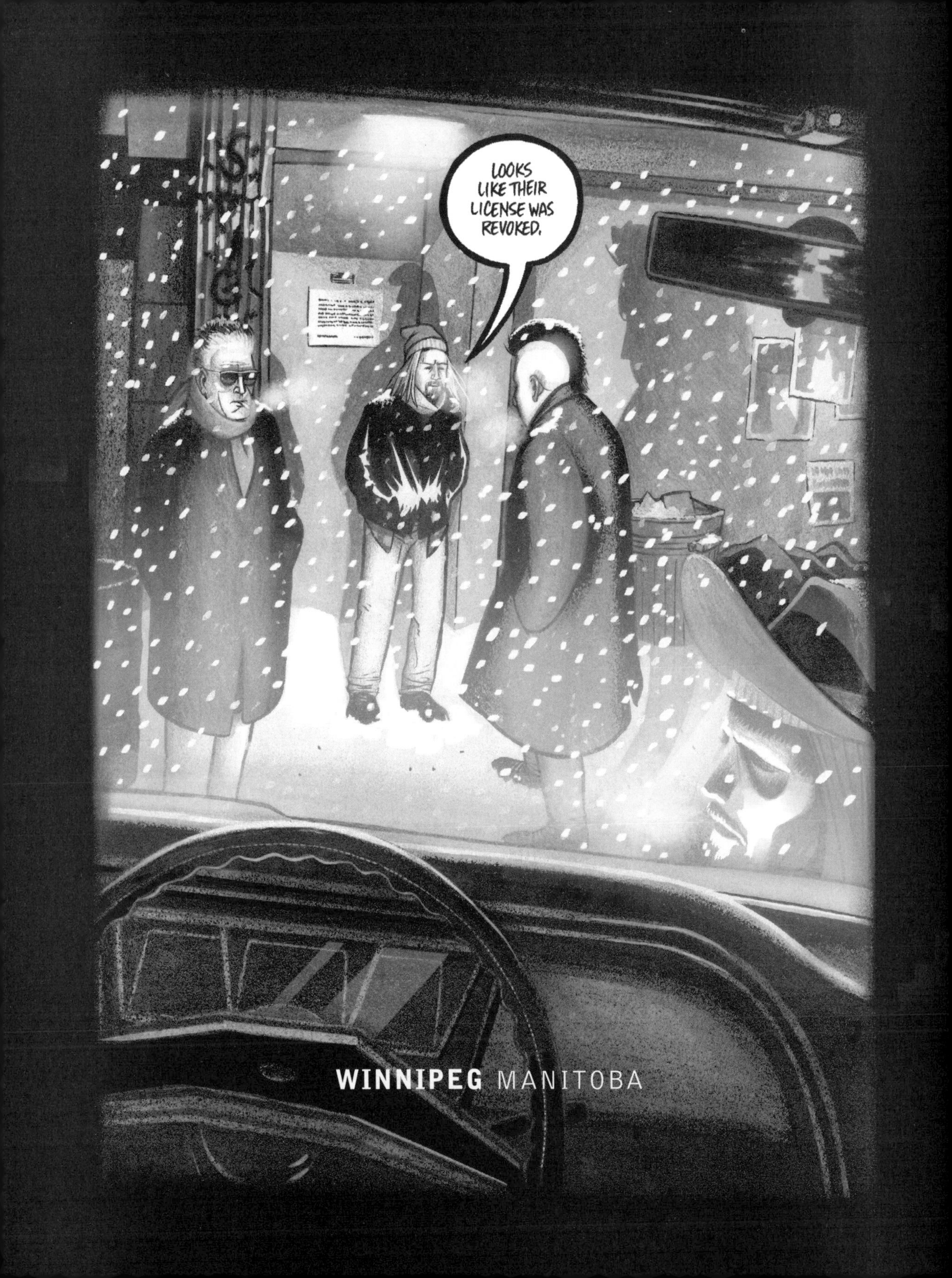

WINNIPEG MANITOBA

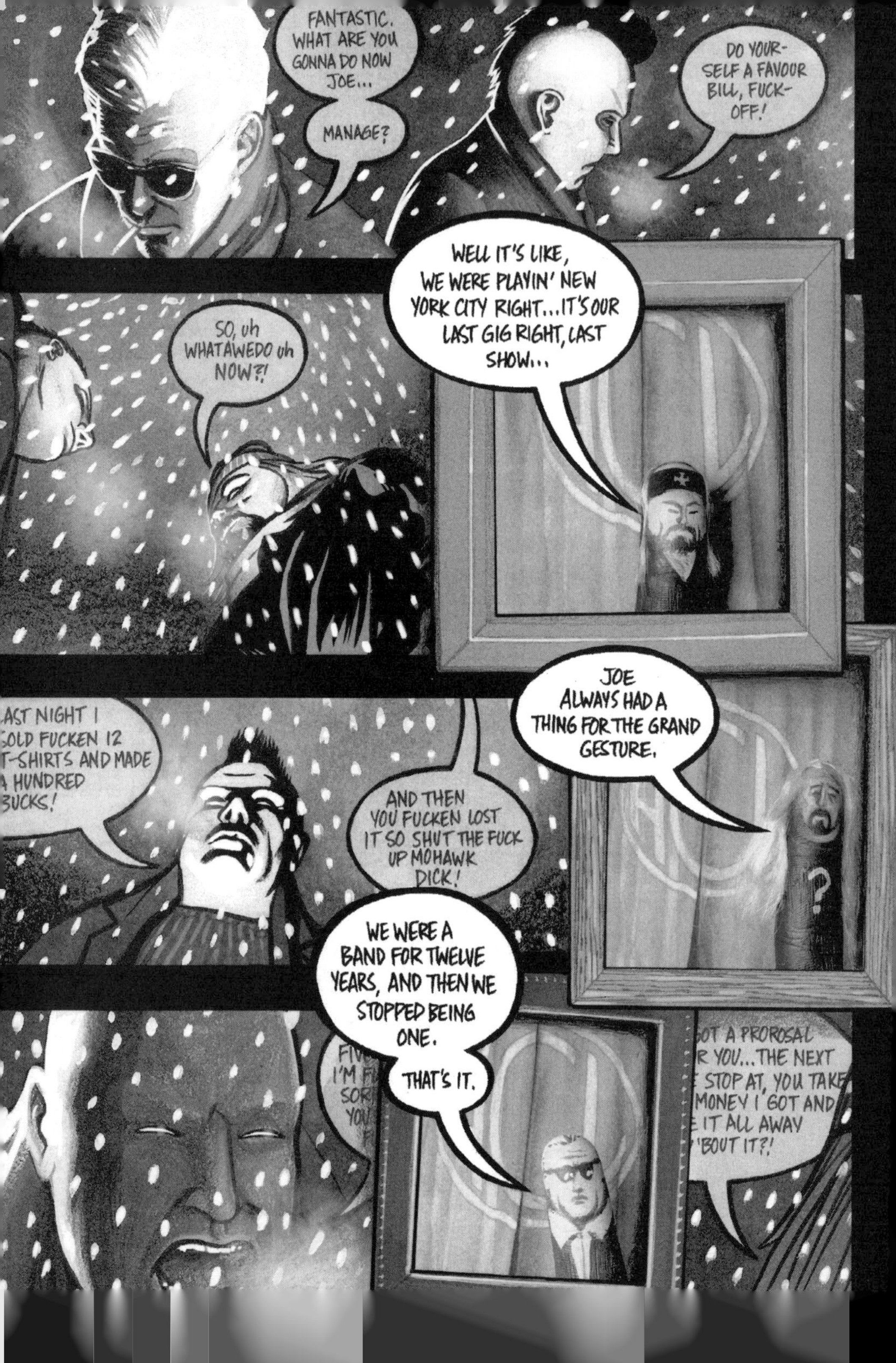
FANTASTIC. WHAT ARE YOU GONNA DO NOW JOE...
MANAGE?
DO YOURSELF A FAVOUR BILL, FUCK-OFF!
WELL IT'S LIKE, WE WERE PLAYIN' NEW YORK CITY RIGHT...IT'S OUR LAST GIG RIGHT, LAST SHOW...
SO, uh WHATAWEDO uh NOW?!
JOE ALWAYS HAD A THING FOR THE GRAND GESTURE.
AST NIGHT I SOLD FUCKEN 12 T-SHIRTS AND MADE HUNDRED BUCKS!
AND THEN YOU FUCKEN LOST IT SO SHUT THE FUCK UP MOHAWK DICK!
WE WERE A BAND FOR TWELVE YEARS, AND THEN WE STOPPED BEING ONE.
THAT'S IT.
GOT A PROROSAL R YOU...THE NEXT STOP AT, YOU TAKE MONEY I GOT AND IT ALL AWAY 'BOUT IT?!

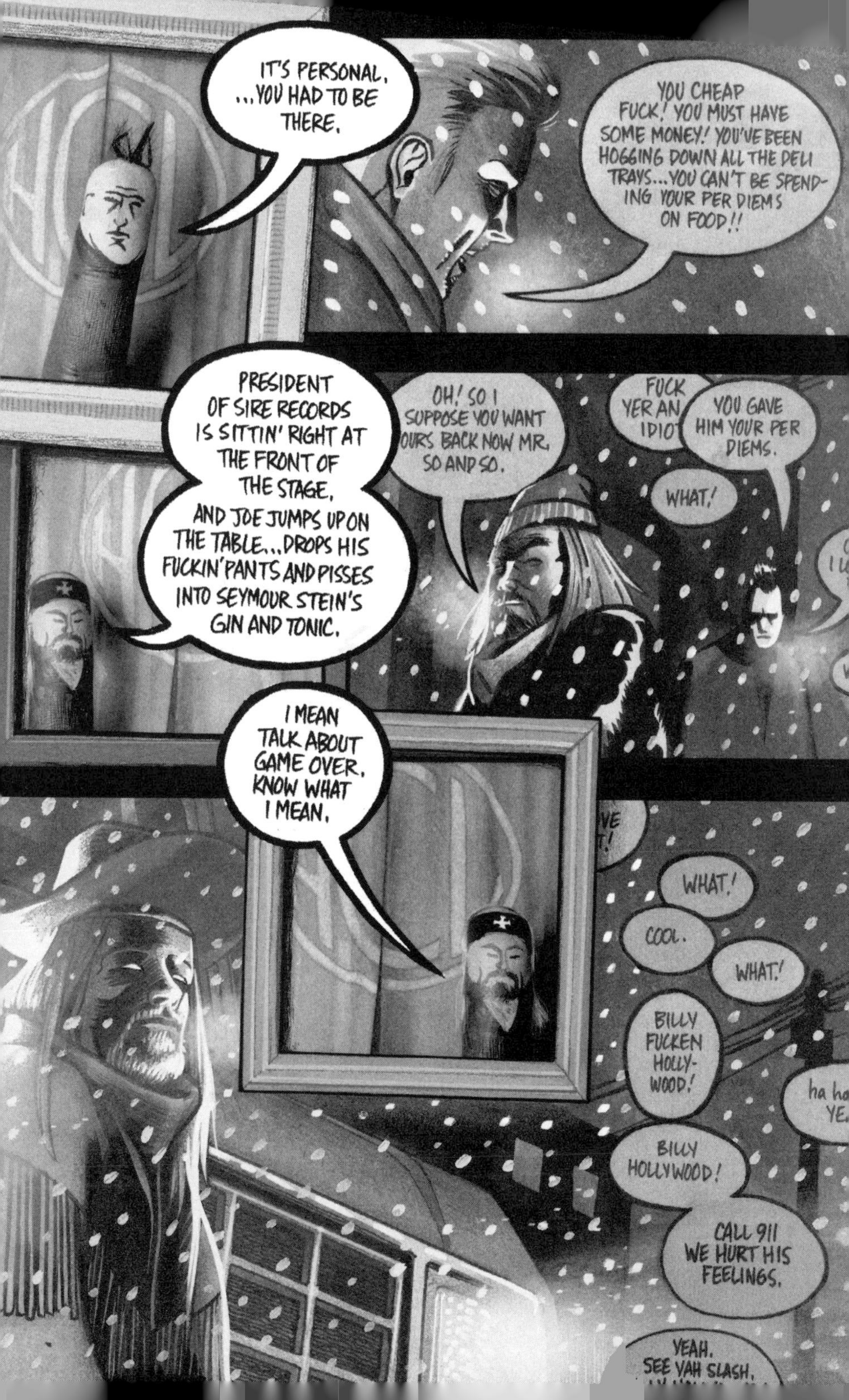
IT'S PERSONAL, ...YOU HAD TO BE THERE.
YOU CHEAP FUCK! YOU MUST HAVE SOME MONEY! YOU'VE BEEN HOGGING DOWN ALL THE DELI TRAYS...YOU CAN'T BE SPENDING YOUR PER DIEMS ON FOOD!!
PRESIDENT OF SIRE RECORDS IS SITTIN' RIGHT AT THE FRONT OF THE STAGE,
AND JOE JUMPS UP ON THE TABLE...DROPS HIS FUCKIN' PANTS AND PISSES INTO SEYMOUR STEIN'S GIN AND TONIC.
OH! SO I SUPPOSE YOU WANT OURS BACK NOW MR. SO AND SO.
FUCK YER AN IDIOT
YOU GAVE HIM YOUR PER DIEMS.
WHAT!
I MEAN TALK ABOUT GAME OVER. KNOW WHAT I MEAN.
WHAT!
COOL.
WHAT!
BILLY FUCKEN HOLLY-WOOD!
BILLY HOLLYWOOD!
CALL 911 WE HURT HIS FEELINGS.
YEAH. SEE YAH SLASH.

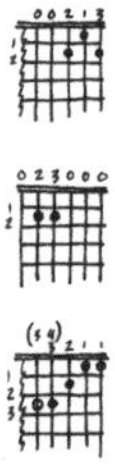

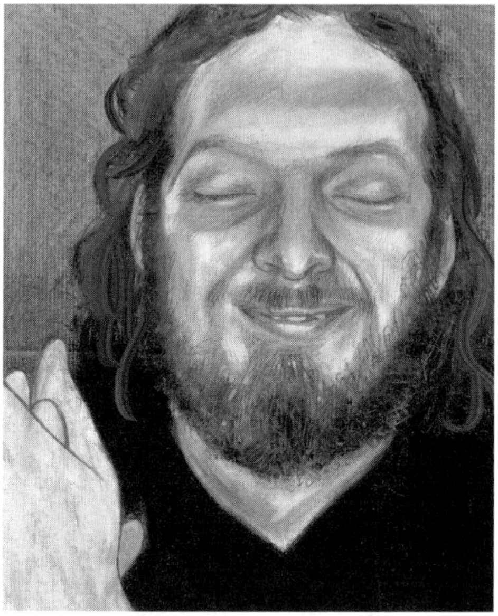

JEFF BIRD

DRIVER, 1984-89 NORTH AMERICAN TOURS

"I've never heard of that band in my entire life."

SSSOMETIMES YYOU LOOK IN THE MIRROR, AAND YOU WONDER WHAT IT WOULD BE LIKE IF I WERE HONEST EVERY MOMENT FFFOR THE REST OF MY LIFE.
SAVE IT FOR YOUR GROUP SESSIONS JOHN.
NNNO. JOE... LLET'S BE HONEST. YOU'D BE NOWHERE WITHOUT BBBILLY.
DO ME A FAVOUR, SHUT-UP!
AAAND BILLY, IIF YOU WERE HONEST WITH YOURSELF YYYYOU'D ADMIT THAT THE JENIFUR GIG'S BEEN CANCELLED. AAAND AND PPIPE?...
JOHNSHUTHEFUCKUP!
WHAT'S THIS ABOUT JENIFUR BILL?

THIS IS JUST AAA LAST TANGO BEFORE AAA LLIFE SPENT AS A GARBAGE MAN.
BILL?
OH! YOU KNOW WHAT YOU ARE?!
YER A SCHIZO MAN ON A FUCKEN HOLIDAY FROM LITHIUM!!
YOU BELONG IN A FUCKEN STRAIGHT JACKET!
WHAT'S THIS ABOUT JENIFUR BILL?
SKAA
REE
EEE
CHH
HOLY FAA
EEEECH
SSSSSSS

SAFUCKINMOOSE!
OK!
LET'S GET A FEW THINGS OUT IN THE OPEN.
PIPE.
THE HOTEL GUY IN REGINA CALLED...YOU SHIT ON THE FUCKEN PILLOW,
WIPE YER ASS WITH THE FUCKEN BEDSPREAD!
NOW WHAT'S THAT? I DON'T GET THAT.
THERE WASN'T ANY TOILET PAPER
NO WHAT'S THAT? THAT'S NOT COOL.

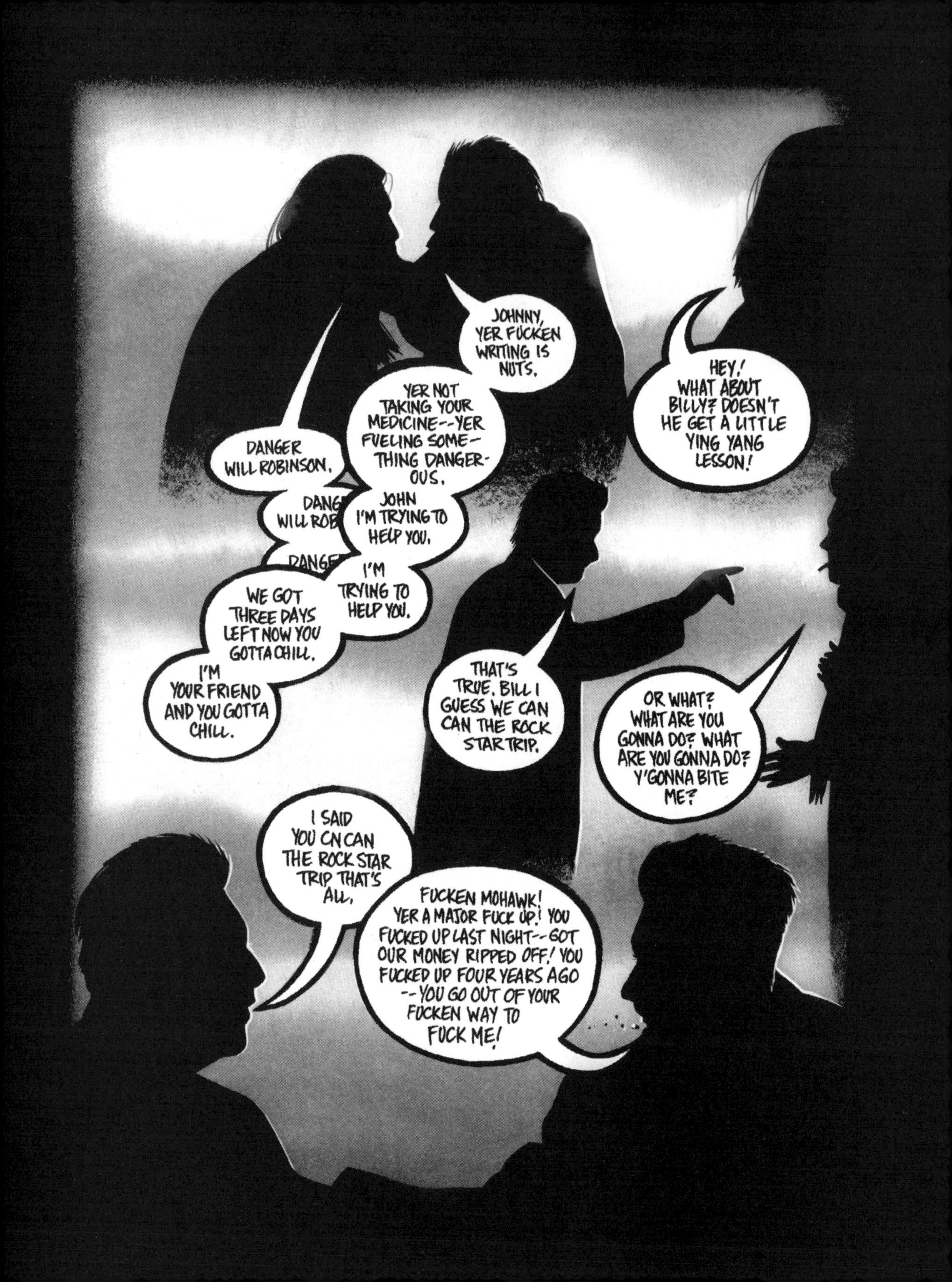
JOHNNY, YER FUCKEN WRITING IS NUTS.
YER NOT TAKING YOUR MEDICINE--YER FUELING SOME-THING DANGER-OUS.
DANGER WILL ROBINSON.
JOHN I'M TRYING TO HELP YOU.
I'M TRYING TO HELP YOU.
WE GOT THREE DAYS LEFT NOW YOU GOTTA CHILL.
I'M YOUR FRIEND AND YOU GOTTA CHILL.
HEY! WHAT ABOUT BILLY? DOESN'T HE GET A LITTLE YING YANG LESSON!
THAT'S TRUE. BILL I GUESS WE CAN CAN THE ROCK STAR TRIP.
OR WHAT? WHAT ARE YOU GONNA DO? WHAT ARE YOU GONNA DO? Y'GONNA BITE ME?
I SAID YOU CN CAN THE ROCK STAR TRIP THAT'S ALL.
FUCKEN MOHAWK! YER A MAJOR FUCK UP! YOU FUCKED UP LAST NIGHT--GOT OUR MONEY RIPPED OFF! YOU FUCKED UP FOUR YEARS AGO--YOU GO OUT OF YOUR FUCKEN WAY TO FUCK ME!

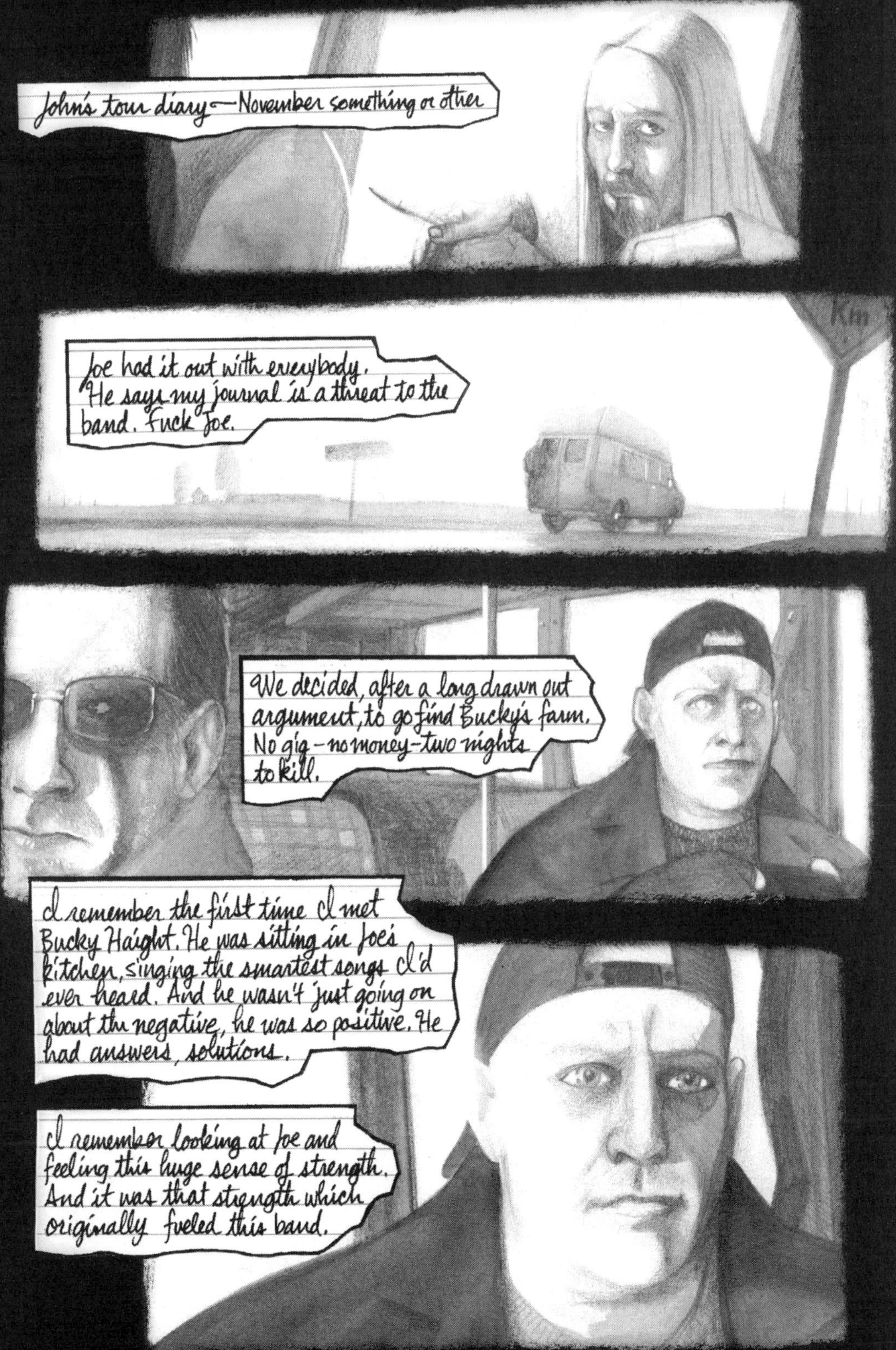
John's tour diary—November something or other
Joe had it out with everybody. He says my journal is a threat to the band. Fuck Joe.
Km
We decided, after a long drawn out argument, to go find Bucky's farm. No gig—no money—two nights to kill.
I remember the first time I met Bucky Haight. He was sitting in Joe's kitchen, singing the smartest songs I'd ever heard. And he wasn't just going on about the negative, he was so positive. He had answers, solutions.
I remember looking at Joe and feeling this huge sense of strength. And it was that strength which originally fueled this band.

ROBERT

PIPEFITTER'S SUB-IN DRUMMER
FROM NORTH VANCOUVER

*"I went to high school with some of
these guys. And when we were in high school
Bucky Haight was the shit. Fucking genius.*

*"We used to take Jay Sweeney's old
man's Buick and go down to New York City
to see Bucky Haight. This is when he was still
playing with Nazis in the Whitehouse. I was
the only one with ID but somehow we used to
weasel our way into the gigs.*

*"Bucky Haight. Yeah Joe just idolized
him. We all did. We never drank. We'd just sit
at the table and take it all in."*

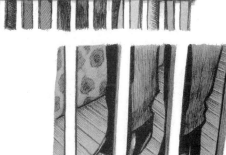

YOU COMIN' IN OR WHAT?

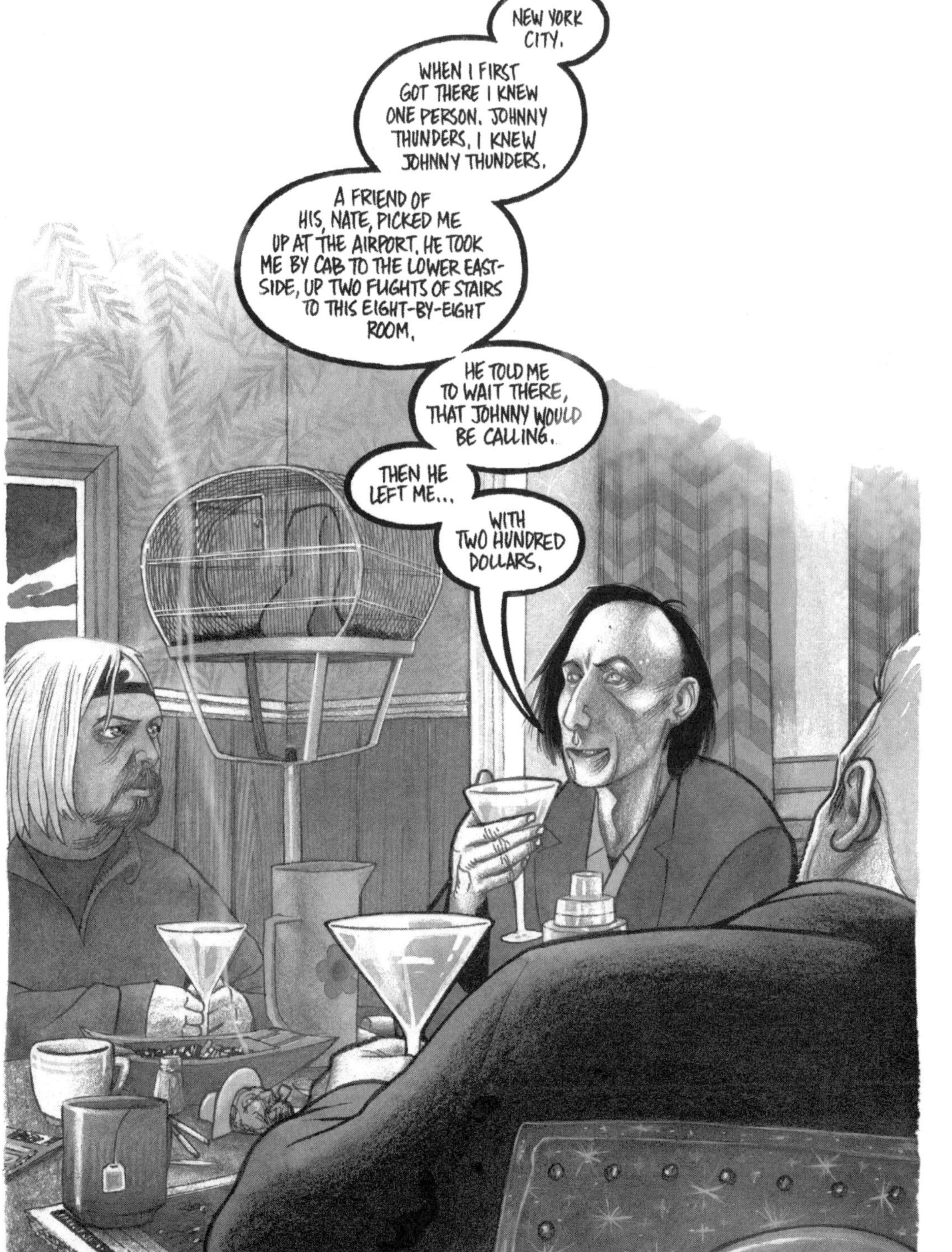
NEW YORK CITY.
WHEN I FIRST GOT THERE I KNEW ONE PERSON. JOHNNY THUNDERS. I KNEW JOHNNY THUNDERS.
A FRIEND OF HIS, NATE, PICKED ME UP AT THE AIRPORT. HE TOOK ME BY CAB TO THE LOWER EAST-SIDE, UP TWO FLIGHTS OF STAIRS TO THIS EIGHT-BY-EIGHT ROOM.
HE TOLD ME TO WAIT THERE, THAT JOHNNY WOULD BE CALLING.
THEN HE LEFT ME...
WITH TWO HUNDRED DOLLARS.

TRUE PUNK TALES, Vol. 37, No. 239, January 1978, published monthly by GOLDEN KEY INC., 18 Gloucester Lane, New York, N.Y. 10018. Second Class postage paid at New York, N.Y., and additional mailing offices. Copyright © 1977, Golden Key Comics Inc. All Rights Reserved. The stories, characters, and incidents mentioned in this magazine are entirely fictional. Any resemblance to actual persons, living or dead, or actual events is purely coincidental. Printed in U.S.A.

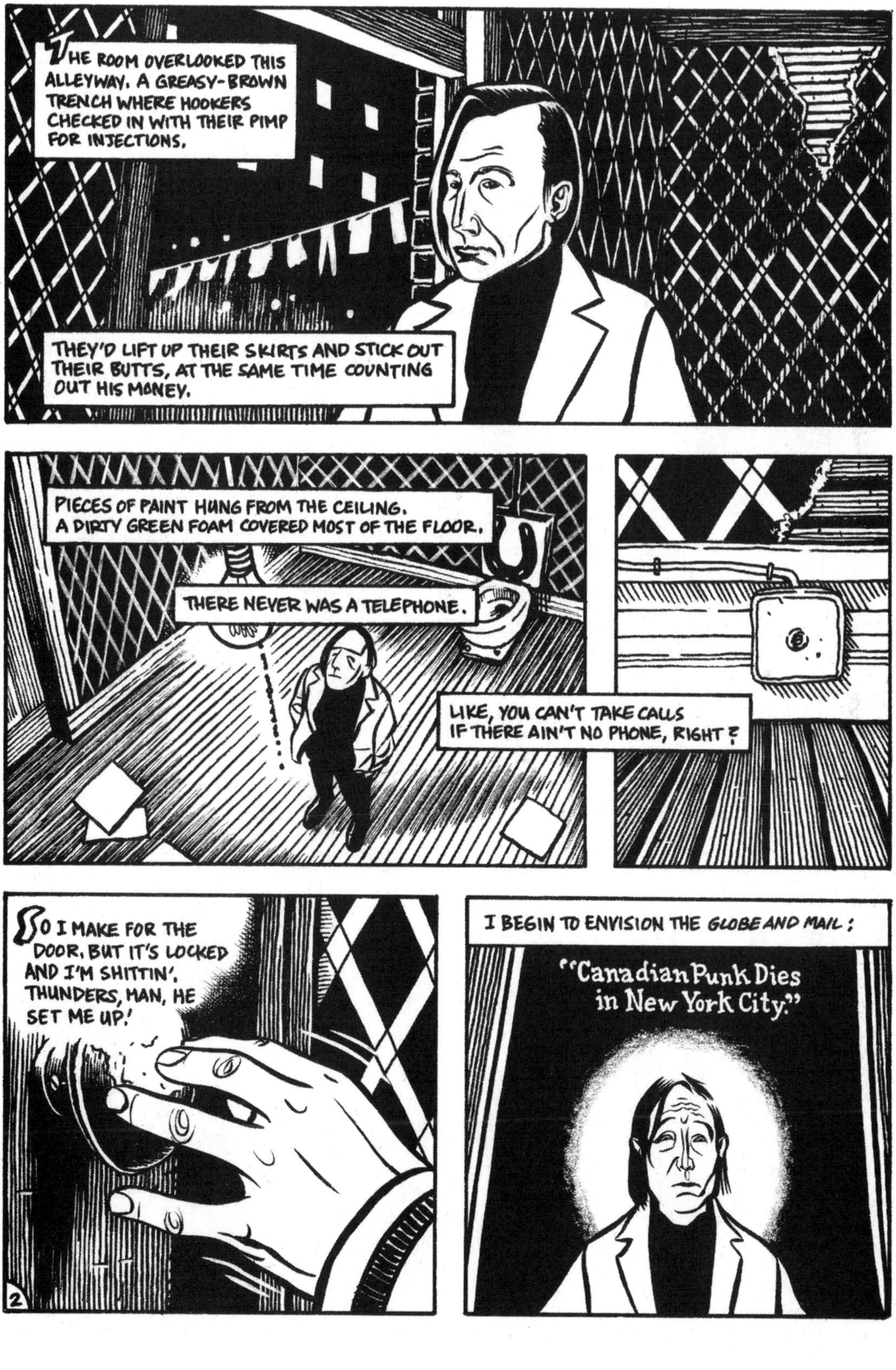
THE ROOM OVERLOOKED THIS ALLEYWAY. A GREASY-BROWN TRENCH WHERE HOOKERS CHECKED IN WITH THEIR PIMP FOR INJECTIONS.
THEY'D LIFT UP THEIR SKIRTS AND STICK OUT THEIR BUTTS, AT THE SAME TIME COUNTING OUT HIS MONEY.
PIECES OF PAINT HUNG FROM THE CEILING. A DIRTY GREEN FOAM COVERED MOST OF THE FLOOR.
THERE NEVER WAS A TELEPHONE.
LIKE, YOU CAN'T TAKE CALLS IF THERE AIN'T NO PHONE, RIGHT?
SO I MAKE FOR THE DOOR, BUT IT'S LOCKED AND I'M SHITTIN'. THUNDERS, MAN, HE SET ME UP!
I BEGIN TO ENVISION THE GLOBE AND MAIL:
"Canadian Punk Dies in New York City."

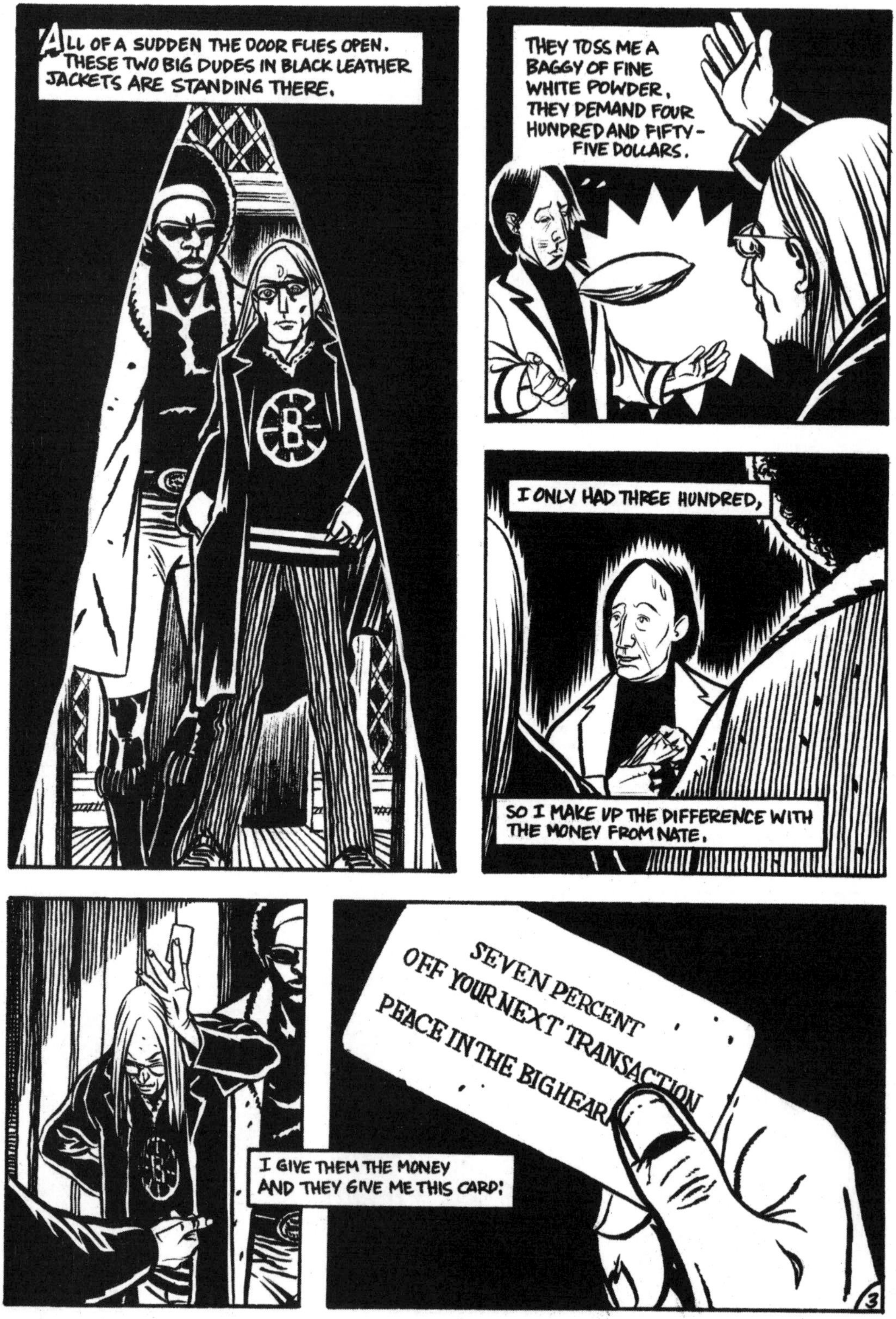
ALL OF A SUDDEN THE DOOR FLIES OPEN. THESE TWO BIG DUDES IN BLACK LEATHER JACKETS ARE STANDING THERE.
THEY TOSS ME A BAGGY OF FINE WHITE POWDER, THEY DEMAND FOUR HUNDRED AND FIFTY-FIVE DOLLARS.
I ONLY HAD THREE HUNDRED,
SO I MAKE UP THE DIFFERENCE WITH THE MONEY FROM NATE.
I GIVE THEM THE MONEY AND THEY GIVE ME THIS CARD:
SEVEN PERCENT
OFF YOUR NEXT TRANSACTION
PEACE IN THE BIG HEAR
3

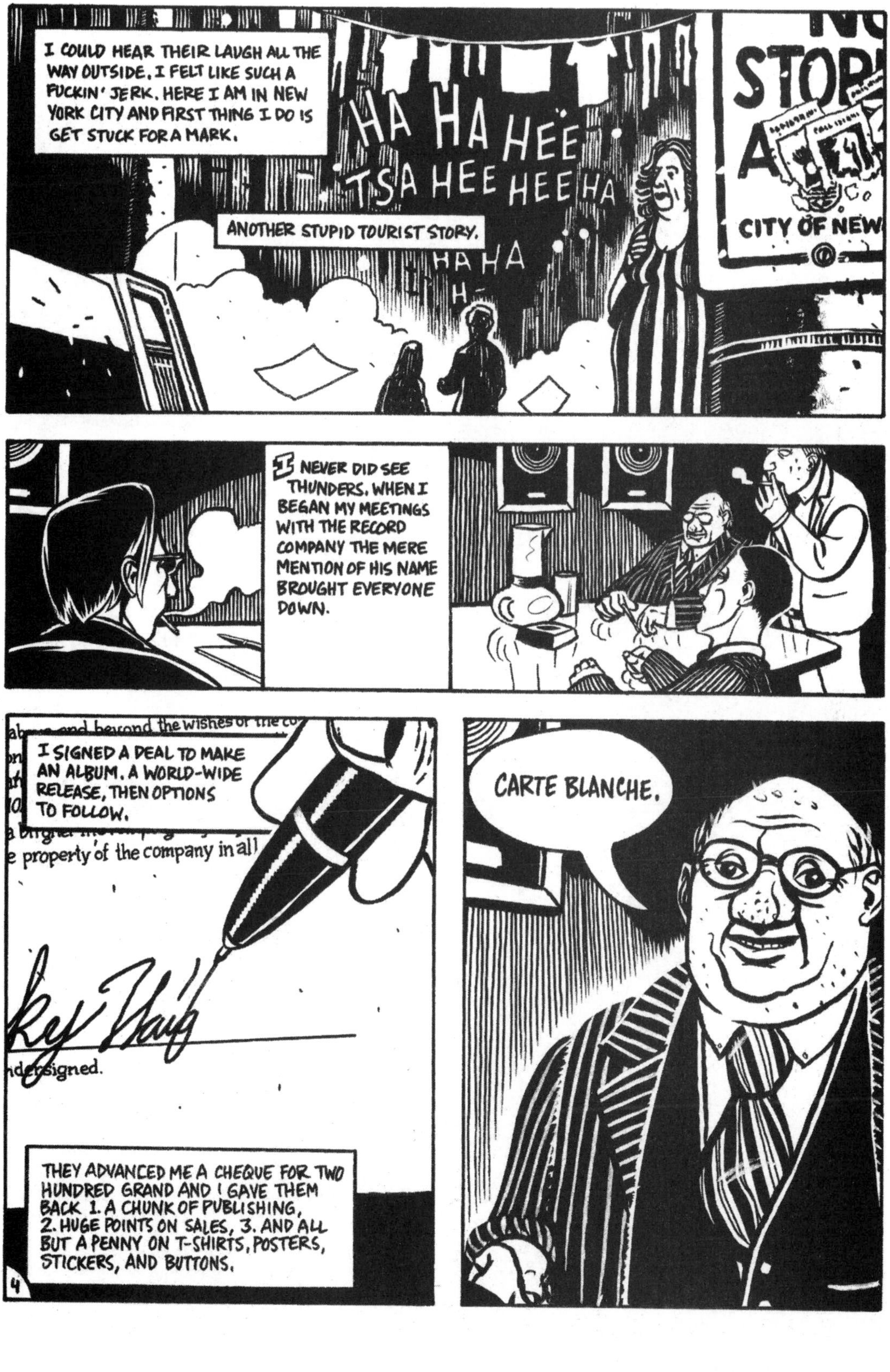

I COULD HEAR THEIR LAUGH ALL THE WAY OUTSIDE. I FELT LIKE SUCH A FUCKIN' JERK. HERE I AM IN NEW YORK CITY AND FIRST THING I DO IS GET STUCK FOR A MARK.
HA HA HEE
TSA HEE HEE HA
ANOTHER STUPID TOURIST STORY.
HA HA
H-
STOP
CITY OF NEW
I NEVER DID SEE THUNDERS. WHEN I BEGAN MY MEETINGS WITH THE RECORD COMPANY THE MERE MENTION OF HIS NAME BROUGHT EVERYONE DOWN.
above and beyond the wishes of the co
I SIGNED A DEAL TO MAKE AN ALBUM. A WORLD-WIDE RELEASE, THEN OPTIONS TO FOLLOW.
property of the company in all
undersigned.
THEY ADVANCED ME A CHEQUE FOR TWO HUNDRED GRAND AND I GAVE THEM BACK 1. A CHUNK OF PUBLISHING, 2. HUGE POINTS ON SALES, 3. AND ALL BUT A PENNY ON T-SHIRTS, POSTERS, STICKERS, AND BUTTONS.
CARTE BLANCHE.

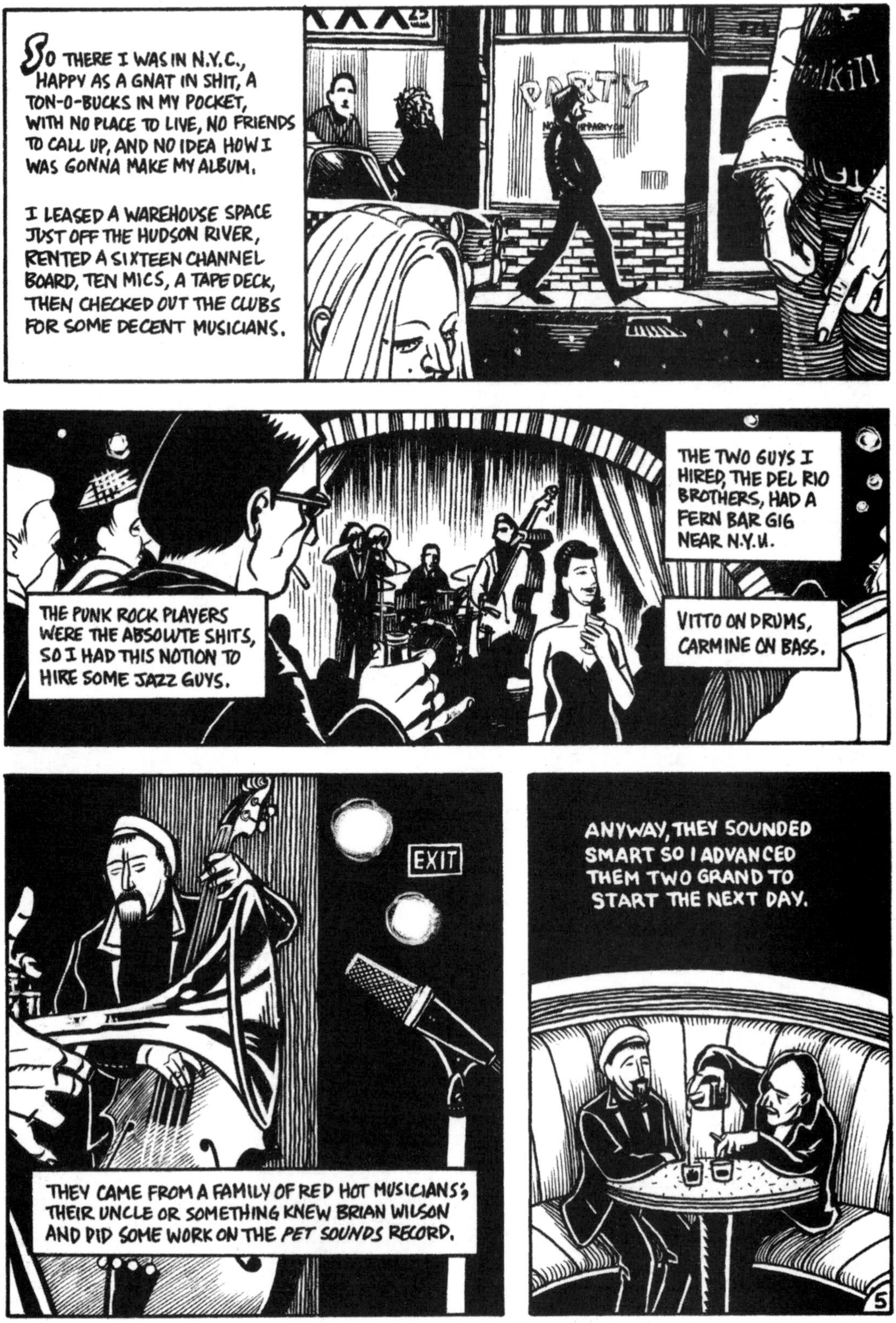
SO THERE I WAS IN N.Y.C., HAPPY AS A GNAT IN SHIT, A TON-O-BUCKS IN MY POCKET, WITH NO PLACE TO LIVE, NO FRIENDS TO CALL UP, AND NO IDEA HOW I WAS GONNA MAKE MY ALBUM.
I LEASED A WAREHOUSE SPACE JUST OFF THE HUDSON RIVER, RENTED A SIXTEEN CHANNEL BOARD, TEN MICS, A TAPE DECK, THEN CHECKED OUT THE CLUBS FOR SOME DECENT MUSICIANS.
PARTY
THE PUNK ROCK PLAYERS WERE THE ABSOLUTE SHITS, SO I HAD THIS NOTION TO HIRE SOME JAZZ GUYS.
THE TWO GUYS I HIRED, THE DEL RIO BROTHERS, HAD A FERN BAR GIG NEAR N.Y.U.
VITTO ON DRUMS, CARMINE ON BASS.
EXIT
THEY CAME FROM A FAMILY OF RED HOT MUSICIANS; THEIR UNCLE OR SOMETHING KNEW BRIAN WILSON AND DID SOME WORK ON THE *PET SOUNDS* RECORD.
ANYWAY, THEY SOUNDED SMART SO I ADVANCED THEM TWO GRAND TO START THE NEXT DAY.

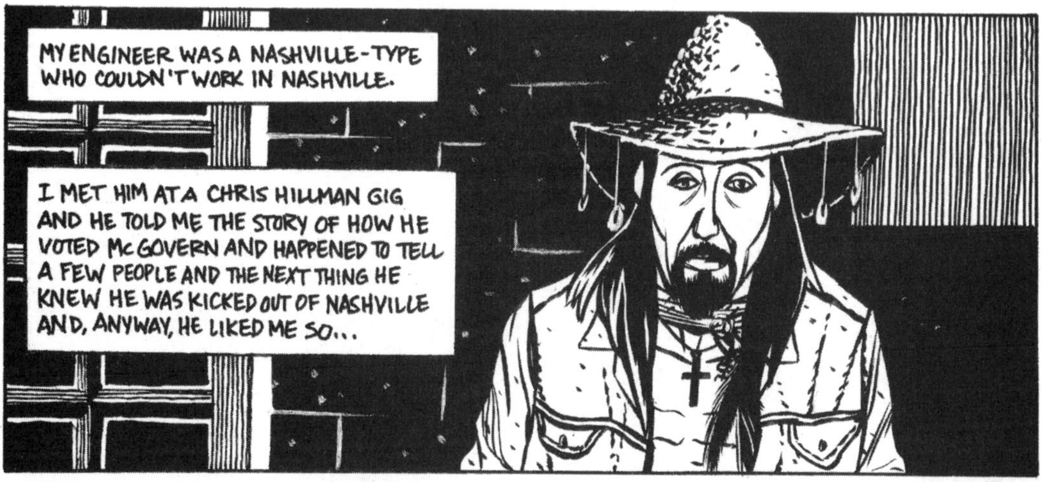
MY ENGINEER WAS A NASHVILLE-TYPE WHO COULDN'T WORK IN NASHVILLE.
I MET HIM AT A CHRIS HILLMAN GIG AND HE TOLD ME THE STORY OF HOW HE VOTED McGOVERN AND HAPPENED TO TELL A FEW PEOPLE AND THE NEXT THING HE KNEW HE WAS KICKED OUT OF NASHVILLE AND, ANYWAY, HE LIKED ME SO...

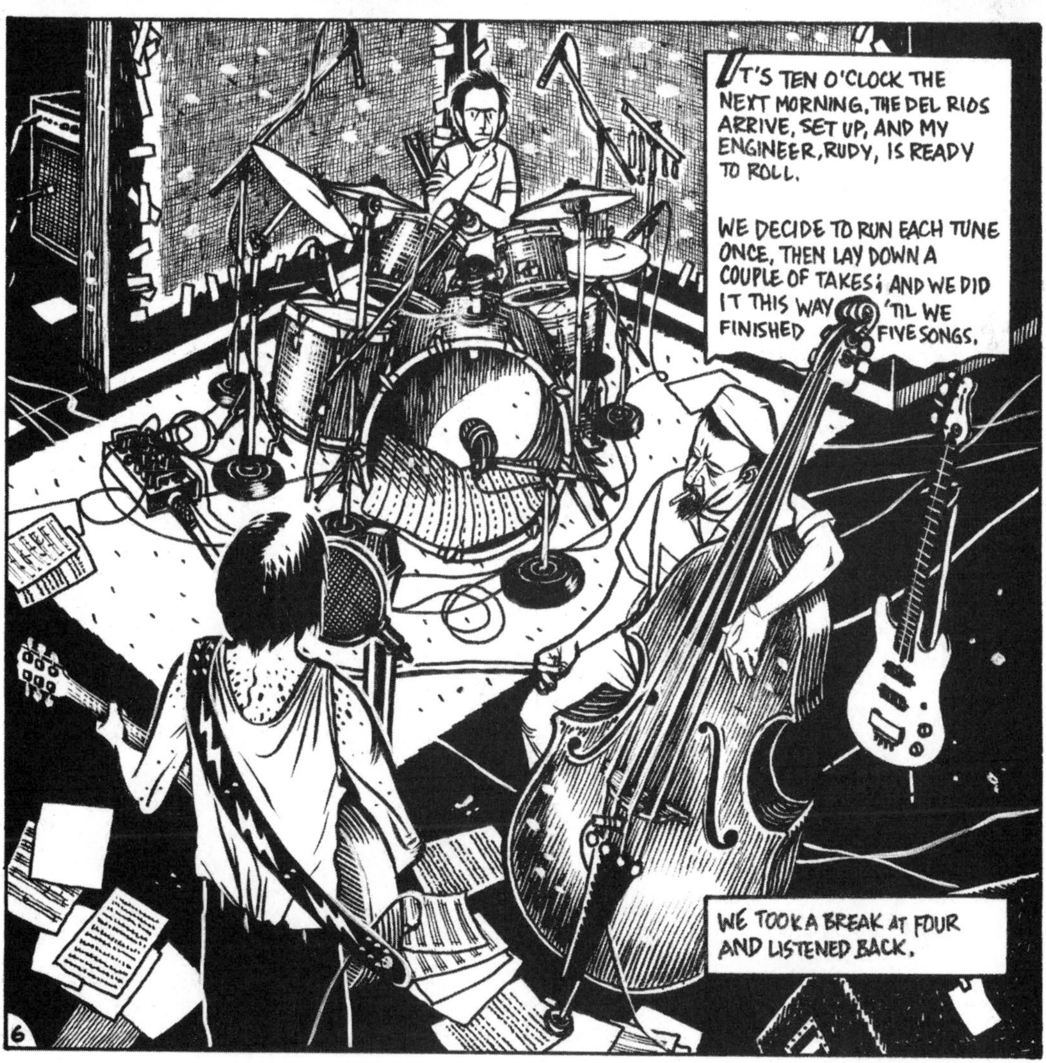
IT'S TEN O'CLOCK THE NEXT MORNING. THE DEL RIOS ARRIVE, SET UP, AND MY ENGINEER, RUDY, IS READY TO ROLL.
WE DECIDE TO RUN EACH TUNE ONCE, THEN LAY DOWN A COUPLE OF TAKES; AND WE DID IT THIS WAY 'TIL WE FINISHED FIVE SONGS.
WE TOOK A BREAK AT FOUR AND LISTENED BACK.

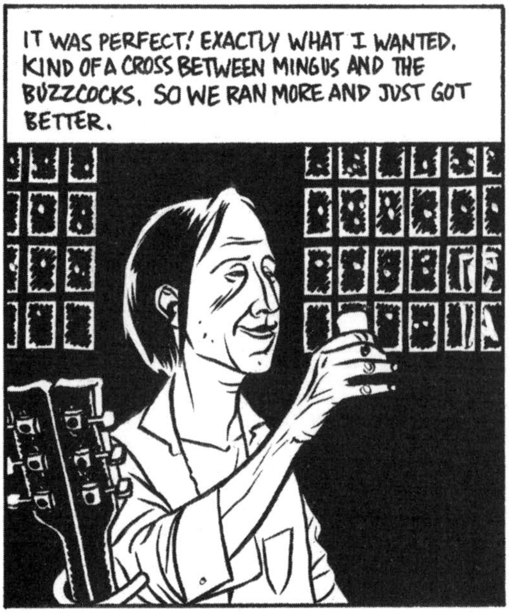
IT WAS PERFECT! EXACTLY WHAT I WANTED. KIND OF A CROSS BETWEEN MINGUS AND THE BUZZCOCKS. SO WE RAN MORE AND JUST GOT BETTER.

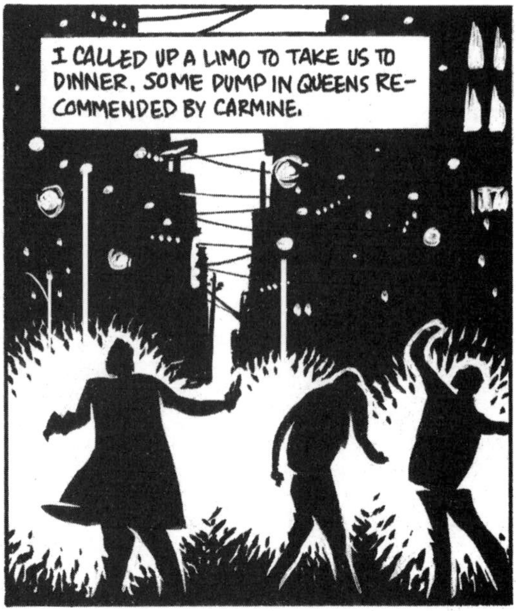
I CALLED UP A LIMO TO TAKE US TO DINNER. SOME DUMP IN QUEENS RE-COMMENDED BY CARMINE.

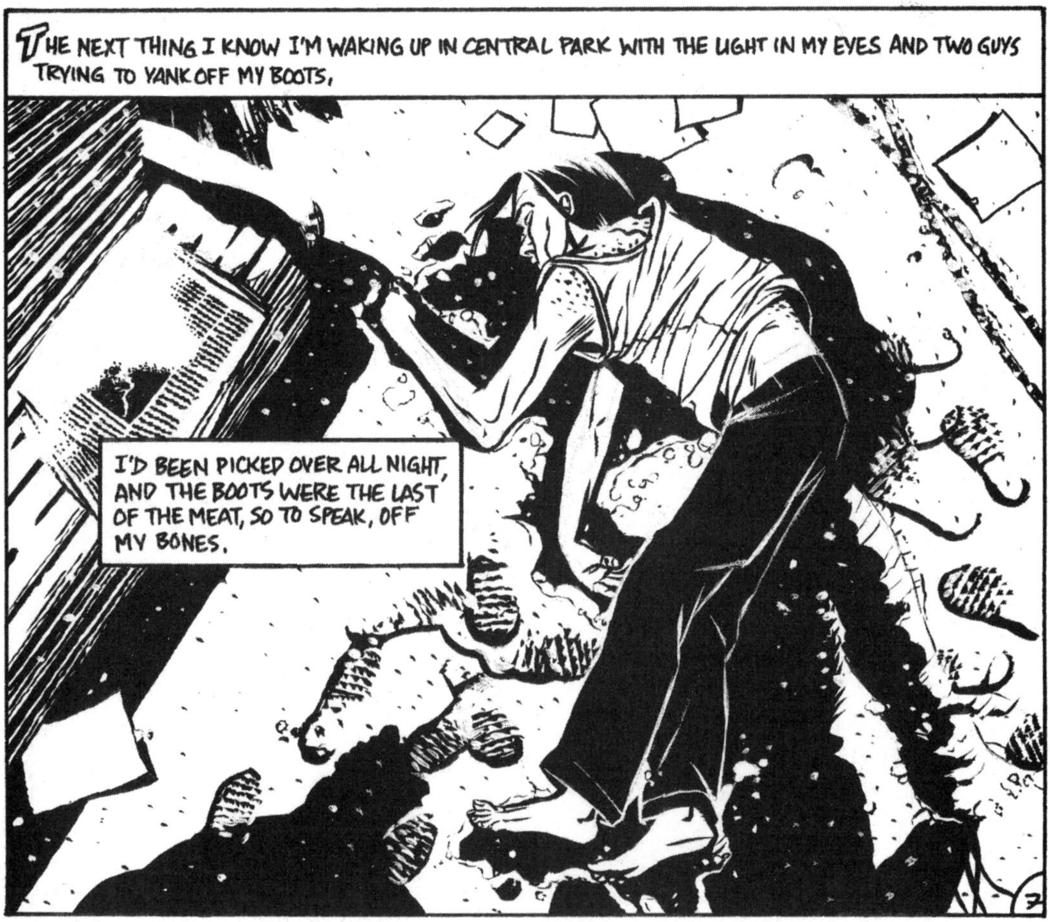
THE NEXT THING I KNOW I'M WAKING UP IN CENTRAL PARK WITH THE LIGHT IN MY EYES AND TWO GUYS TRYING TO YANK OFF MY BOOTS.
I'D BEEN PICKED OVER ALL NIGHT, AND THE BOOTS WERE THE LAST OF THE MEAT, SO TO SPEAK, OFF MY BONES.

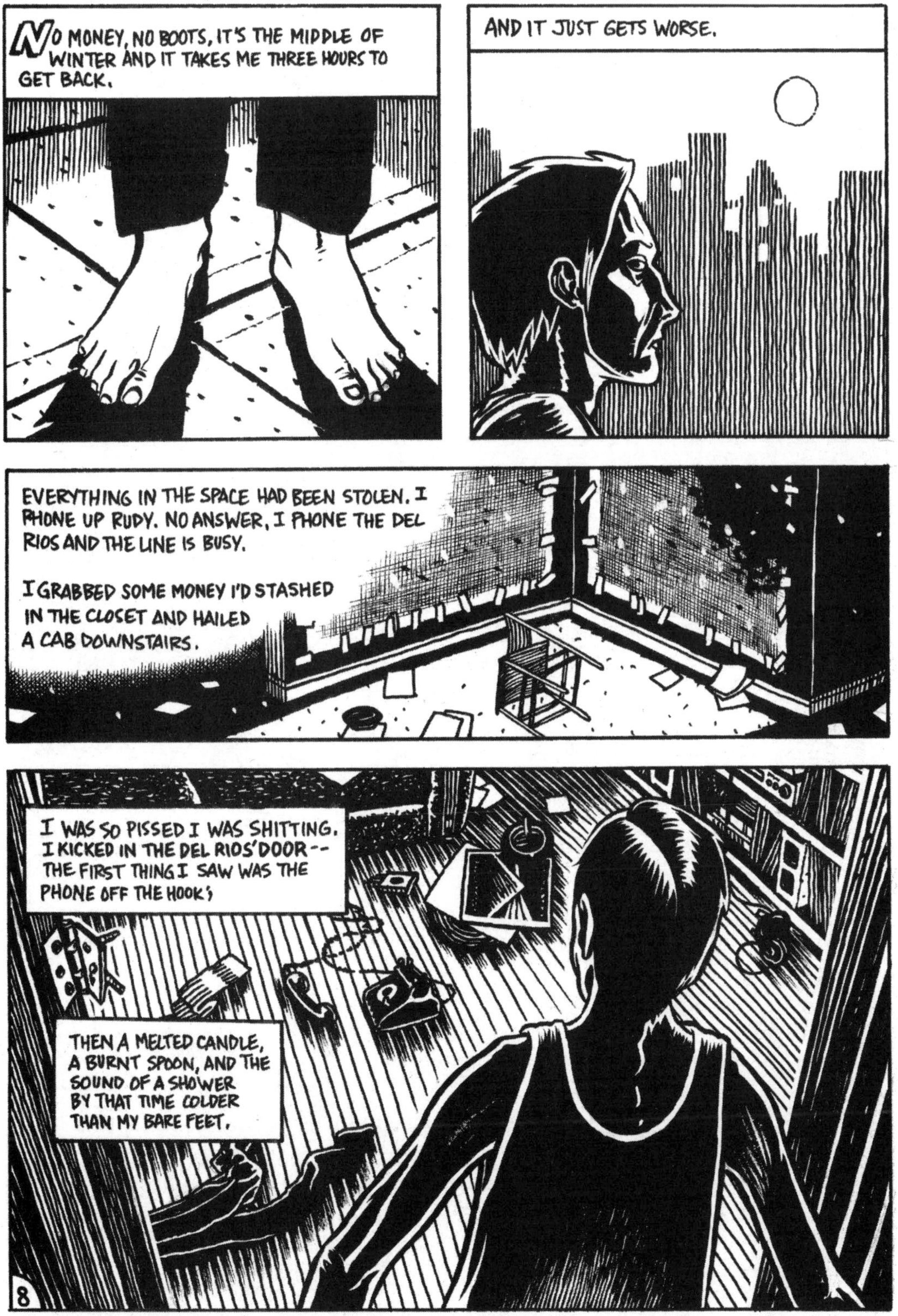
NO MONEY, NO BOOTS, IT'S THE MIDDLE OF WINTER AND IT TAKES ME THREE HOURS TO GET BACK.
AND IT JUST GETS WORSE.
EVERYTHING IN THE SPACE HAD BEEN STOLEN. I PHONE UP RUDY. NO ANSWER, I PHONE THE DEL RIOS AND THE LINE IS BUSY.
I GRABBED SOME MONEY I'D STASHED IN THE CLOSET AND HAILED A CAB DOWNSTAIRS.
I WAS SO PISSED I WAS SHITTING. I KICKED IN THE DEL RIOS' DOOR -- THE FIRST THING I SAW WAS THE PHONE OFF THE HOOK;
THEN A MELTED CANDLE, A BURNT SPOON, AND THE SOUND OF A SHOWER BY THAT TIME COLDER THAN MY BARE FEET.

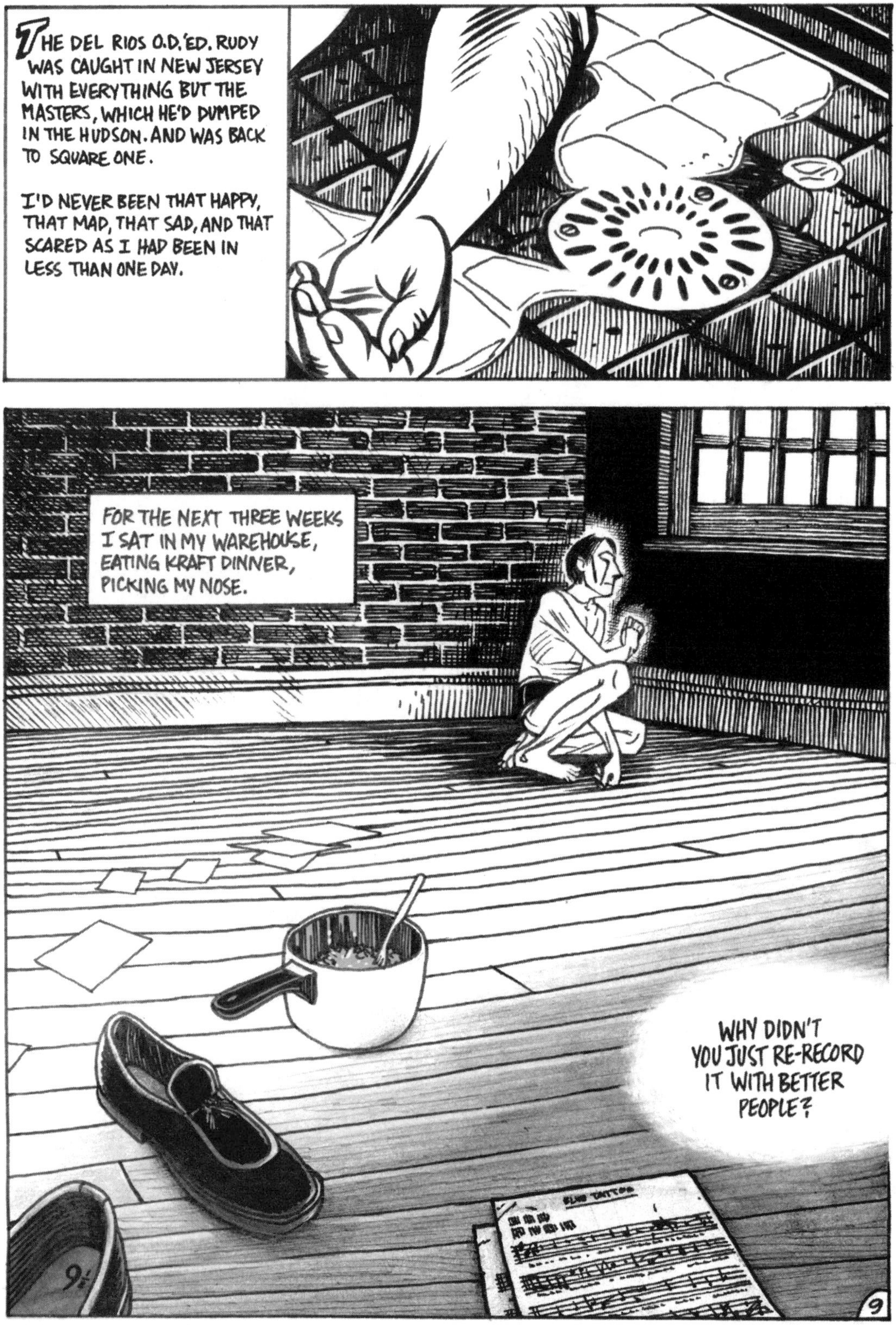
THE DEL RIOS O.D.'ED. RUDY WAS CAUGHT IN NEW JERSEY WITH EVERYTHING BUT THE MASTERS, WHICH HE'D DUMPED IN THE HUDSON. AND WAS BACK TO SQUARE ONE.
I'D NEVER BEEN THAT HAPPY, THAT MAD, THAT SAD, AND THAT SCARED AS I HAD BEEN IN LESS THAN ONE DAY.
FOR THE NEXT THREE WEEKS I SAT IN MY WAREHOUSE, EATING KRAFT DINNER, PICKING MY NOSE.
WHY DIDN'T YOU JUST RE-RECORD IT WITH BETTER PEOPLE?
9

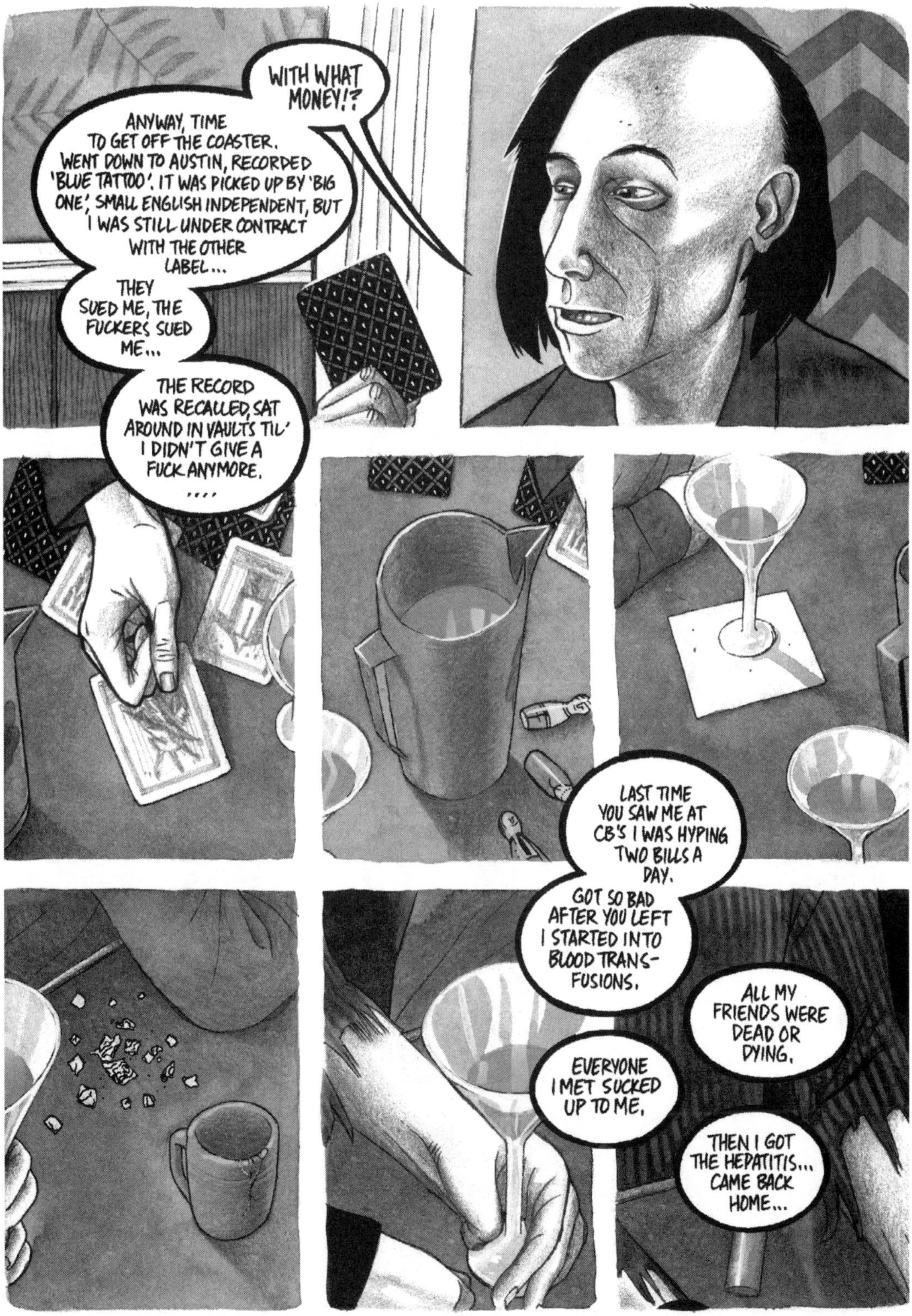
ANYWAY, TIME TO GET OFF THE COASTER. WENT DOWN TO AUSTIN, RECORDED 'BLUE TATTOO'. IT WAS PICKED UP BY 'BIG ONE', SMALL ENGLISH INDEPENDENT, BUT I WAS STILL UNDER CONTRACT WITH THE OTHER LABEL...
WITH WHAT MONEY!?
THEY SUED ME, THE FUCKERS SUED ME...
THE RECORD WAS RECALLED, SAT AROUND IN VAULTS TIL' I DIDN'T GIVE A FUCK ANYMORE.
....
LAST TIME YOU SAW ME AT CB'S I WAS HYPING TWO BILLS A DAY.
GOT SO BAD AFTER YOU LEFT I STARTED INTO BLOOD TRANS-FUSIONS.
ALL MY FRIENDS WERE DEAD OR DYING.
EVERYONE I MET SUCKED UP TO ME.
THEN I GOT THE HEPATITIS... CAME BACK HOME...

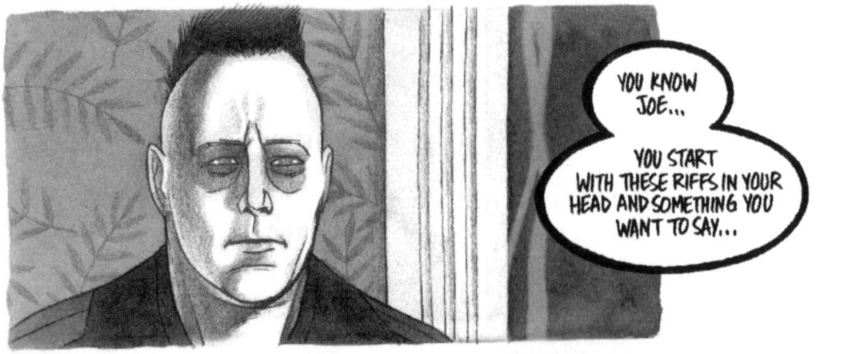
YOU KNOW JOE...
YOU START WITH THESE RIFFS IN YOUR HEAD AND SOMETHING YOU WANT TO SAY...

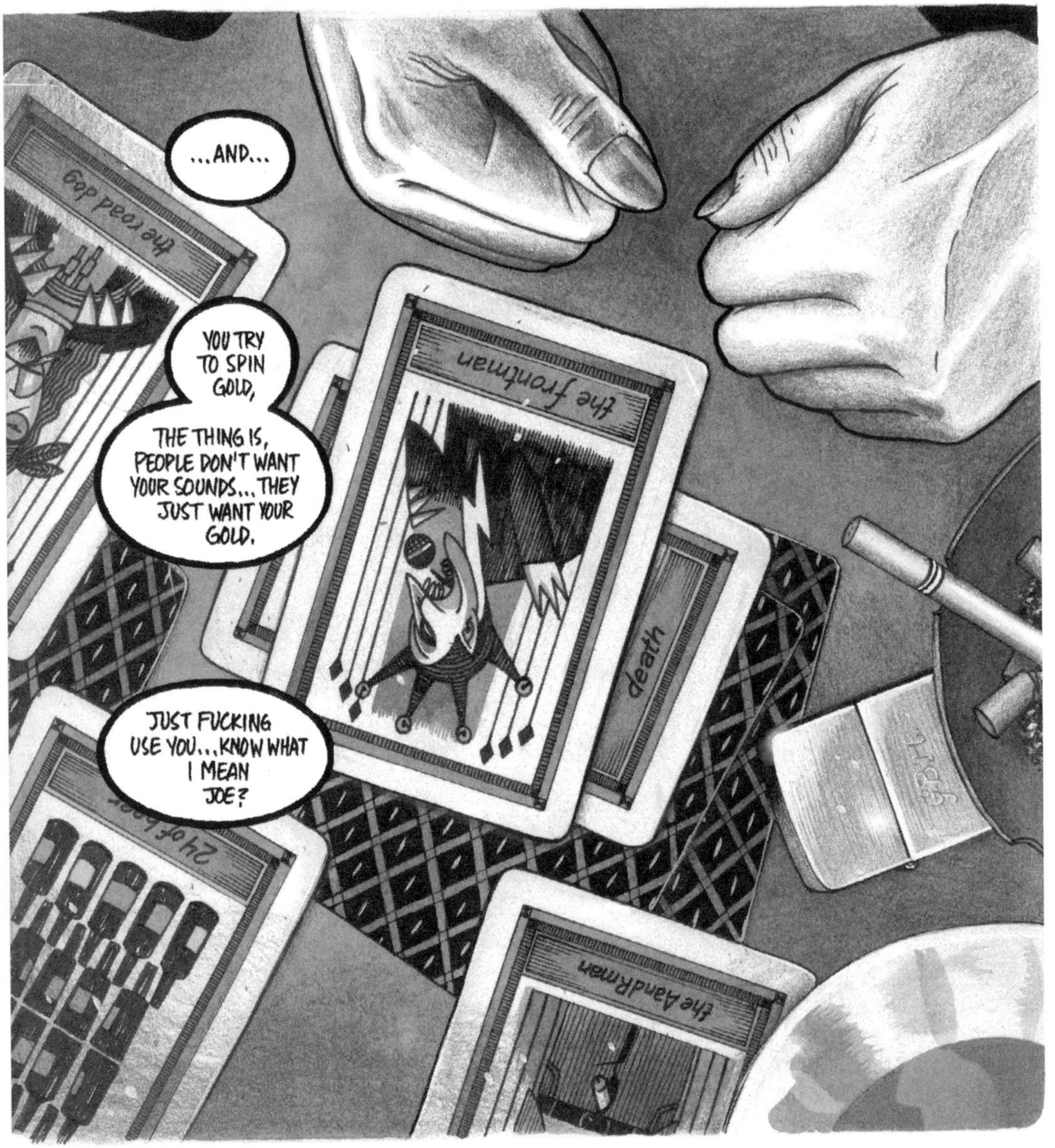
...AND...
YOU TRY TO SPIN GOLD,
THE THING IS, PEOPLE DON'T WANT YOUR SOUNDS... THEY JUST WANT YOUR GOLD.
JUST FUCKING USE YOU... KNOW WHAT I MEAN JOE?
the road dog
the frontman
death
24 of beer
the roadman

<u>John's tour diary</u>

The visit with Bucky was not what I expected.
He was living on this farm in the prairies, this native
woman, Niomi, looked after him. I reckoned he be healthier, but
he looked as bad as he did in the eighties. Most of the time we

spent sitting in the kitchen, listening, drinking his booze and
eating his food. He had a funny way of putting things where
everything's funny and sad all at once.

I remember looking over at Joe, wondering
what was going on in his head. There was this
blank ugly stare, this guilty yet glazed look in
his eyes. This was a Joe I'd never quite seen before. It was
as if he was lobotomized. There was nothing left.
Nothing.
Joe had lied about Bucky.
He was never shot. There were no hunters.

COUNTRY BLUEGRASS BAR

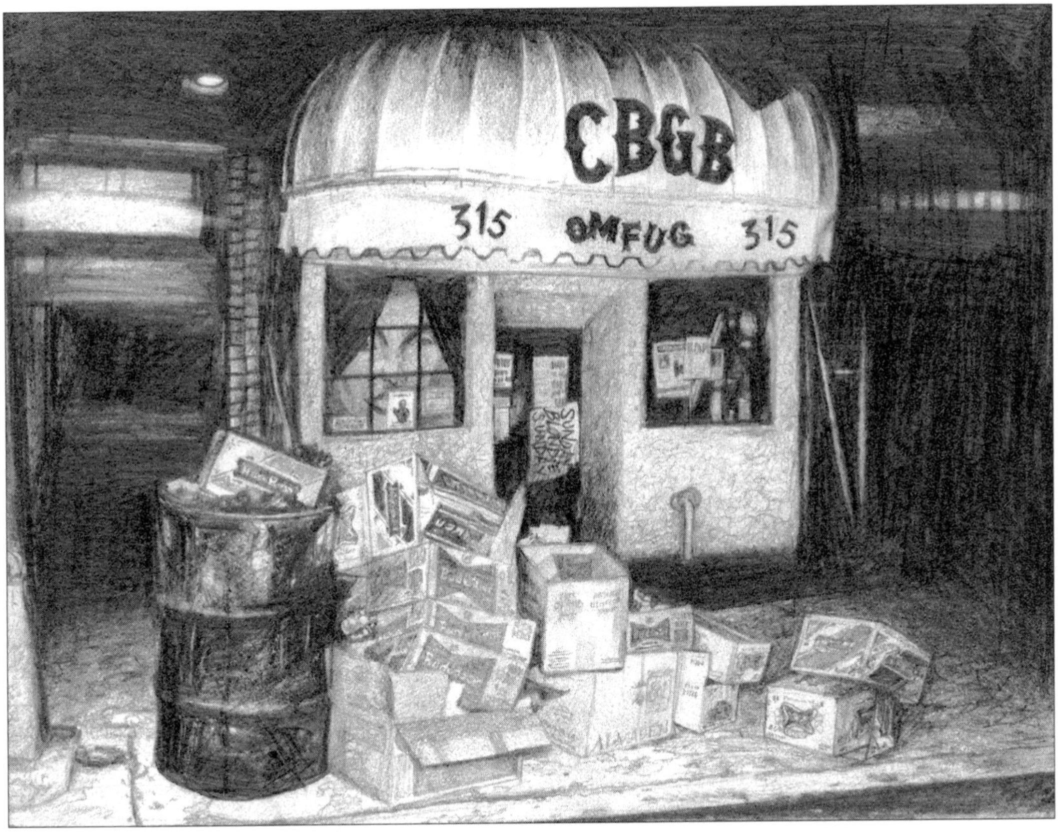
CBGB
315 OMFUG 315

The Birthplace of Punk

NEW YORK CITY CIRCA 1977

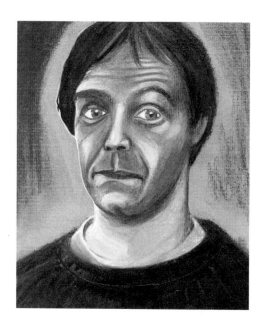

LEWIS MELVILLE

MUSICIAN/PRODUCER

SON OF A BITCH TO THE CORE (EP)—1978

U.S. OUT OF NORTH AMERICA—1981

"Really it was the only way Joe would be able to get Billy back. I don't think he actually expected to get away with it. Bucky would have found out sooner or later. He's not that isolated from the world.

"How else could they have afforded to tour?"

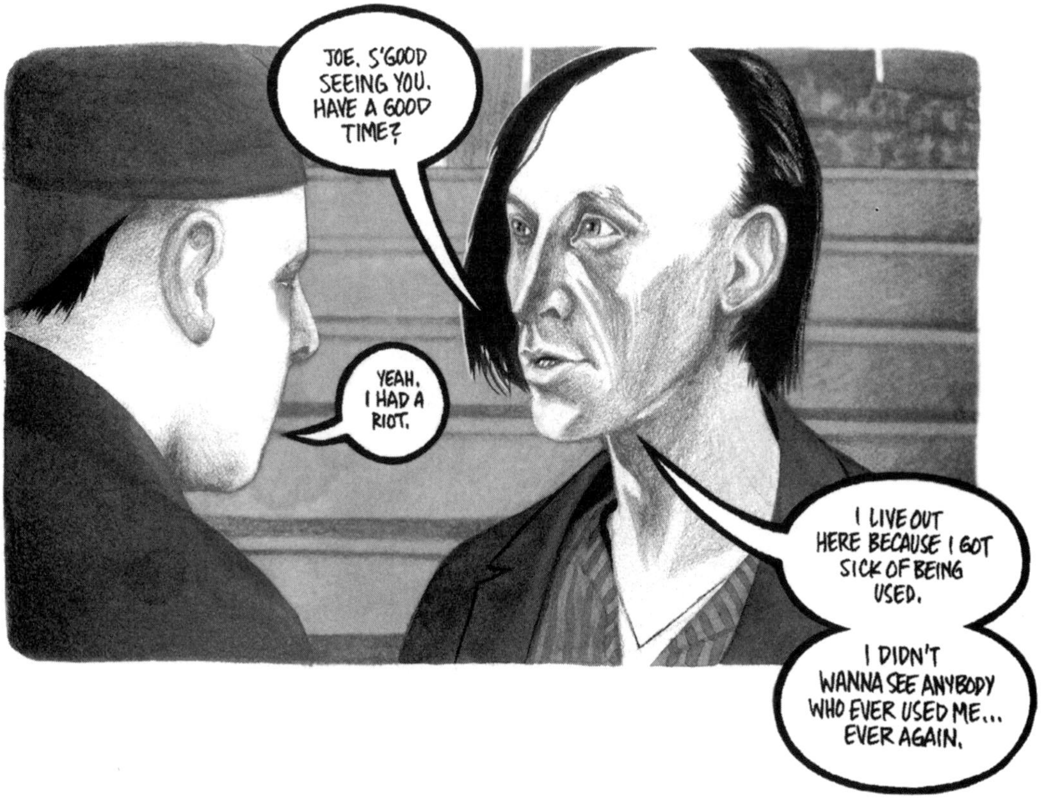
JOE. S'GOOD SEEING YOU. HAVE A GOOD TIME?
YEAH. I HAD A RIOT.
I LIVE OUT HERE BECAUSE I GOT SICK OF BEING USED.
I DIDN'T WANNA SEE ANYBODY WHO EVER USED ME... EVER AGAIN.

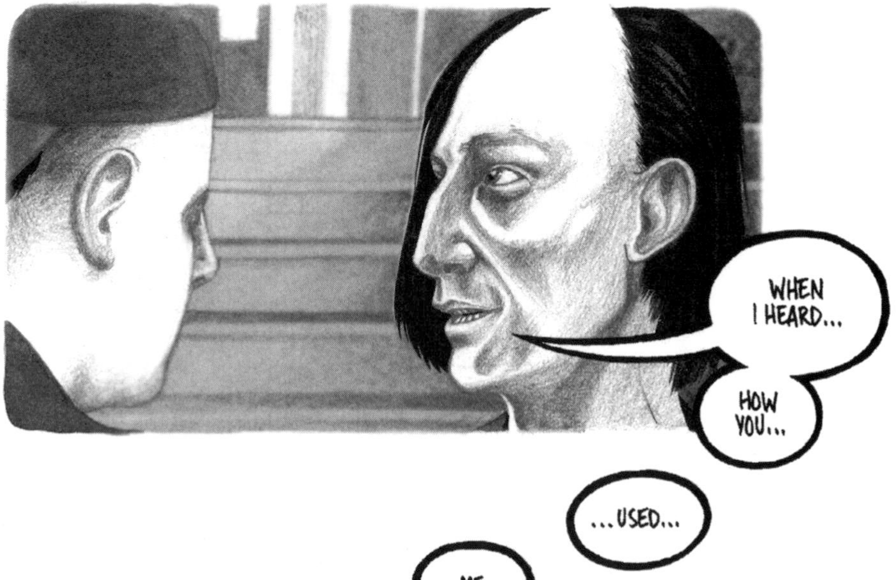
WHEN I HEARD...
HOW YOU...
...USED...
...ME...

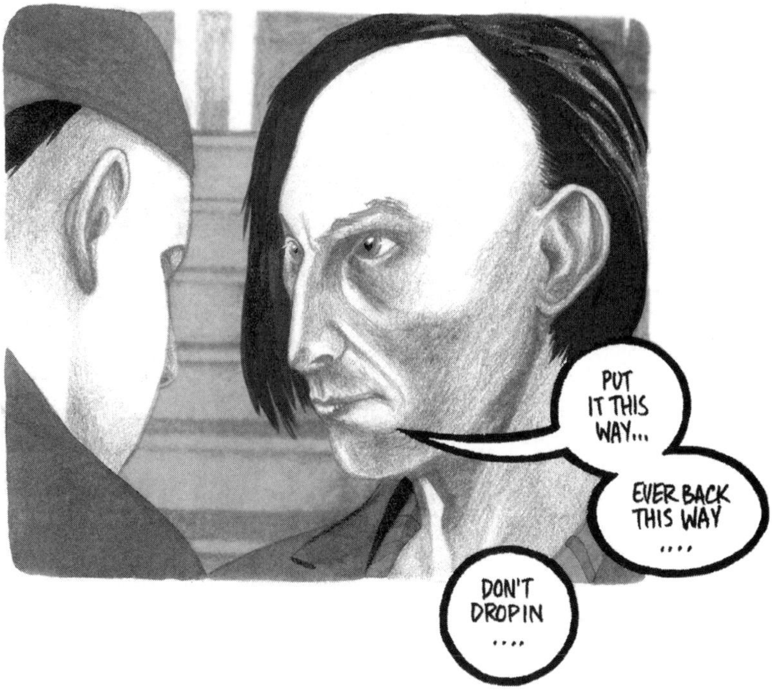
PUT IT THIS WAY...
EVER BACK THIS WAY ....
DON'T DROP IN ....

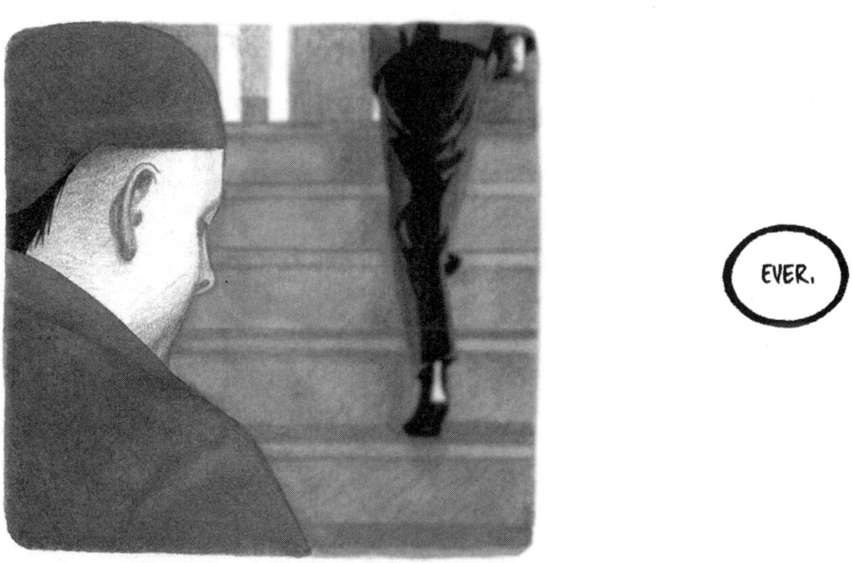
EVER.

Blue Tattoo

It hurt so bad when you got it
It went straight to your head
It drove you insane
But now all that's forgotten
And you can go on
Without any pain

A blue tattoo on your shoulder
In the shape of a heart
In the middle of my name
And that's how I remember
All of the bad things
That you couldn't change

Blue Tattoo
Blue Tattoo

You had no time for corruption
You felt the world
Was an unsafe place
You worked towards a solution
But the best you could do
Was to send me away

A blue tattoo on my shoulder
In the shape of the world
In the middle of your name
And that's how I remember
All of the good things
You took to your grave

Blue Tattoo
Blue Tattoo

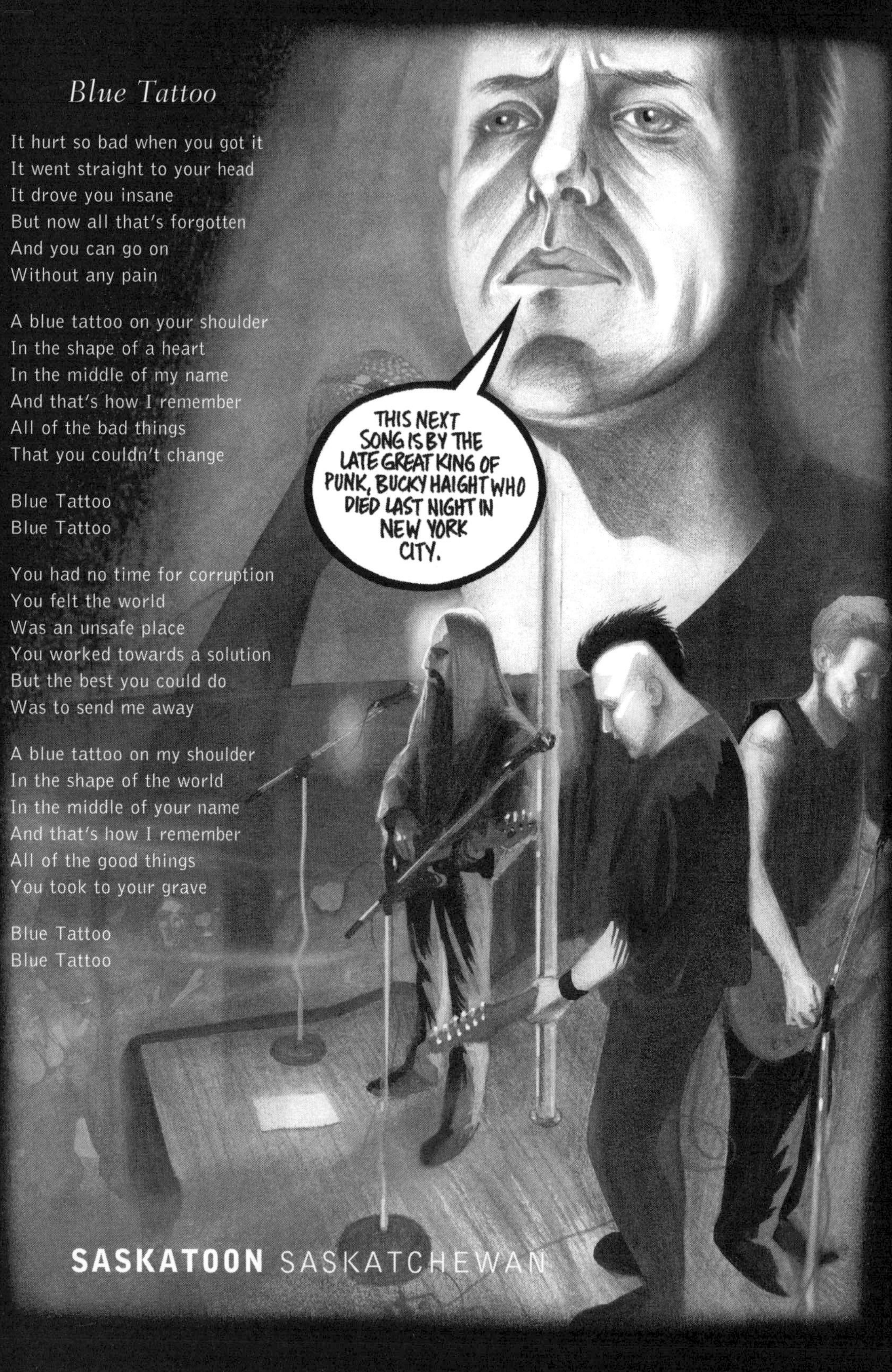

SASKATOON SASKATCHEWAN

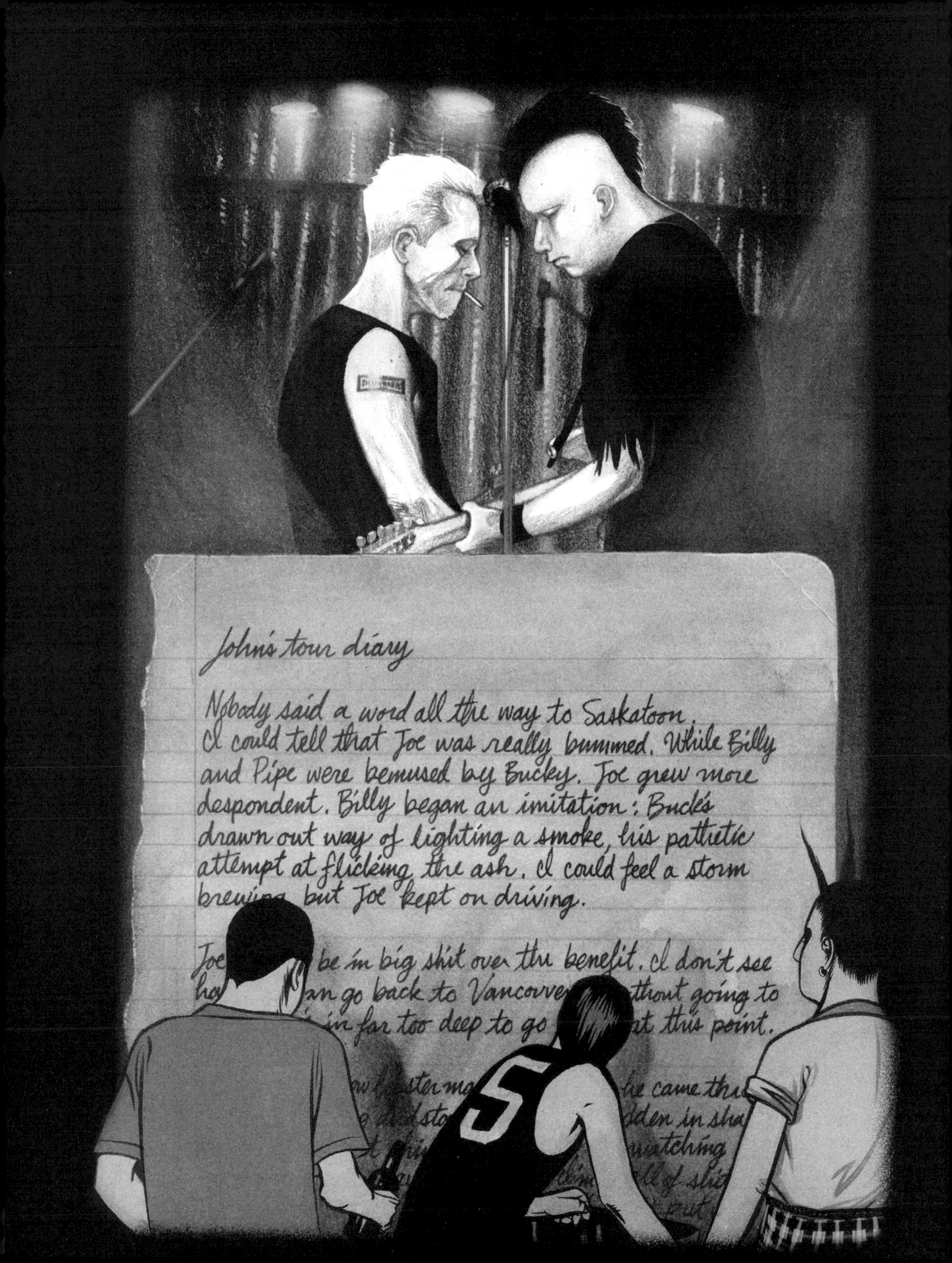
John's tour diary
Nobody said a word all the way to Saskatoon.
I could tell that Joe was really bummed. While Billy and Pipe were bemused by Bucky, Joe grew more despondent. Billy began an imitation: Buck's drawn out way of lighting a smoke, his pathetic attempt at flicking the ash. I could feel a storm brewi
but Joe kept on driving.
be in big shit over the benefit. I don't see
an go back to Vancouver
thout going to
in far too deep to go
at this point.

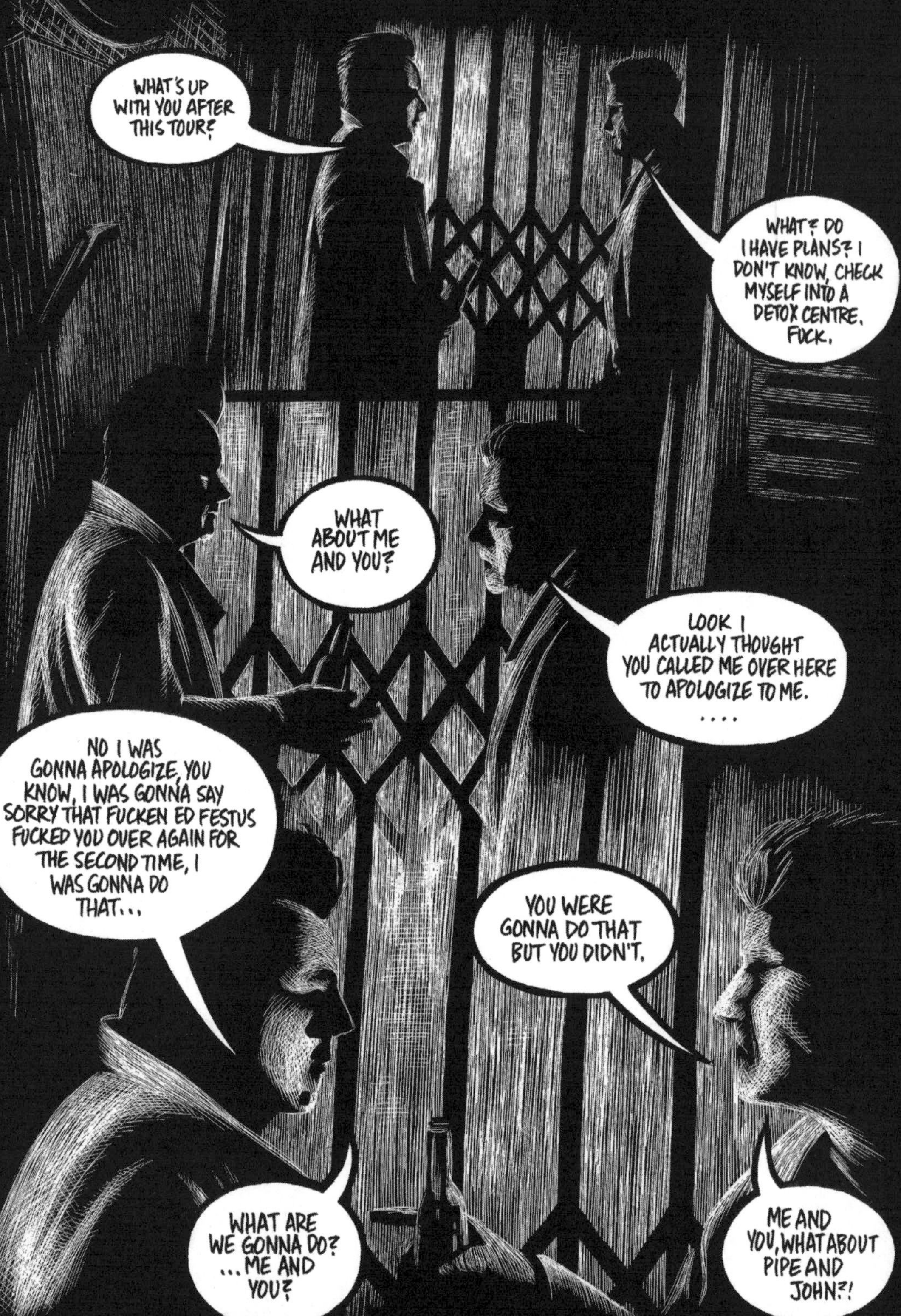
WHAT'S UP WITH YOU AFTER THIS TOUR?
WHAT? DO I HAVE PLANS? I DON'T KNOW, CHECK MYSELF INTO A DETOX CENTRE. FUCK.
WHAT ABOUT ME AND YOU?
LOOK I ACTUALLY THOUGHT YOU CALLED ME OVER HERE TO APOLOGIZE TO ME. ....
NO I WAS GONNA APOLOGIZE, YOU KNOW, I WAS GONNA SAY SORRY THAT FUCKEN ED FESTUS FUCKED YOU OVER AGAIN FOR THE SECOND TIME, I WAS GONNA DO THAT...
YOU WERE GONNA DO THAT BUT YOU DIDN'T.
WHAT ARE WE GONNA DO? ... ME AND YOU?
ME AND YOU, WHAT ABOUT PIPE AND JOHN?!

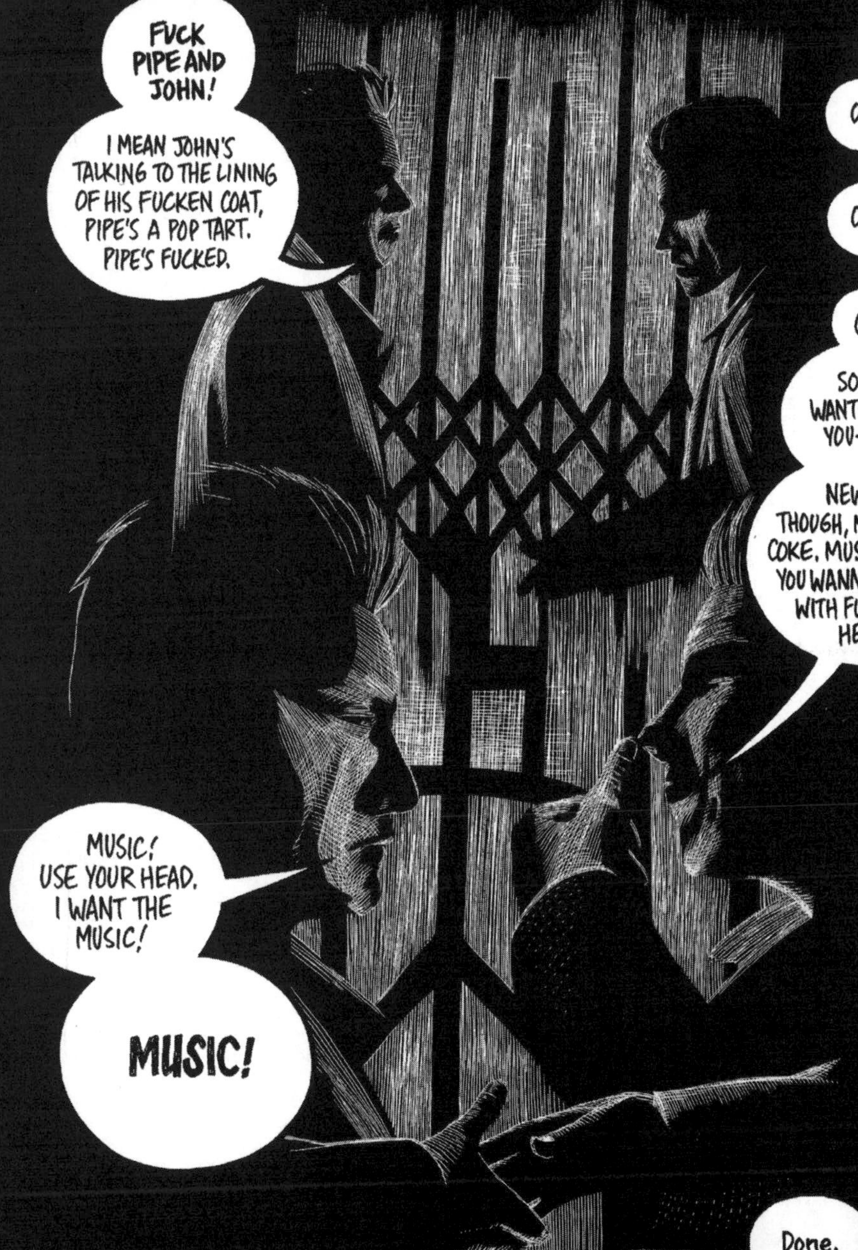
FUCK PIPE AND JOHN!
I MEAN JOHN'S TALKING TO THE LINING OF HIS FUCKEN COAT, PIPE'S A POP TART. PIPE'S FUCKED.
OK.
OK.
OK.
OK.
OK.
OK.
SO YOU WANT YOU-ME YOU-ME...
NEW DEAL THOUGH, MUSIC NO COKE. MUSIC NO COKE. YOU WANNA HANG OUT WITH FUCKEN COKE HEADS?...
MUSIC! USE YOUR HEAD. I WANT THE MUSIC!
MUSIC!
Done.

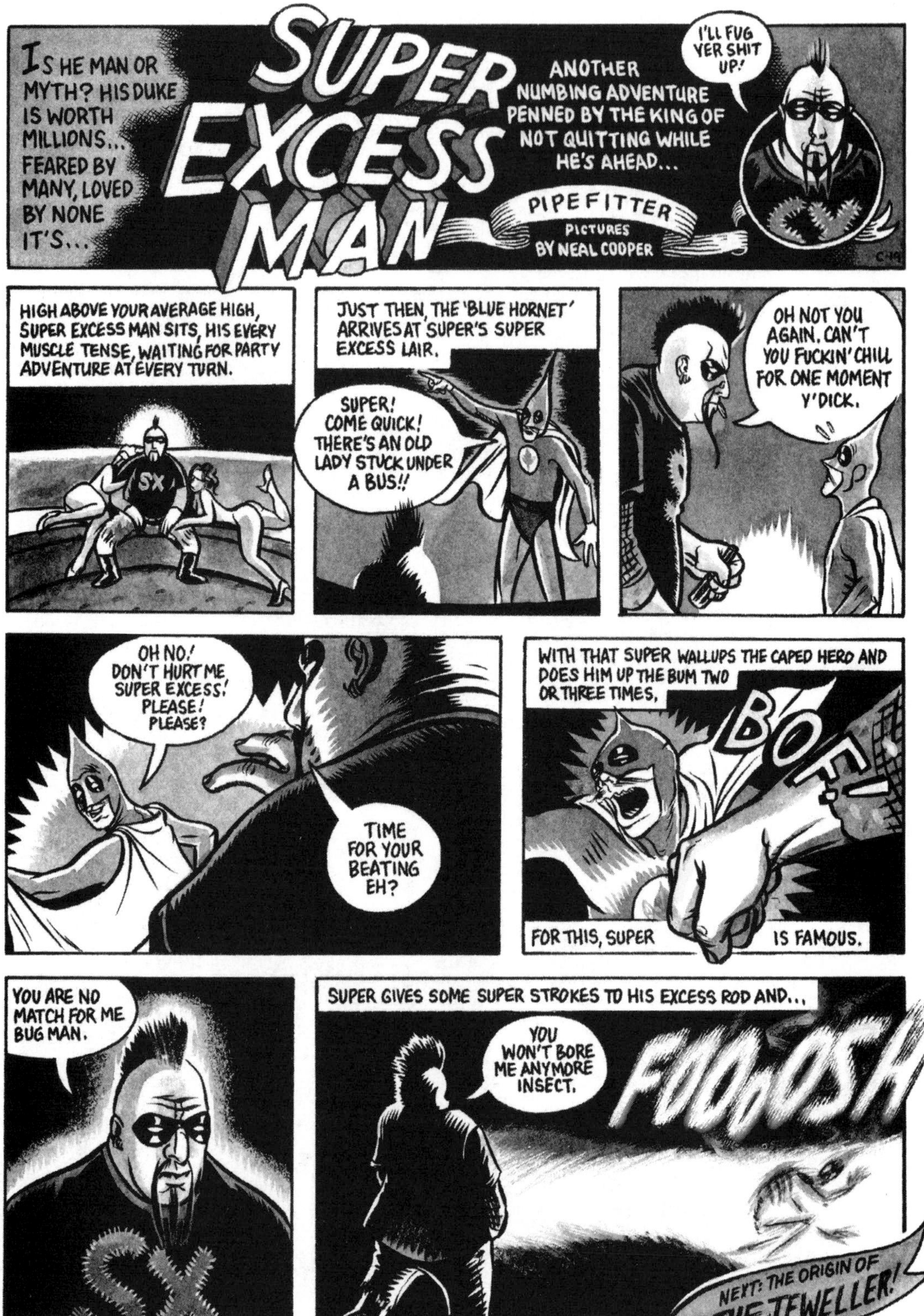
IS HE MAN OR MYTH? HIS DUKE IS WORTH MILLIONS... FEARED BY MANY, LOVED BY NONE IT'S...
SUPER EXCESS MAN
ANOTHER NUMBING ADVENTURE PENNED BY THE KING OF NOT QUITTING WHILE HE'S AHEAD...
PIPEFITTER
PICTURES BY NEAL COOPER
I'LL FUG YER SHIT UP!
HIGH ABOVE YOUR AVERAGE HIGH, SUPER EXCESS MAN SITS, HIS EVERY MUSCLE TENSE, WAITING FOR PARTY ADVENTURE AT EVERY TURN.
SX
JUST THEN, THE 'BLUE HORNET' ARRIVES AT SUPER'S SUPER EXCESS LAIR.
SUPER! COME QUICK! THERE'S AN OLD LADY STUCK UNDER A BUS!!
OH NOT YOU AGAIN. CAN'T YOU FUCKIN' CHILL FOR ONE MOMENT Y'DICK.
OH NO! DON'T HURT ME SUPER EXCESS! PLEASE! PLEASE?
TIME FOR YOUR BEATING EH?
WITH THAT SUPER WALLUPS THE CAPED HERO AND DOES HIM UP THE BUM TWO OR THREE TIMES,
BOF!
FOR THIS, SUPER IS FAMOUS.
YOU ARE NO MATCH FOR ME BUG MAN.
SUPER GIVES SOME SUPER STROKES TO HIS EXCESS ROD AND...
YOU WON'T BORE ME ANYMORE INSECT.
FOOoOSH
NEXT: THE ORIGIN OF THE JEWELLER!

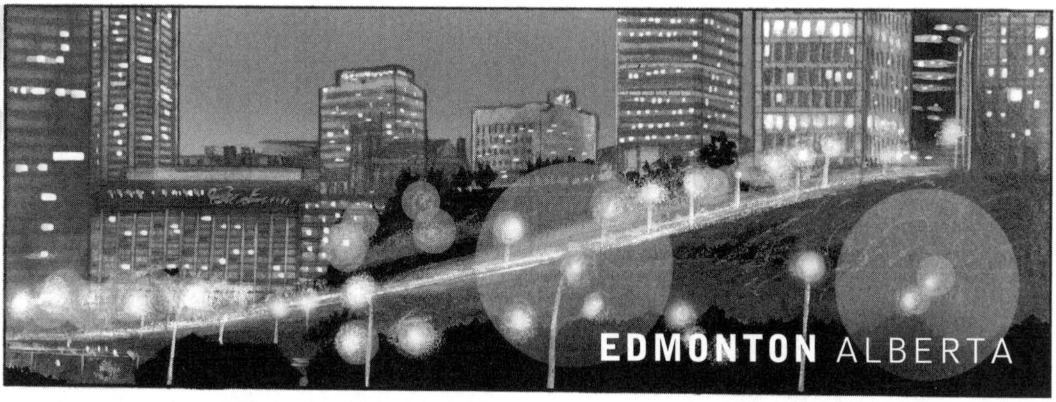
EDMONTON ALBERTA

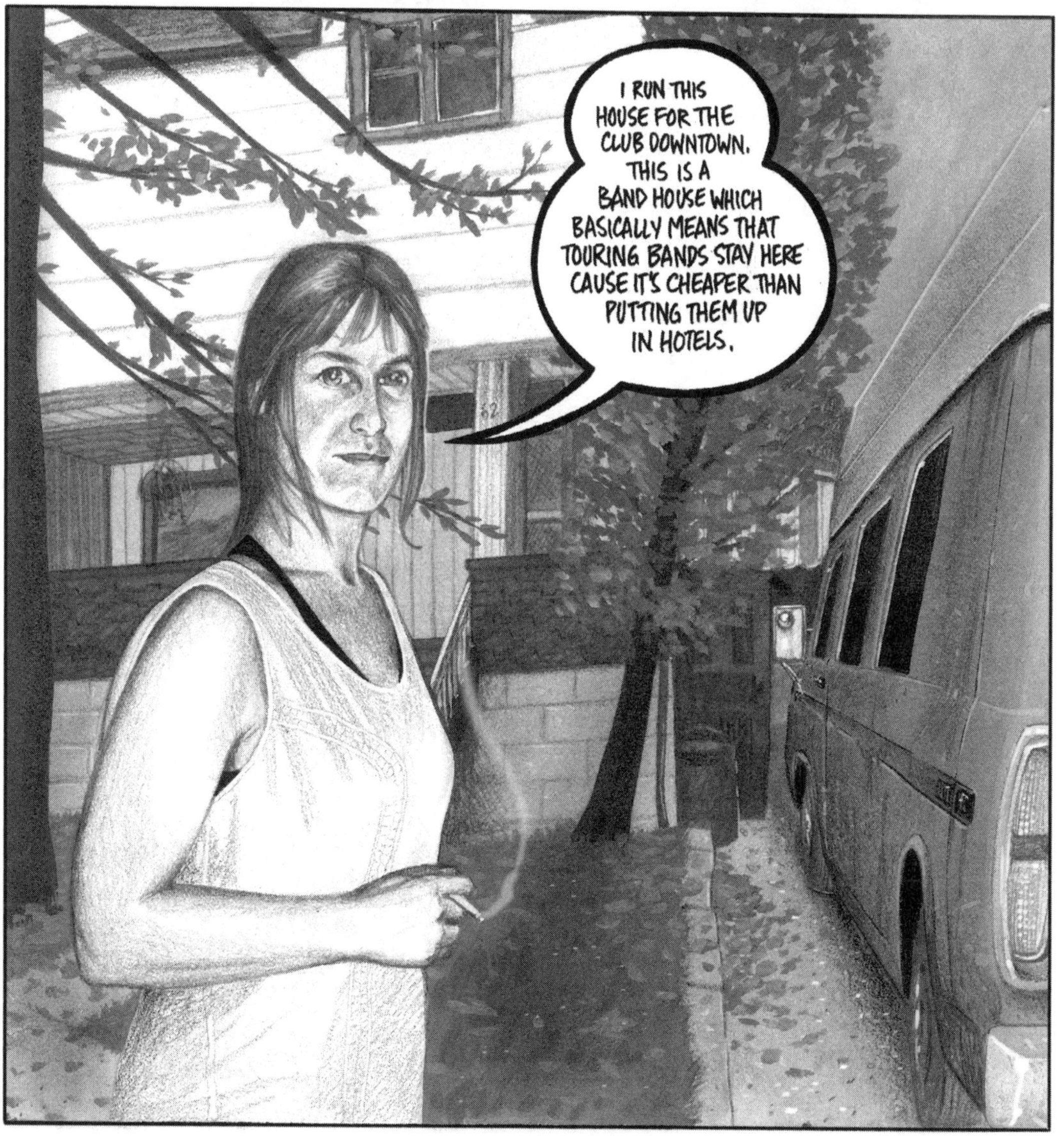
I RUN THIS HOUSE FOR THE CLUB DOWNTOWN. THIS IS A BAND HOUSE WHICH BASICALLY MEANS THAT TOURING BANDS STAY HERE CAUSE IT'S CHEAPER THAN PUTTING THEM UP IN HOTELS.

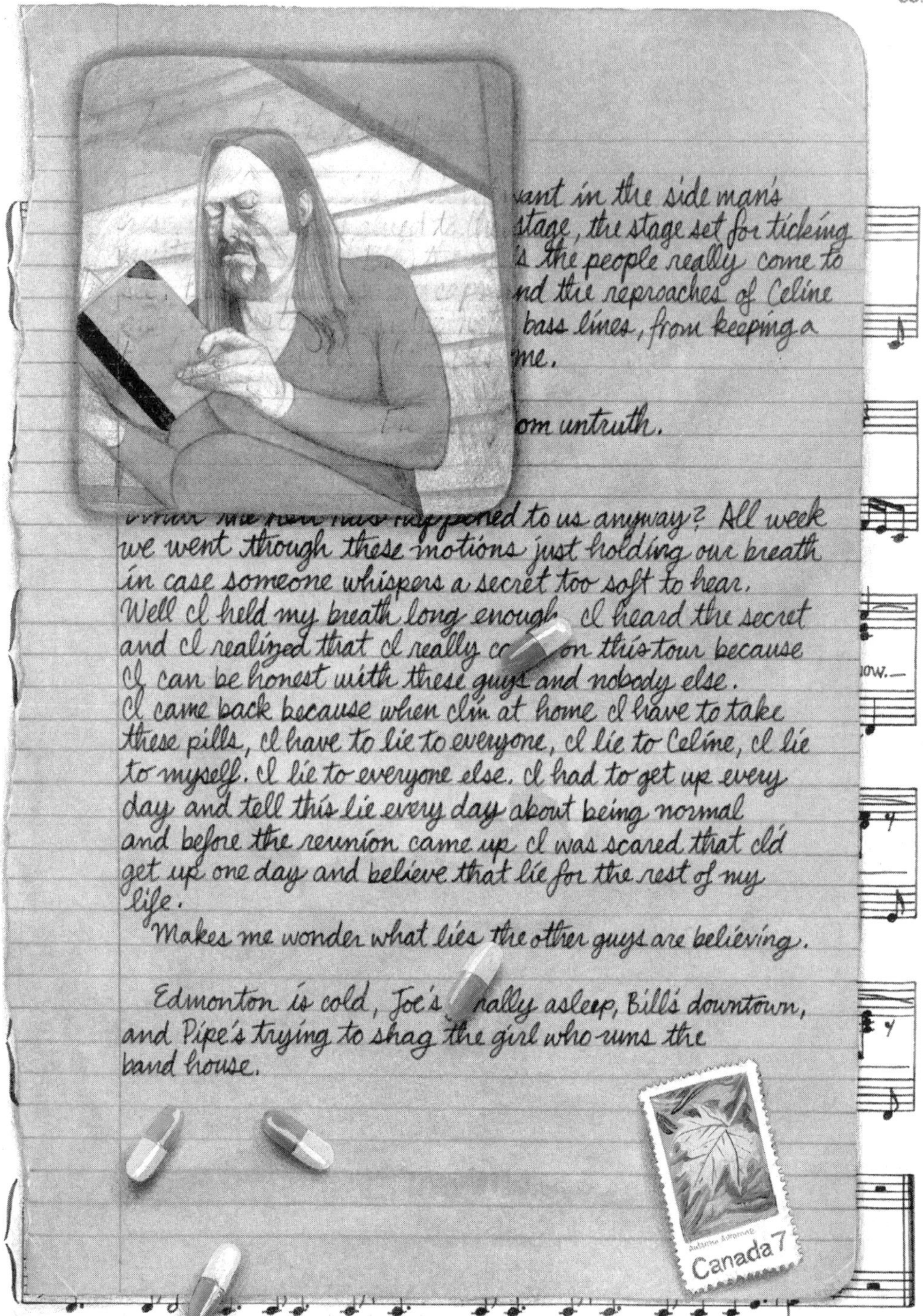

ant in the side man's
stage, the stage set for ticking
's the people really come to
nd the reproaches of Celine
bass lines, from keeping a
me.

om untruth.

What the fuck has happened to us anyway? All week
we went through these motions just holding our breath
in case someone whispers a secret too soft to hear.
Well I held my breath long enough I heard the secret
and I realized that I really co   on this tour because
I can be honest with these guys and nobody else.
I came back because when I'm at home I have to take
these pills, I have to lie to everyone, I lie to Celine, I lie
to myself. I lie to everyone else. I had to get up every
day and tell this lie every day about being normal
and before the reunion came up I was scared that I'd
get up one day and believe that lie for the rest of my
life.

Makes me wonder what lies the other guys are believing.

Edmonton is cold, Joe's   nally asleep, Bill's downtown,
and Pipe's trying to shag the girl who runs the
band house.

Canada 7

MESSAGE

Date .... Time ....

To BILLY TALLENT

WHILE YOU WERE OUT

From ....

TELEPHONE ....

Telephoned		Please call	
Called to see you		Will call again	
Wants to see you		Returned your call	

MESSAGE PHONE ED FESTUS COLLECT!

Operator .... URGENT

46-501 pink
46-502 yellow

Hilroy

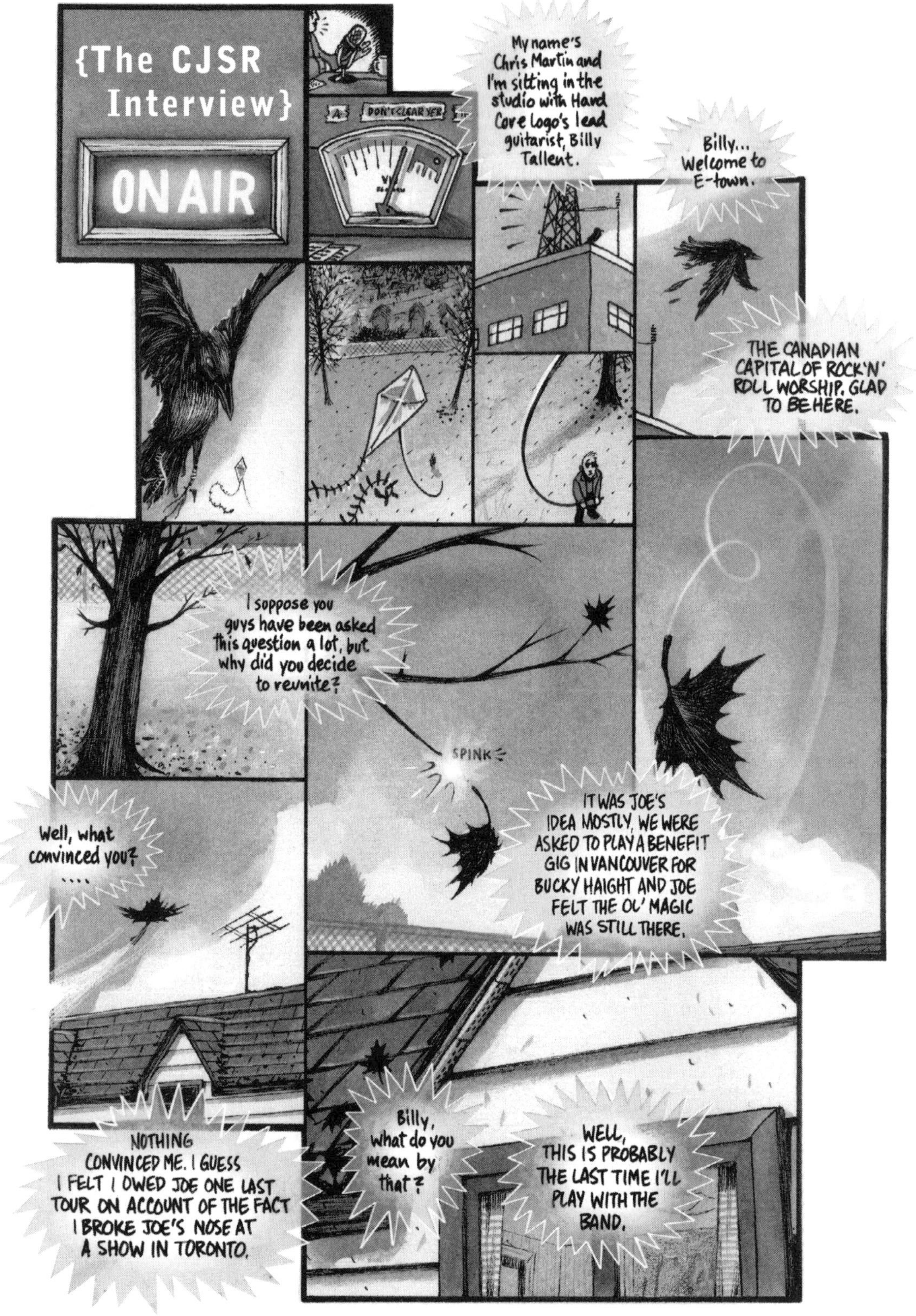
{The CJSR Interview}
ON AIR
DON'T CLEAR YER
My name's Chris Martin and I'm sitting in the studio with Hard Core Logo's lead guitarist, Billy Tallent.
Billy... Welcome to E-town.
THE CANADIAN CAPITAL OF ROCK'N' ROLL WORSHIP. GLAD TO BE HERE.
I suppose you guys have been asked this question a lot, but why did you decide to reunite?
SPINK
IT WAS JOE'S IDEA MOSTLY, WE WERE ASKED TO PLAY A BENEFIT GIG IN VANCOUVER FOR BUCKY HAIGHT AND JOE FELT THE OL' MAGIC WAS STILL THERE.
Well, what convinced you? ....
NOTHING CONVINCED ME. I GUESS I FELT I OWED JOE ONE LAST TOUR ON ACCOUNT OF THE FACT I BROKE JOE'S NOSE AT A SHOW IN TORONTO.
Billy, what do you mean by that?
WELL, THIS IS PROBABLY THE LAST TIME I'LL PLAY WITH THE BAND.

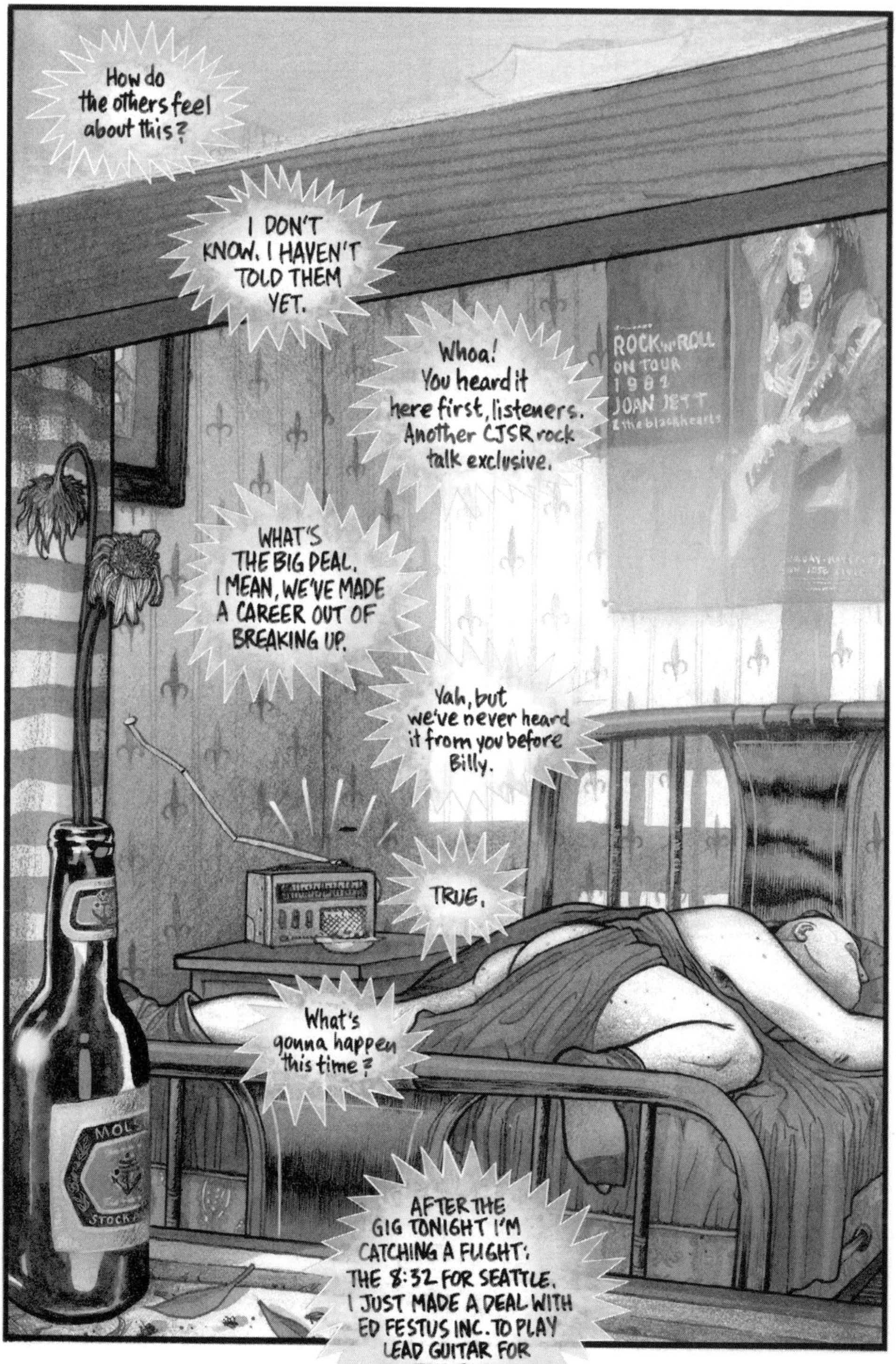

How do the others feel about this?
I DON'T KNOW. I HAVEN'T TOLD THEM YET.
Whoa! You heard it here first, listeners. Another CJSR rock talk exclusive.
ROCK n' ROLL ON TOUR 1981 JOAN JETT & the blackhearts
WHAT'S THE BIG DEAL. I MEAN, WE'VE MADE A CAREER OUT OF BREAKING UP.
Yah, but we've never heard it from you before Billy.
TRUE.
What's gonna happen this time?
AFTER THE GIG TONIGHT I'M CATCHING A FLIGHT: THE 8:32 FOR SEATTLE. I JUST MADE A DEAL WITH ED FESTUS INC. TO PLAY LEAD GUITAR FOR JENIFUR.

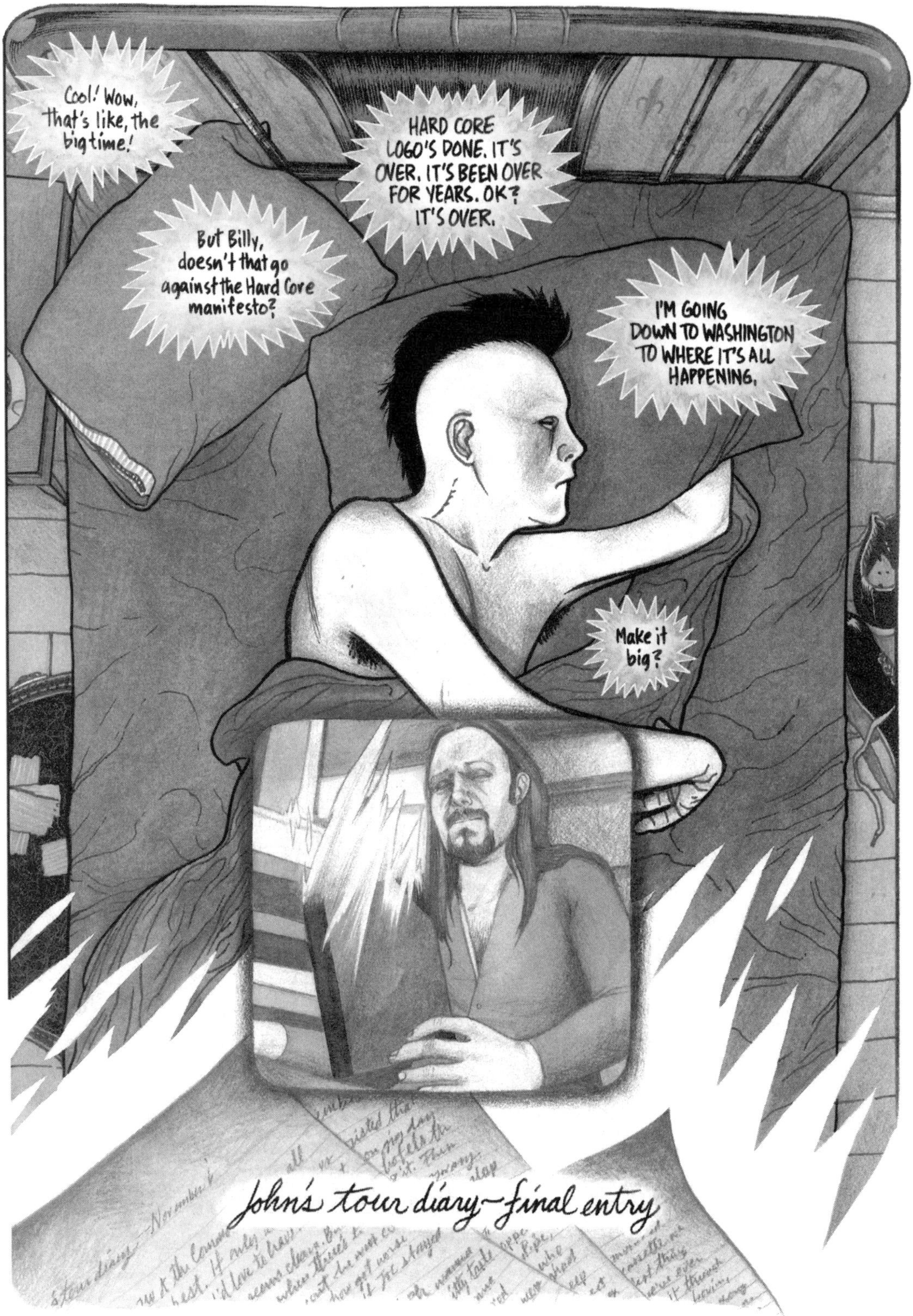

Cool! Wow, that's like, the big time!
HARD CORE LOGO'S DONE. IT'S OVER. IT'S BEEN OVER FOR YEARS. OK? IT'S OVER.
But Billy, doesn't that go against the Hard Core manifesto?
I'M GOING DOWN TO WASHINGTON TO WHERE IT'S ALL HAPPENING.
Make it big?
John's tour diary~final entry

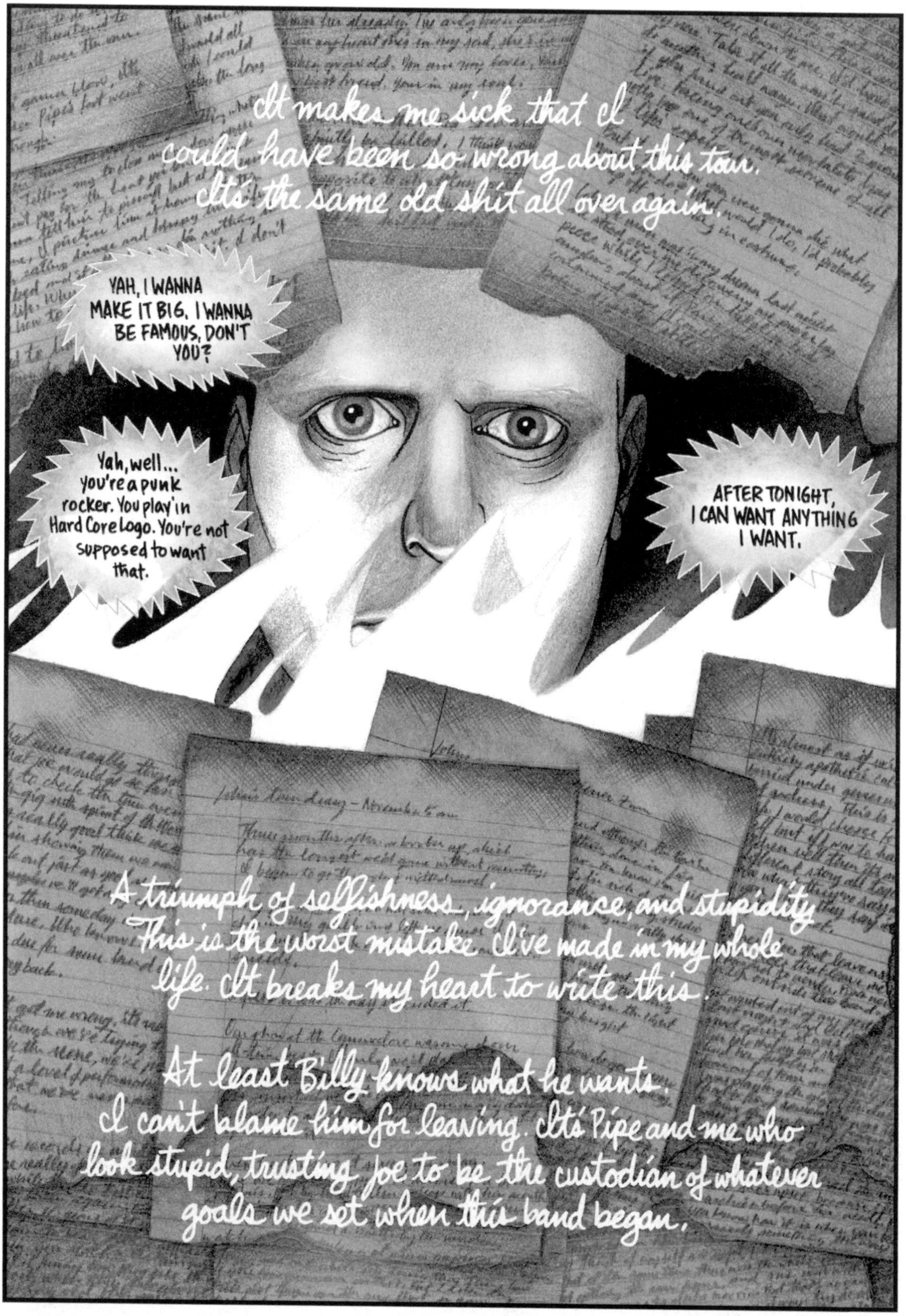

It makes me sick that I could have been so wrong about this tour. It's the same old shit all over again.
YAH, I WANNA MAKE IT BIG. I WANNA BE FAMOUS, DON'T YOU?
Yah, well... you're a punk rocker. You play in Hard Core Logo. You're not supposed to want that.
AFTER TONIGHT, I CAN WANT ANYTHING I WANT.
A triumph of selfishness, ignorance, and stupidity. This is the worst mistake I've made in my whole life. It breaks my heart to write this.
At least Billy knows what he wants. I can't blame him for leaving. It's Pipe and me who look stupid, trusting Joe to be the custodian of whatever goals we set when this band began.

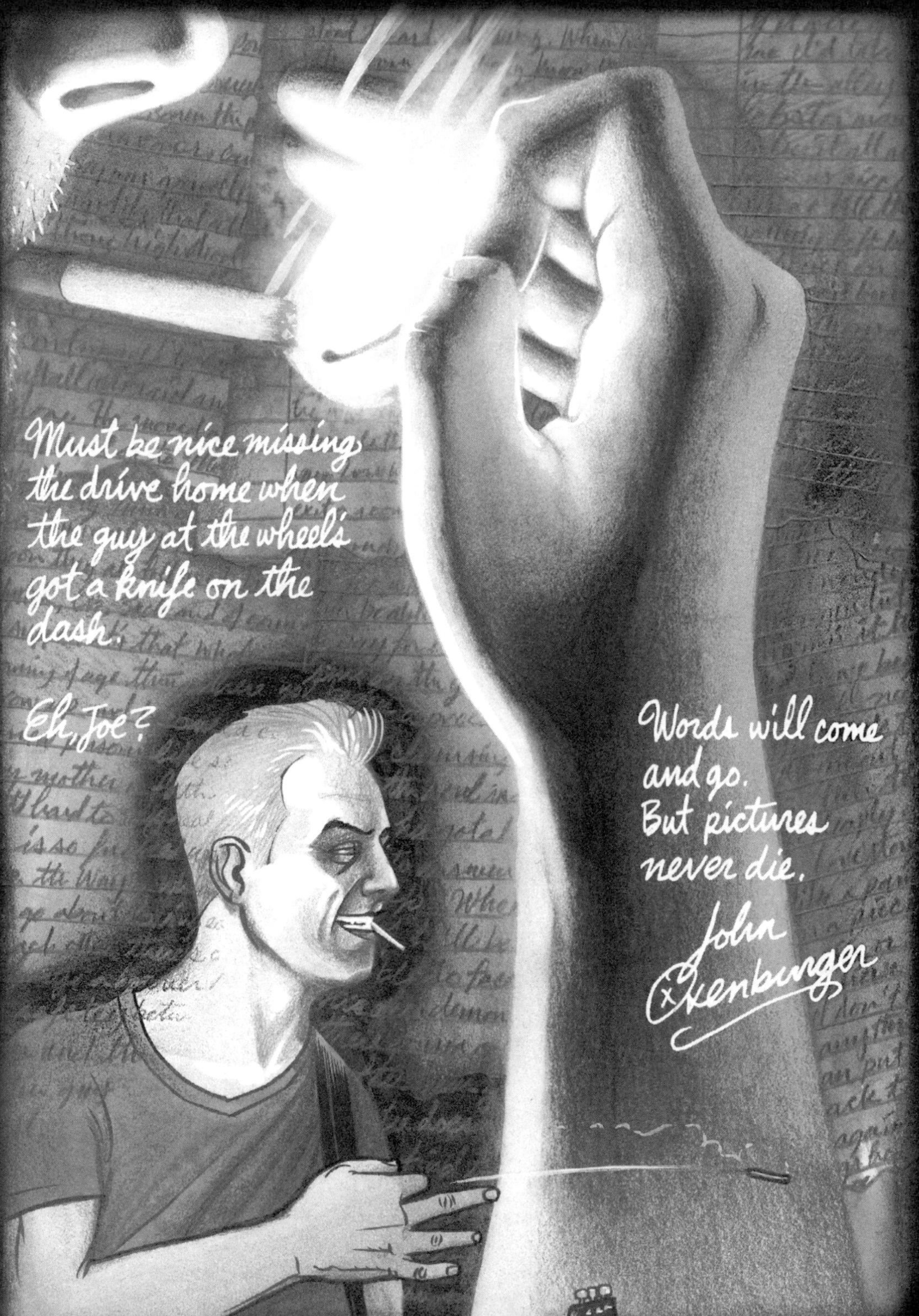
Must be nice missing the drive home when the guy at the wheel's got a knife on the dash.
Eh, Joe?
Words will come and go. But pictures never die.
John Oxenburger

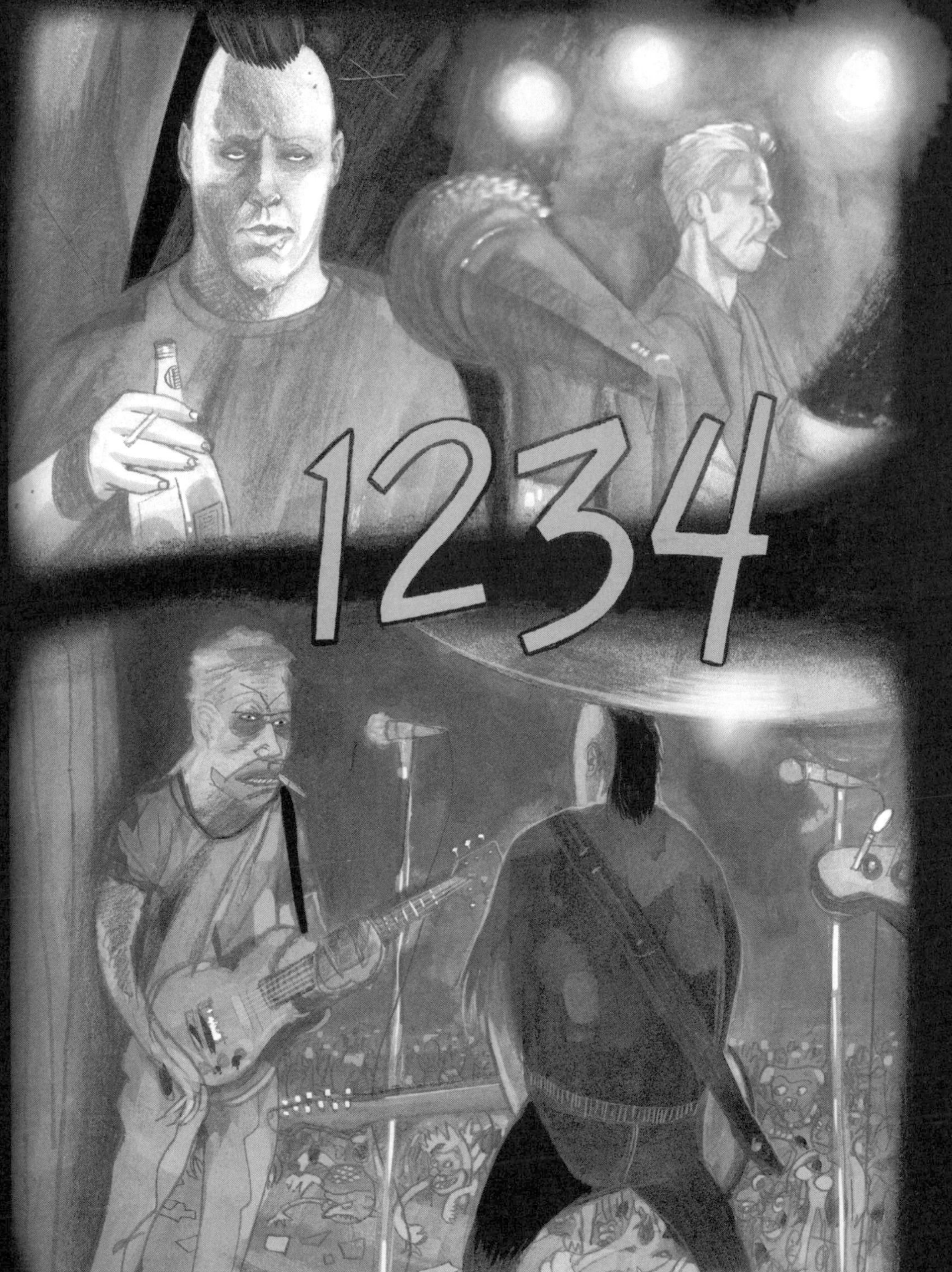
1234

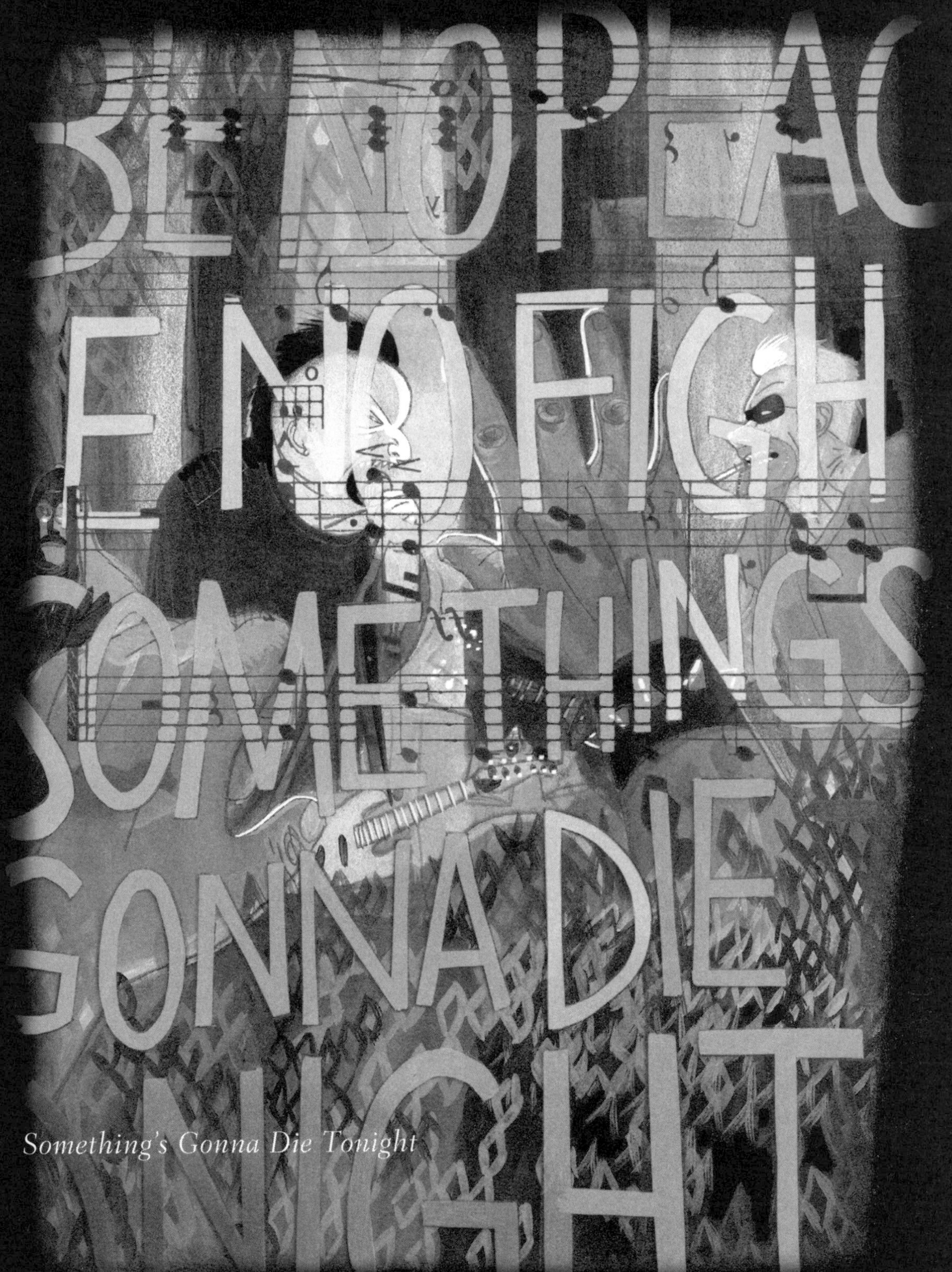
BE NO PLAC
E NO FIGH
SOMETHINGS
GONNA DIE
NIGHT

Something's Gonna Die Tonight

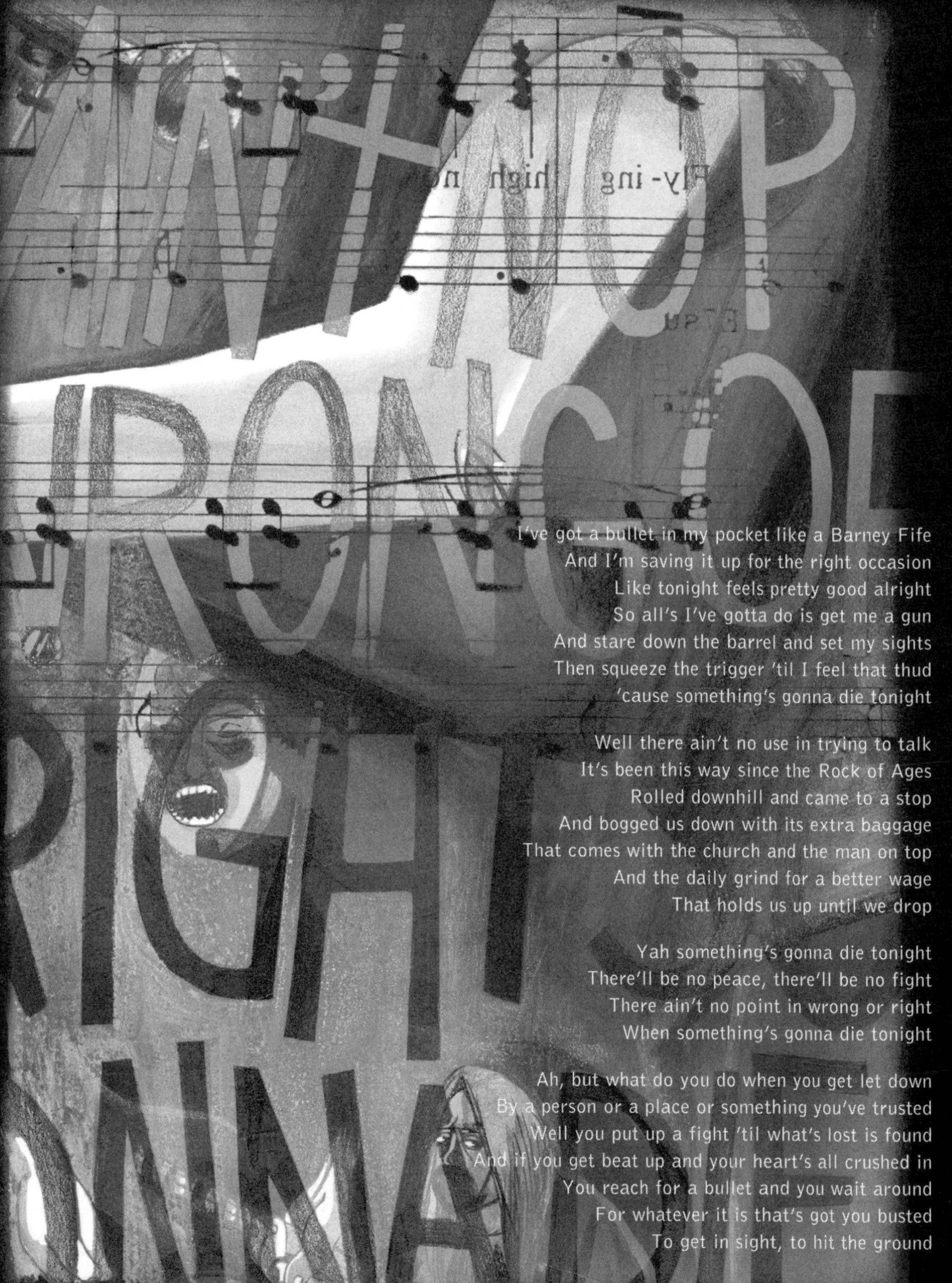

I've got a bullet in my pocket like a Barney Fife
And I'm saving it up for the right occasion
Like tonight feels pretty good alright
So all's I've gotta do is get me a gun
And stare down the barrel and set my sights
Then squeeze the trigger 'til I feel that thud
'cause something's gonna die tonight

Well there ain't no use in trying to talk
It's been this way since the Rock of Ages
Rolled downhill and came to a stop
And bogged us down with its extra baggage
That comes with the church and the man on top
And the daily grind for a better wage
That holds us up until we drop

Yah something's gonna die tonight
There'll be no peace, there'll be no fight
There ain't no point in wrong or right
When something's gonna die tonight

Ah, but what do you do when you get let down
By a person or a place or something you've trusted
Well you put up a fight 'til what's lost is found
And if you get beat up and your heart's all crushed in
You reach for a bullet and you wait around
For whatever it is that's got you busted
To get in sight, to hit the ground

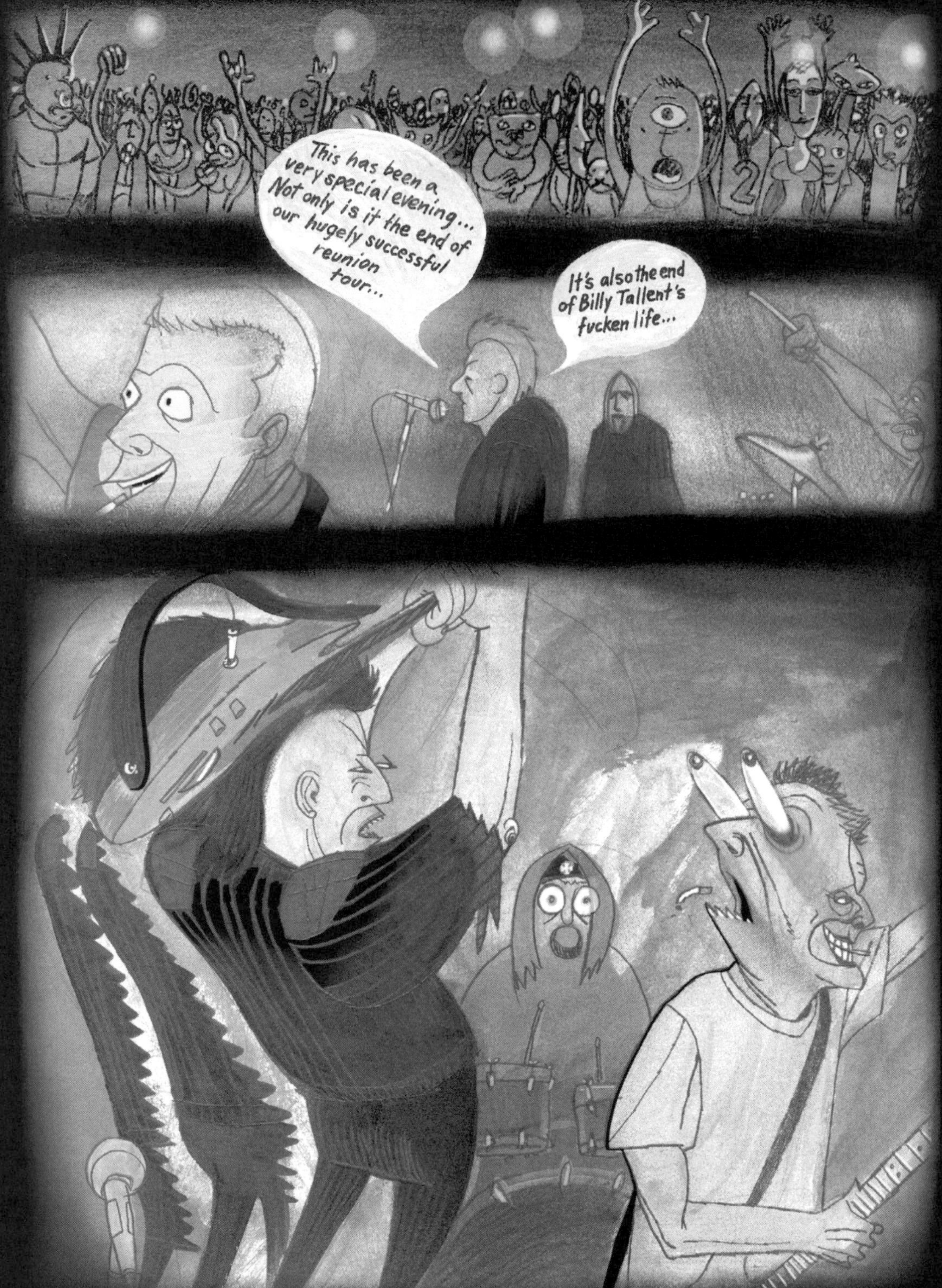
This has been a very special evening... Not only is it the end of our hugely successful reunion tour...
It's also the end of Billy Tallent's fucken life...

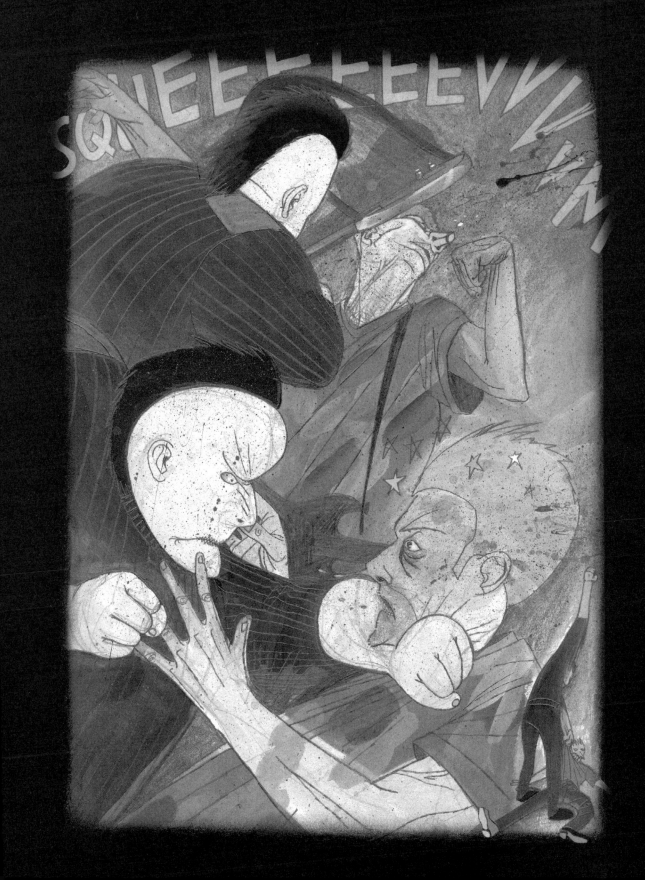

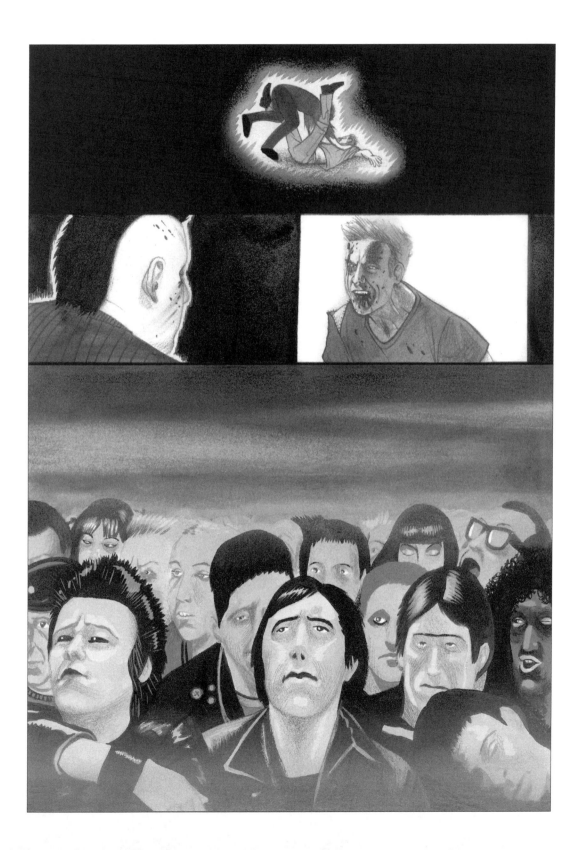

IN THE IT'S LOVE
IN THE END IT'S LOVE

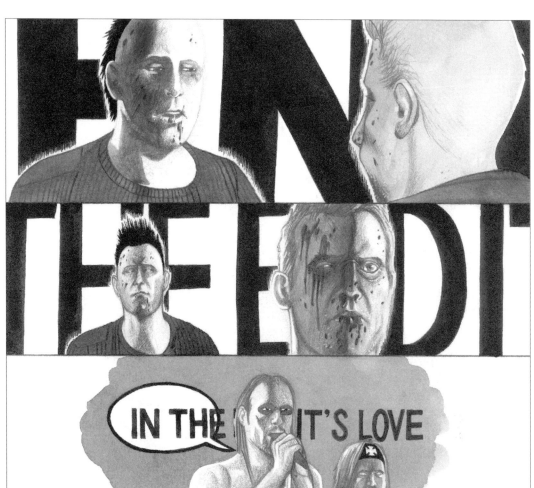

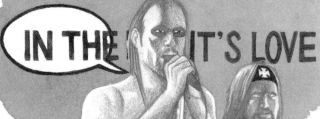

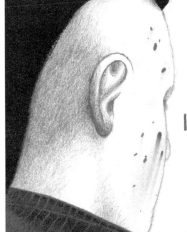

and in the end . . .

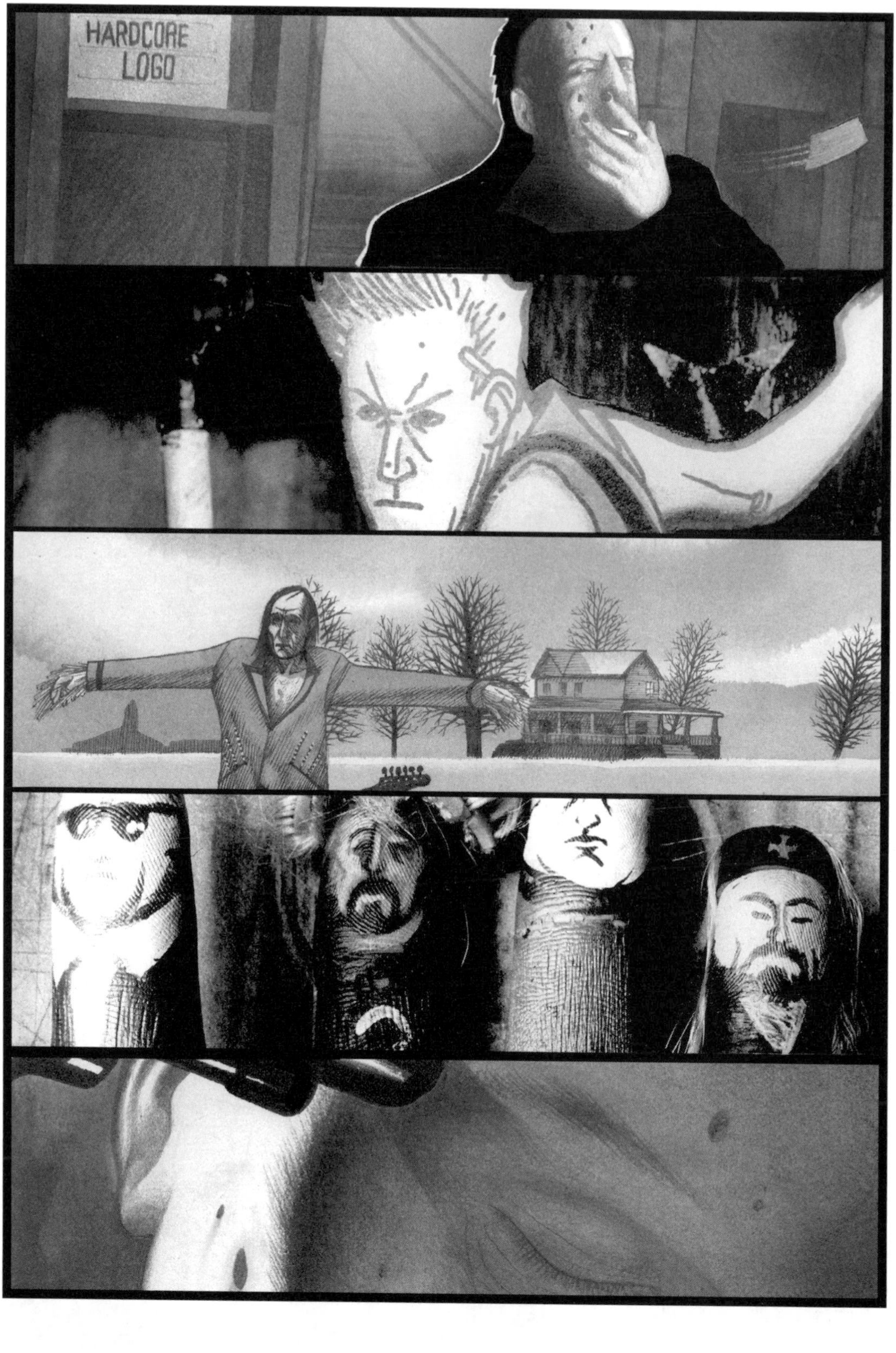
HARDCORE
LOGO

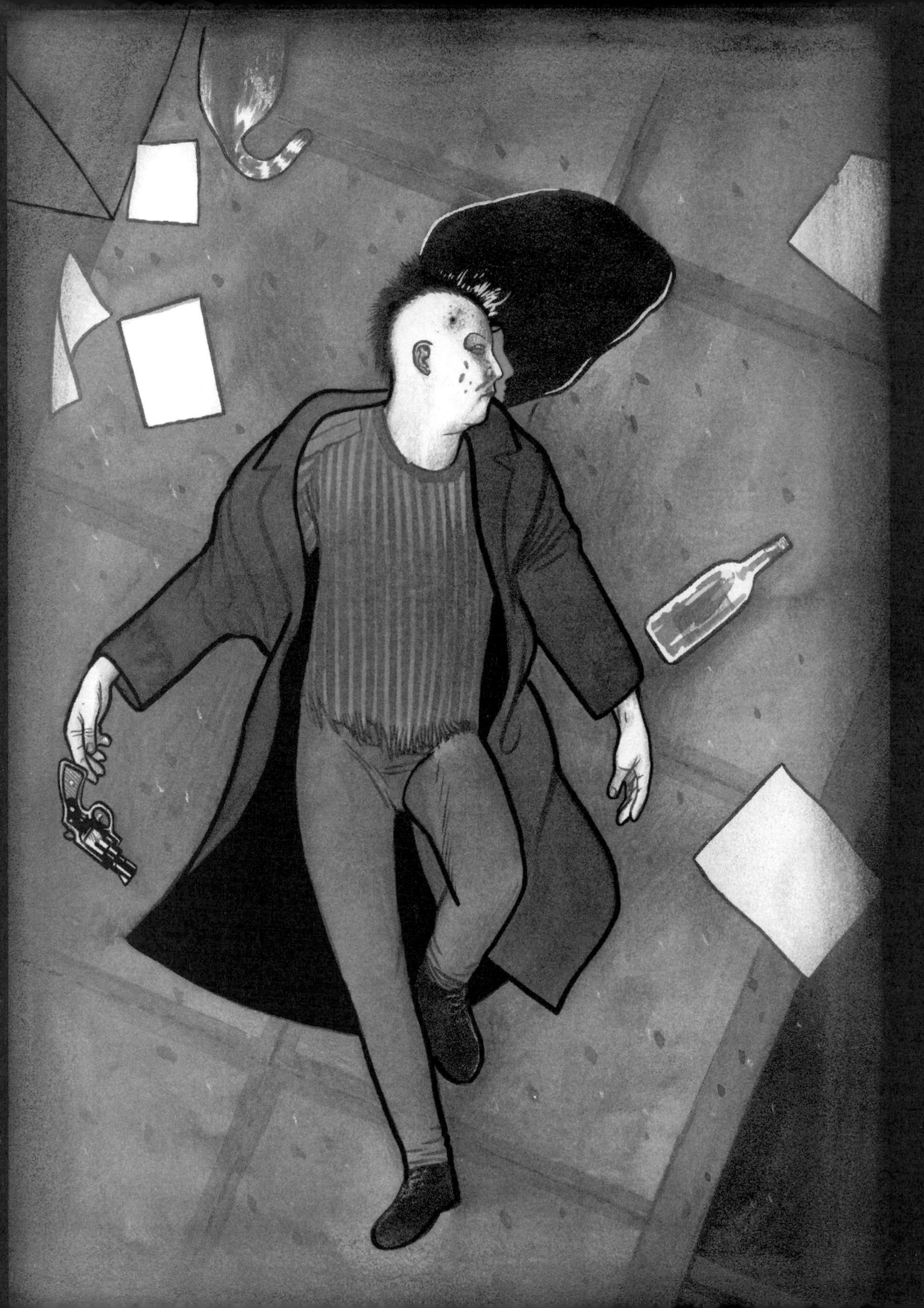

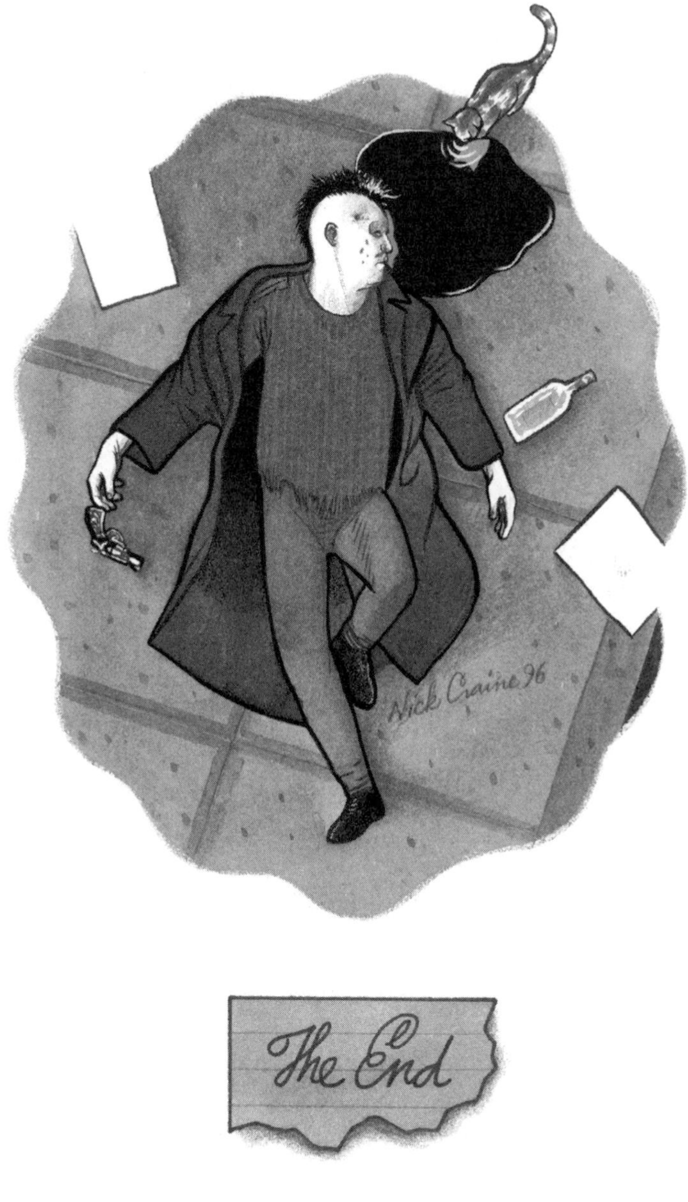
Nick Craine 96
The End

cut on the dotted line

GUITAR
CHORD
BOOK

YOU CAN PLAY EVERY SONG

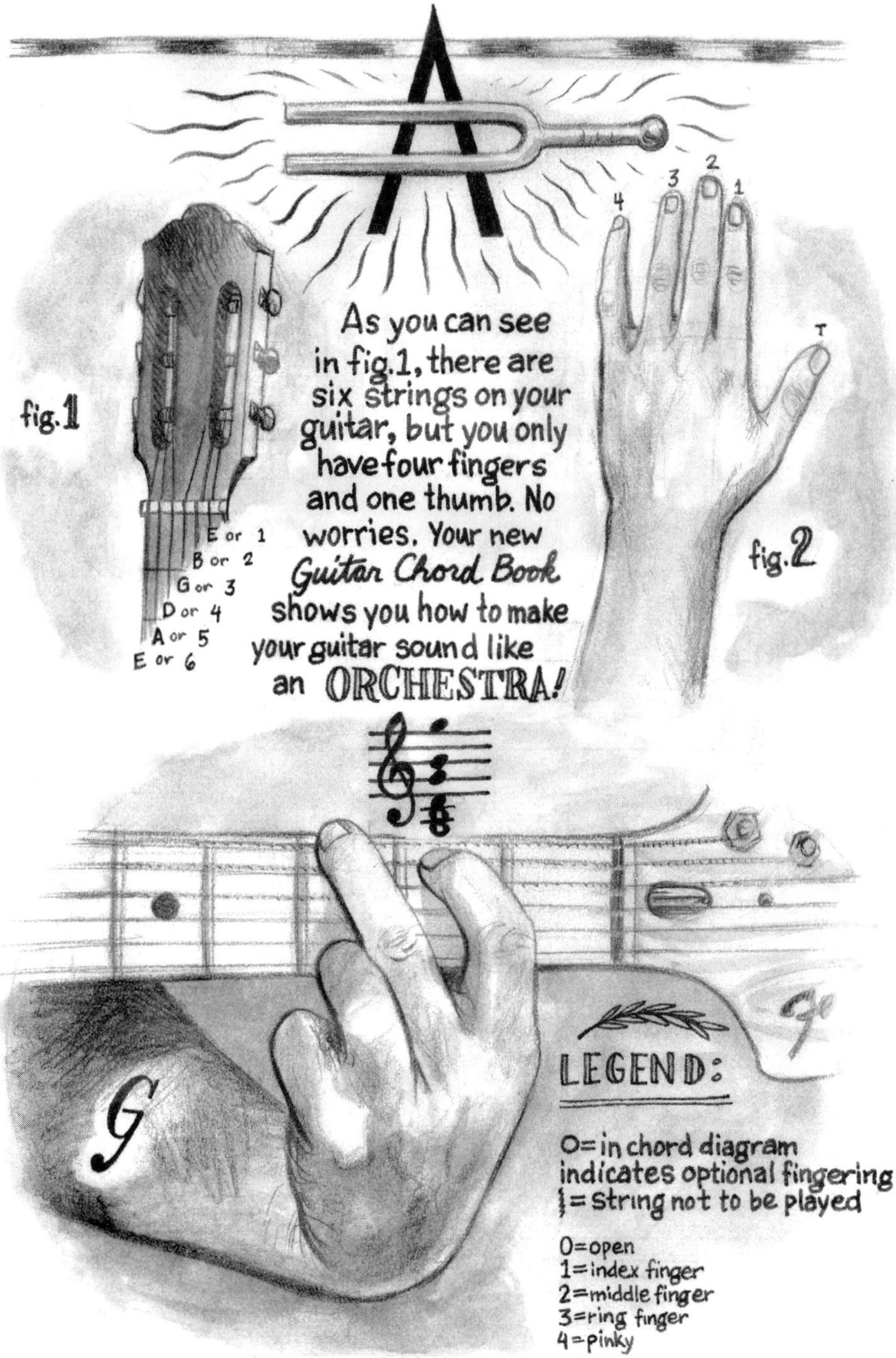
A
4
3
2
1
T
fig.1
fig.2
As you can see in fig.1, there are six strings on your guitar, but you only have four fingers and one thumb. No worries. Your new *Guitar Chord Book* shows you how to make your guitar sound like an ORCHESTRA!
E or 1
B or 2
G or 3
D or 4
A or 5
E or 6
G
LEGEND:
O= in chord diagram indicates optional fingering
}= string not to be played
0=open
1=index finger
2=middle finger
3=ring finger
4=pinky

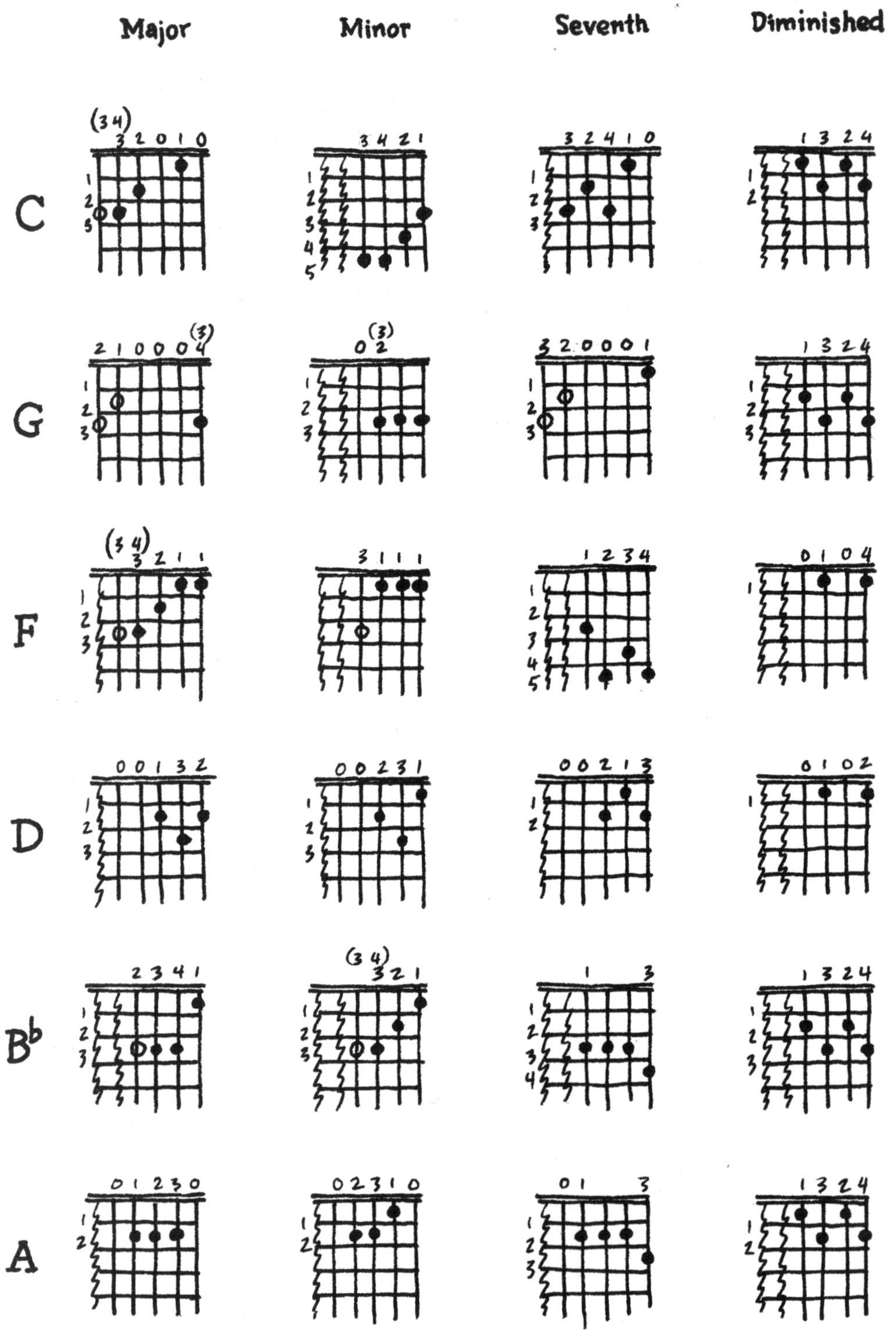
Major
Minor
Seventh
Diminished
C
G
F
D
B♭
A

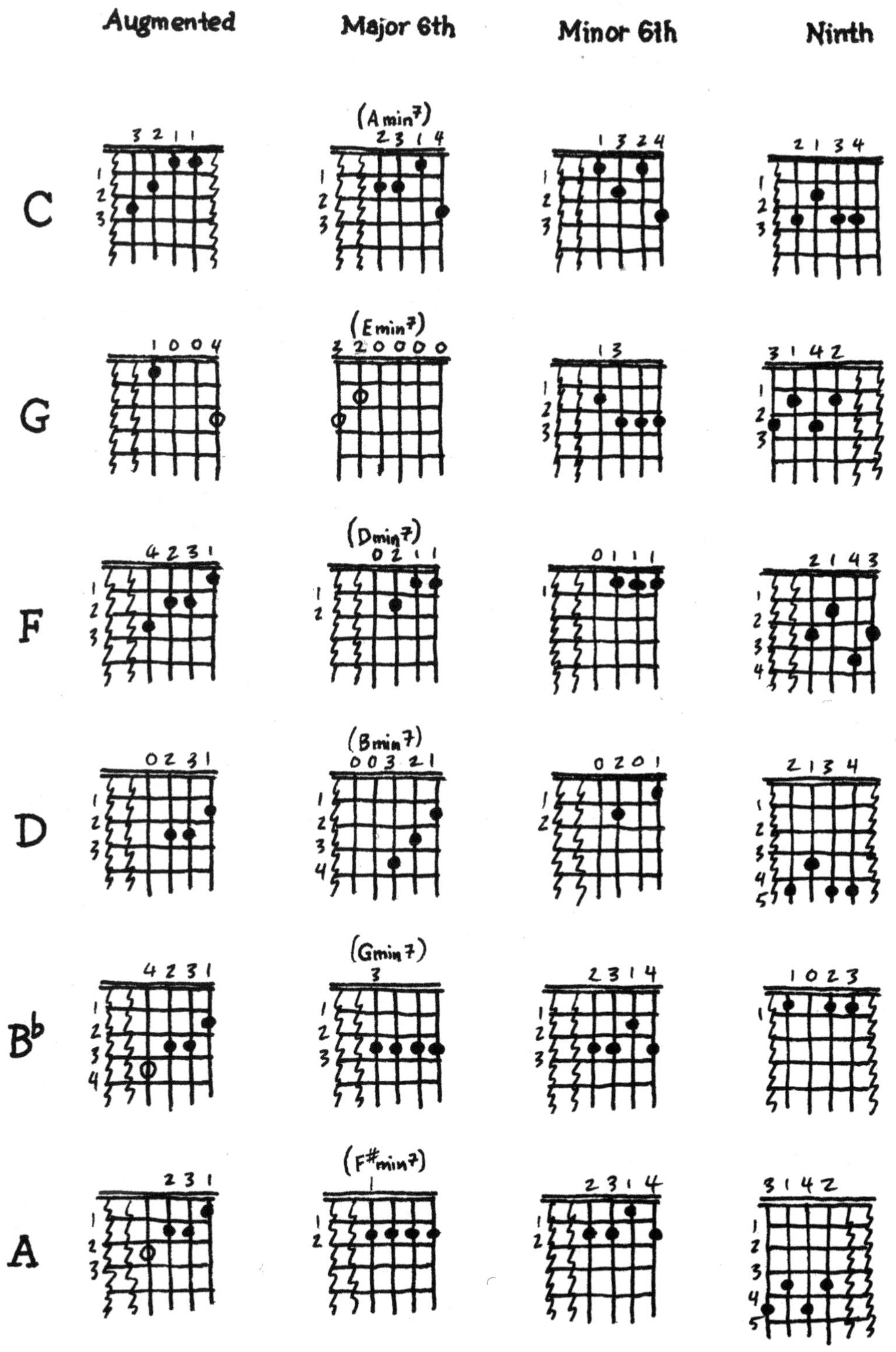
Augmented
Major 6th
Minor 6th
Ninth
C
(Amin7)
G
(Emin7)
F
(Dmin7)
D
(Bmin7)
B♭
(Gmin7)
A
(F#min7)

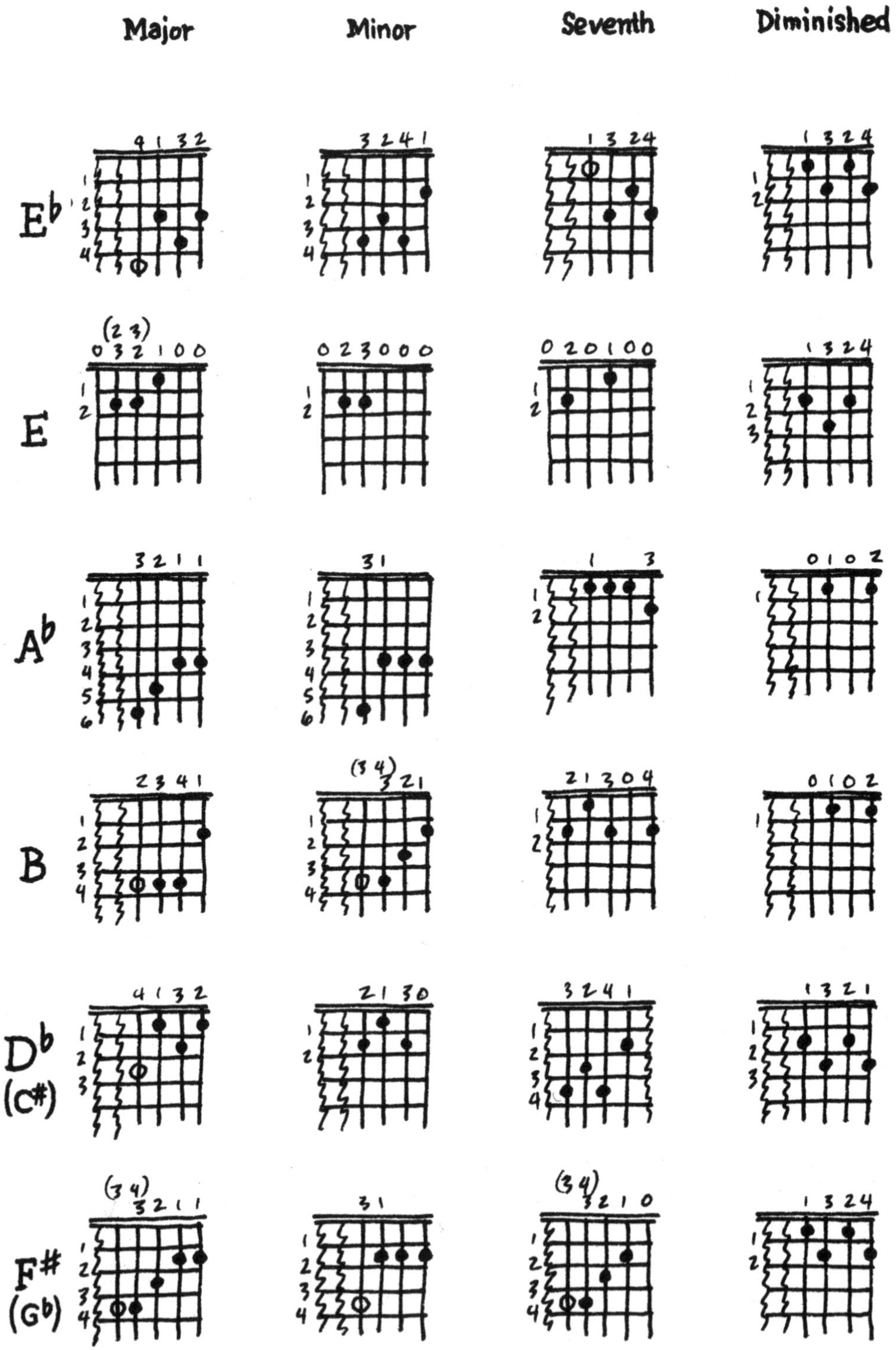
Major
Minor
Seventh
Diminished
E♭
E
A♭
B
D♭
(C#)
F#
(G♭)

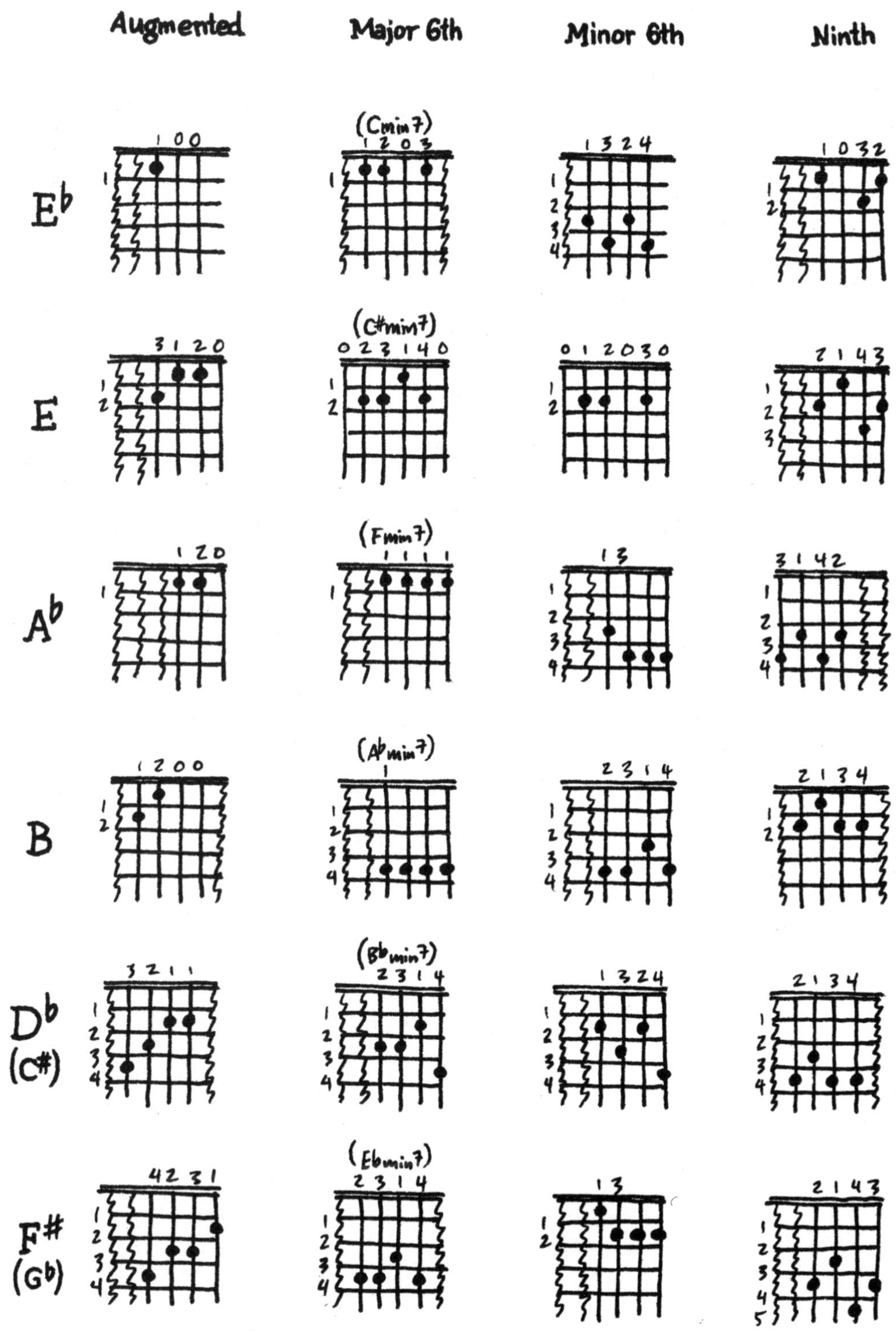
Augmented
Major 6th
Minor 6th
Ninth
E♭
(Cmin7)
E
(C#min7)
A♭
(Fmin7)
B
(A♭min7)
D♭
(C#)
(B♭min7)
F#
(G♭)
(E♭min7)

ANANSI

"Rock'n'Roll is Fat and Ugly," pages 17-18, 20, 23;
"Blue Tattoo," page 94;
"Something's Gonna Die Tonight," page 109:
used by permission: Hard Core Logo Music,
Colonel Festus Publishing, socan, 1993.

Text from "Bucky Got Drunk and Told Stories" sequence, pages 77-87;
"Post-Show Interview" sequence, pages 43-46;
"Mary the Fan", page 56;
and parts of "John's Tour Diary,"
pages 34, 35, 36, 38, 40, 41, 42, 47, 49, 73, 89, 95, 100, 105, 106:
from *Hard Core Logo*, Michael Turner,
Arsenal Pulp Press: Vancouver, 1993.

The feature film *Hard Core Logo* is a co-production
between Shadow Shows and Terminal City Pictures
and produced by Ed Festus Productions.
Directed by Bruce McDonald
Screenplay by Noel S. Baker
Based on the book *Hard Core Logo* by Michael Turner.

THANKS TO
Karen DiCicco, Mary Humpfries, Sara Soskolne, Michael Turner,
Bruce McDonald, Noel Baker, Michael Timmins, Martha Sharpe,
Kelly Joseph, Patrick Whistler, Sarah MacLachlan, Maria Golikova,
Cindy Ma, Matt Williams, Erin Mallory, Alysia Shewchuk, Lynn Crosbie,
Bart Beaty, Dylan Horrocks, Sandy Kaplansky, Tom Carroll, Janie Yoon,
Peter Georgelos, Gail Madill, Peter Canakis, Scott Merritt, Justin Hosker,
and to my musical brothers and sisters, Jeff, Sue, Pat, Harry, Lewis, Sheila,
Tristan, Spike, Dave, Mark, Kate, Michael, Sam, Jon, and Victor.

ADDITIONAL THANKS TO
Mike Watt and the Trashteria, Gail Manning and Staedtler Canada,
Arches Papers, and Windsor & Newton.

Photo credit: Nick Craine

ONE MORE SHOT
An Afterword

The sun is setting over a crest of Canadian Shield as clouds of midges wobble circles in the fading evening. We're on location somewhere near Shebeshekong, Ontario, occupying an entire hunting lodge. It's the first week of principal photography for *Dance Me Outside*. Bruce McDonald jumps on Gooch's motorcycle and guns it through the snaky gravel roads and endless pine and cedar. The producer, Brian Dennis, is losing his shit. There's a flurry of walkie-talkie crackle and panicked barking back and forth. The production company does not have joyride insurance.

That's Bruce: mischievously running his finger through the formal "cake icing" of the film set hierarchy, doing his best to consolidate the rebel and the craftsman. That seems to be the MO of his career. He's a seeker of adventure, a risk taker. More at home with a biker gang than he is with his art school peer group. And me? I'm another in a long line of creatives who fell under Bruce's spell, swept up in his enthusiasm for a project. Take Hugh Dillon. I don't think Hugh could foresee what lay ahead when he was launching snot balls across stages with his Headstoned bandmates. Bruce's collaboration with Hugh on *Hard Core Logo* transformed him from a rock-and-roll front man into a commercially successful artist. Take Adam Beach as the slacker Frank Fencepost. Or there's Noel Baker, a young and inexperienced screenwriter who, from my sketchy memory, just happened to canvas Bruce's Gloucester Lane office in person when they were optioning the rights to Turner's novel. Take the fantastic Ellen Page. The nearly unknown actress became DiCaprio's *Inception* co-star a mere three years after the incredible Jimi-Hendrix-meets-Cubism *The Tracey Fragments*. When time accordions and we see the thread foreshortened, it's clear: one common trait that all these encounters share is Bruce's

"The loudest book I've ever read about the hell-fire that is today's music business." —ART BERGMANN
HARD CORE LOGO
MICHAEL TURNER

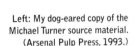

Left: My dog-eared copy of the Michael Turner source material. (Arsenal Pulp Press, 1993.)

Right: An early Hugh Dillon/ Clarence Gaskill study from the preliminary sketchbook for *Dance Me Outside: The Illustrated Screenplay*.

705

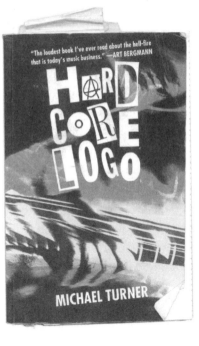

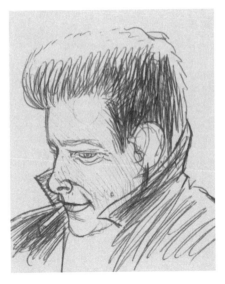

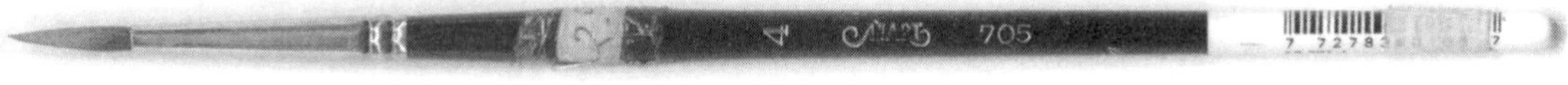

The brush I used for work on the graphic novel adaptation of *Hard Core Logo*.

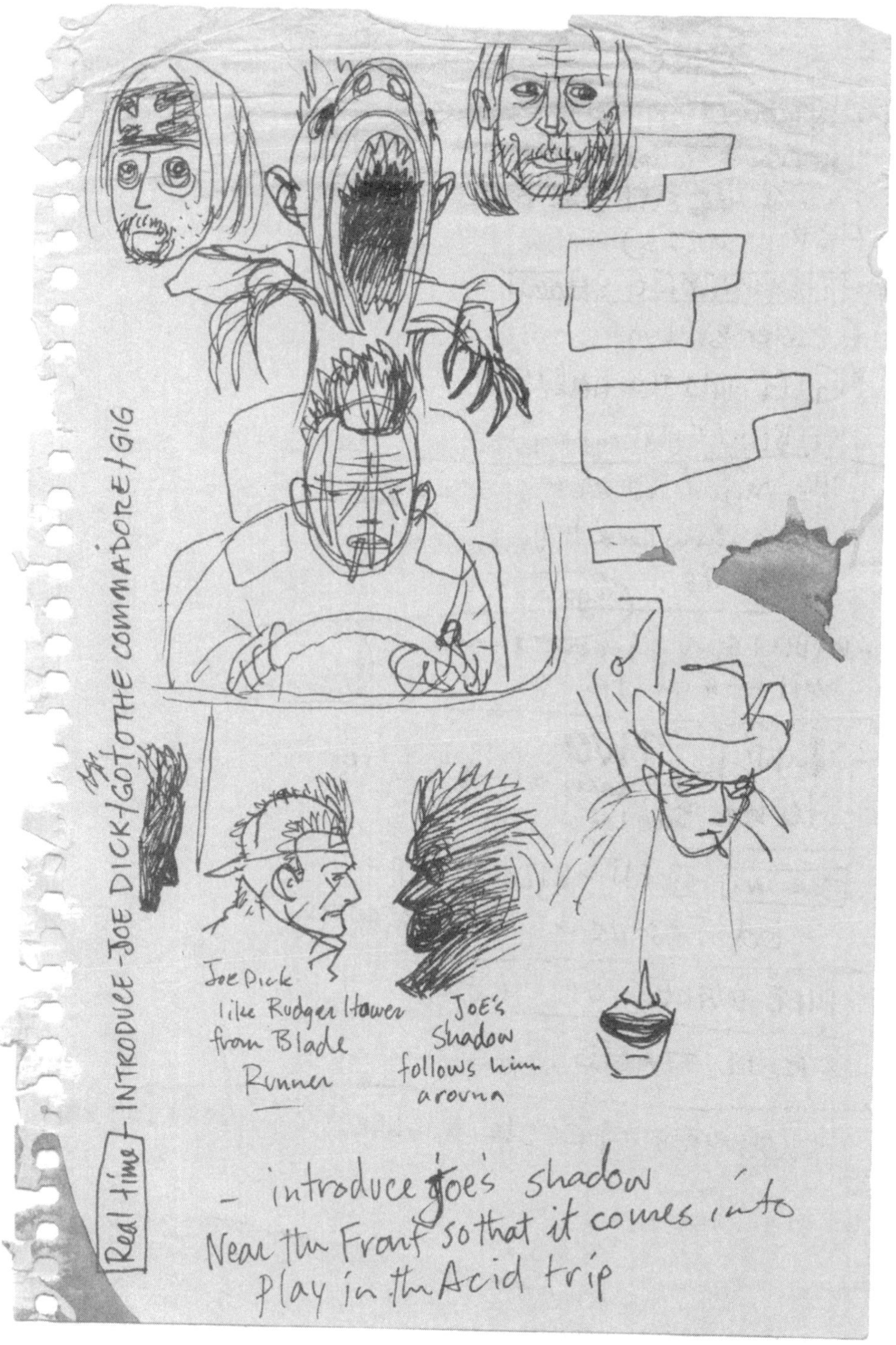
Real time - INTRODUCE - JOE DICK / GO TO THE COMMADORE / GIG
Joe Dick like Rudger Hower from Blade Runner
Joe's Shadow follows him arouna
- introduce joe's shadow Near the Front so that it comes into play in the Acid trip

Early band concepts.

heart, good will, and beguiling skills as a con artist, the essential toolset of any great filmmaker.

Bruce's work is, on one hand, a portrayal of a dream borne of the imagination, but it's also about being part of a gang. Dreaming is easy, but crystallizing a vision into a film is a most difficult exercise in quasi-military hierarchy. This in concert with a host of unforeseen circumstances and one whose reliance on outside forces is often accompanied by that unwelcome party guest that always stays till the lights come up: *compromise*.

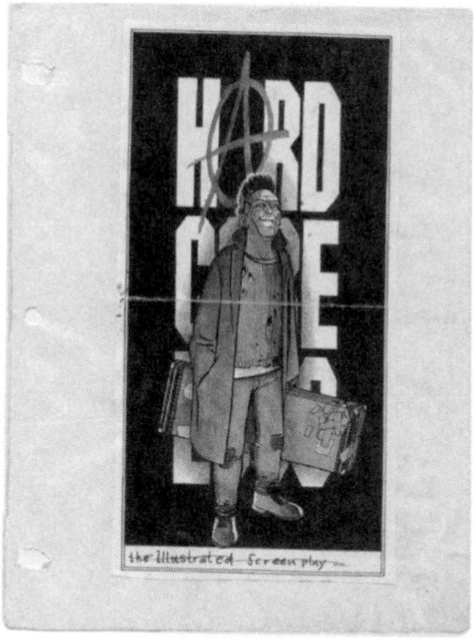
the illustrated Screenplay

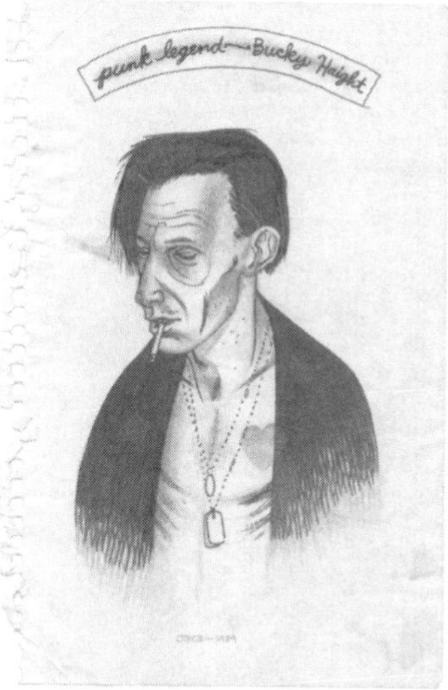
punk legend—Bucky Haight

Left: An early Joe Dick study.

Right: An early Bucky Haight study.

Both *Hard Core Logo: Portrait of a Thousand Punks* and *Dance Me Outside: The Illustrated Screenplay* are exercises in adaptation. In my attempts to turn a dynamic audiovisual experience into a silent narrative built from static images, it became clear that, unlike the filmmaker, I had only the constraints of time and effort. I have such high admiration at the forces required to bring these films into existence. The creation of a graphic novel is never set back by bad weather. There's never an actor who shows up late or

Opposite: Here's who was playing Vancouver during the *Hard Core Logo* shoot, from the pages of the *Georgia Straight*. I saw Mary Margaret O'Hara for the first time here. We also saw Jewel minutes before she broke out (me and about ten other people) at the club that was set dressed as Hard Core Logo's Calgary stop.

BUCKY nods. NAOMI joins him, slips an arm around him.

                    BUCKY   *I moved out here . . . .*
        Guys, you're ever back this
        way...

                    ~~NAOMI~~
        ~~Don't drop in.~~

JOE and BUCKY hug. JOE gets in and starts the van. They nod good-
bye and close the rear door. A final angle on Bucky's perfectly
good legs.

TITLE: "BLUE TATTOO"

                    JOE (VO)
                 (into a mike)
        Hello Saskatoon ~~people! We're Hard
        Core Logo. Our buddy Eliot's given
        us the stage to warm you up for
        tomorrow night when it'll cost ya
        ten bucks to see us.~~

INT. AMIGOS CLUB IN SASKATOON - NIGHT

The band are on stage. JOE is drunk and more drugged-out than ever
as he totters at the mike.

                    JOE (cont'd)
        Here's a song by Bucky Haight, the
        legendary punk king who died last **NIGHT**
        ~~year~~ in New York City.

Joe taps out a beat and the band follow him into the deeply moving
"BLUE TATTOO."

                    JOE SINGS:
        IT HURT SO BAD WHEN YOU GOT IT   *you had no time for*
        IT WENT RIGHT TO YOUR HEAD   *corruption*
        IT DROVE YOU INSANE   *You thought the world*
        BUT NOW ALL THAT'S FORGOTTEN   *was an unsafe place*
        AND YOU CAN GO ON
        WITHOUT ANY PAIN   *You work towards a*
        A BLUE TATTOO ON YOUR SHOULDER   *solution*
        IN THE SHAPE OF A HEART   *Best you could do was*
        IN THE MIDDLE OF MY NAME   *to send me away*
        AND THAT'S HOW I REMEMBER
        ALL OF THE BAD THINGS
        THAT YOU COULDN'T CHANGE
        BLUE TATTOO
        BLUE TATTOO

                *Em D
        C Em C Em G Dm
        F C F C G F C - Am G*

My notes on Noel Baker's script for the *Hard Core Logo* film.

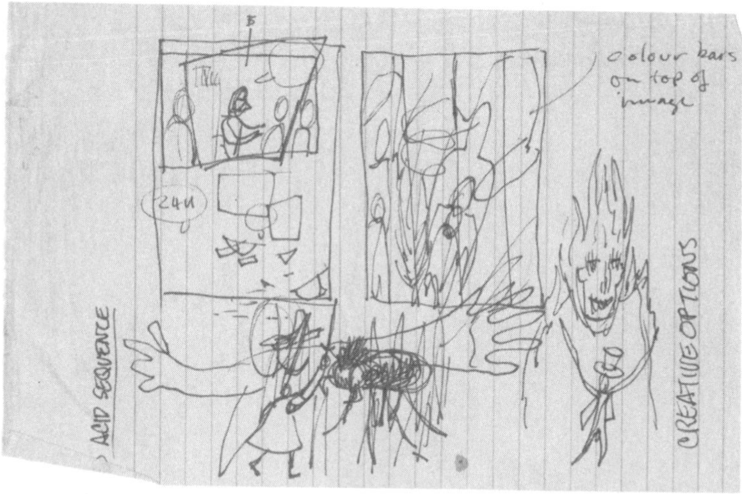
colour bars on top of image
ACID SEQUENCE
CREATIVE OPTIONS

My notes on the acid-trip sequence deleted from the graphic novel. After a year and a half of work, I was beginning to run out of both time and effort. I myself have never taken acid, but I would have loved to include this sequence; it would have been so fun to draw.

intoxicated. The craft services truck doesn't drive off the edge of the Canadian Shield. I don't have a writer sitting on my shoulder, refusing to proceed because we don't share the same vision. I don't require permits. There isn't some green production assistant who nearly destroys the camera rig by tearing it down prematurely (me). No communities have to be negotiated with, no egos assuaged, no points of view championed. I am left to my task like a lonely hitchhiker on the flats of the Alberta prairie, in some ways equally daunting because of the endless possibilities.

As a result, I took many liberties with the adaptation. I illustrated Turner's wonderful passage wherein Bucky gets drunk and tells road stories. The graphic novel dispenses with the narrative device of the documentary filmmaker, offering limitless freedom to include a first-person flashback to Bucky early in his career. Conversely, passages that hinged on the filmmaker revealing critical plot points had to be reworked to function without the mockumentary framework, such as Joe and Billy's post-interview moment, when Bruce vengefully drops the Jenifur bomb to Joe on

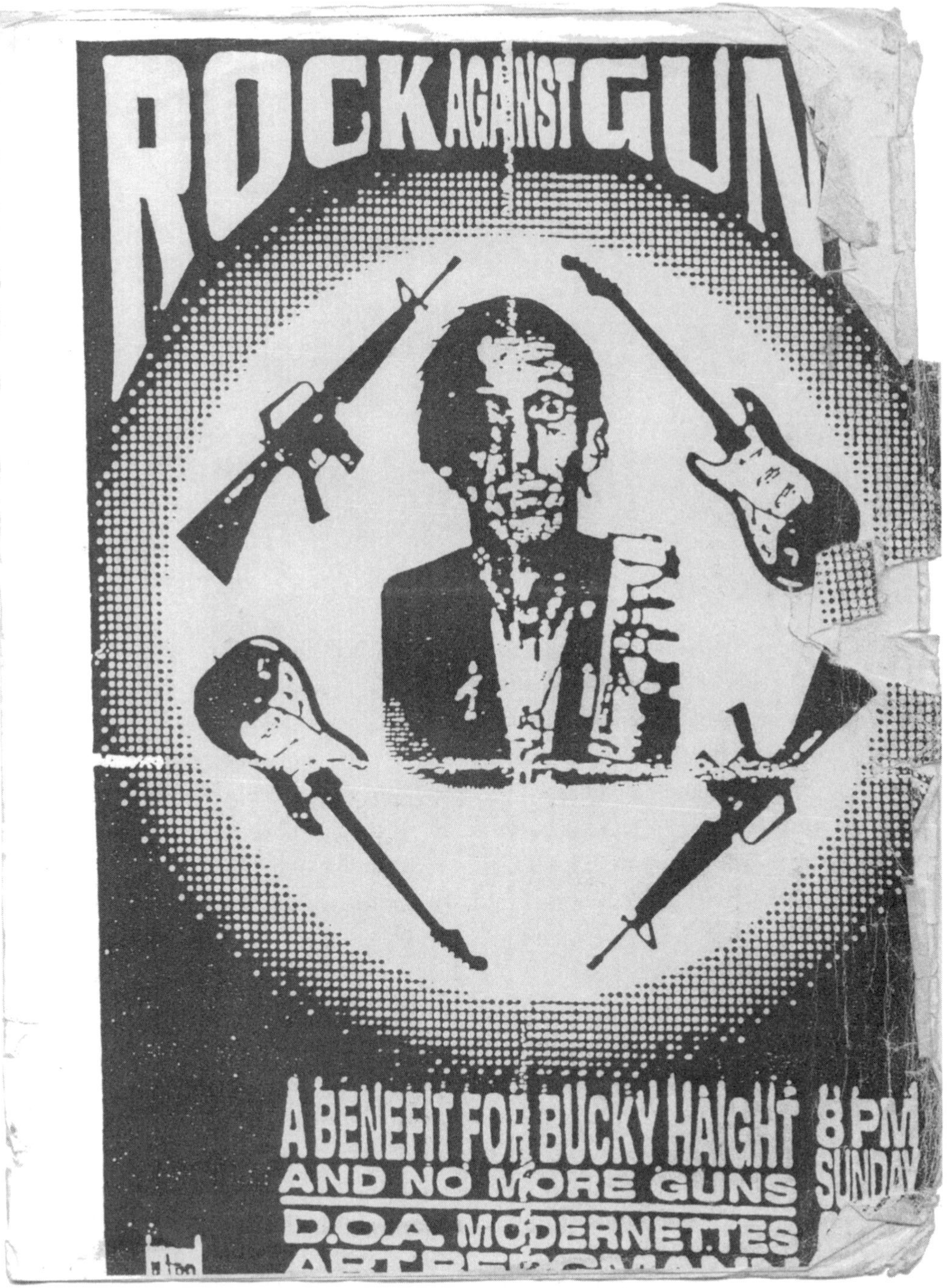
ROCK AGAINST GUN
A BENEFIT FOR BUCKY HAIGHT
AND NO MORE GUNS
8 PM
SUNDAY
D.O.A. MODERNETTES

The gig poster for the Rock Against Guns benefit Hard Core Logo reunion show at the Commodore. At the time, the line between reality and fiction was beginning to blur. Many of the extras in attendance thought Hard Core Logo was indeed a real band. Some even talked about owning their LPs. Other "real" performers on the bill included D.O.A., The Modernettes, and Art Bergmann.

camera. It cost me nothing to "shoot" New York City circa 1977 or fill Central Park with snow or rent a warehouse and create a believable live-off-the-floor recording situation. The inclusion of this passage reintroduced the mythical punk rock lore quality that Turner's source material so elegantly portrayed.

Similarly, the confrontation on page 56 comes to a head: John, Pipe, and Billy get it from Joe, who has had it up to here with the possible threat of Billy's selling out and leaving the band. As an illustrator, I spared no expense hiring an animal trainer and putting a moose on the road as a catalyst for the argument. As I was working on the first draft of the *Hard Core Logo* graphic novel, I was also on the road with my own band, Black Cabbage. Having spent enough time crisscrossing the province and indeed Canada, I learned that watching for moose is a constant concern for the touring musician.

Below: A Black Cabbage gig poster that was influential in the lead-up to my *Hard Core Logo* adaptation.

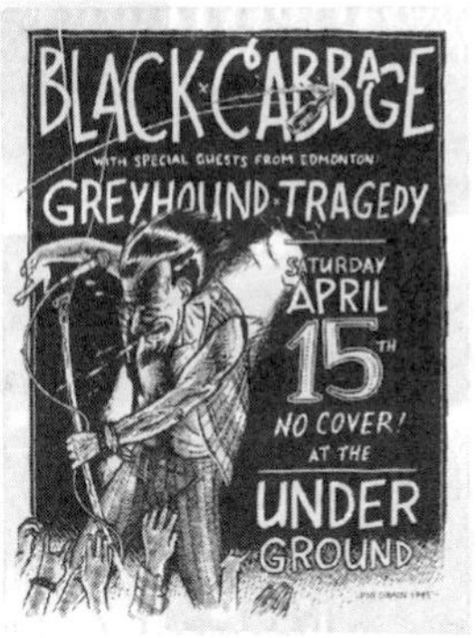
BLACK CABBAGE
WITH SPECIAL GUESTS FROM EDMONTON
GREYHOUND TRAGEDY
SATURDAY
APRIL
15TH
NO COVER!
AT THE
UNDER
GROUND

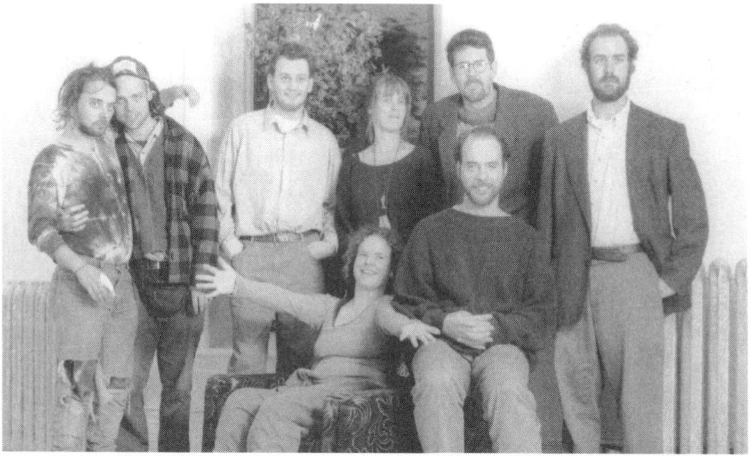

Left: Black Cabbage. Left to right: Sam Cino, Mike O'Connell, Nick Craine, Kate Richmond (seated), Sheila Gruner, Michael Barclay (seated), Dave Withers, and Tristan O'Malley. (Soundman Jon Halliwell not pictured.) Photo credit: Trina Koster.

In the film, Joe and the boys tour the country in an old meat truck. Our eight-member band (plus our soundman, Jon Halliwell) lived in our old Ford Econoline, and I knew every inch of its interior by heart. We nearly died in that van on several occasions, so my emotional attachment to the vessel was deep and real. I imagined Michael Turner and his Hard Rock Miners carving along this road map of the touring Canadian rock band. I was a real life John Oxenburger, scribbling away in my bound ream of blank paper, sketching thumbnails that would become pages of this book. The parallels to my own experience as a musician were beginning to stack up. Our drummer, Sam Cino, *was* Pipefitter. When Sam saw me sketching, he immediately pitched me "Super Excess Man," word for word. The sketch included in this book is the original from our time on the road.

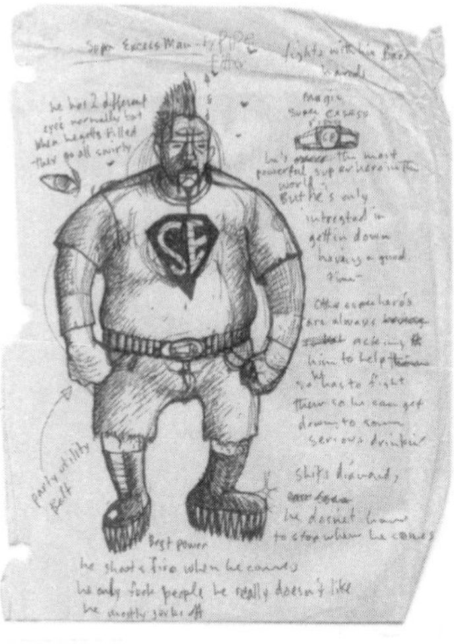

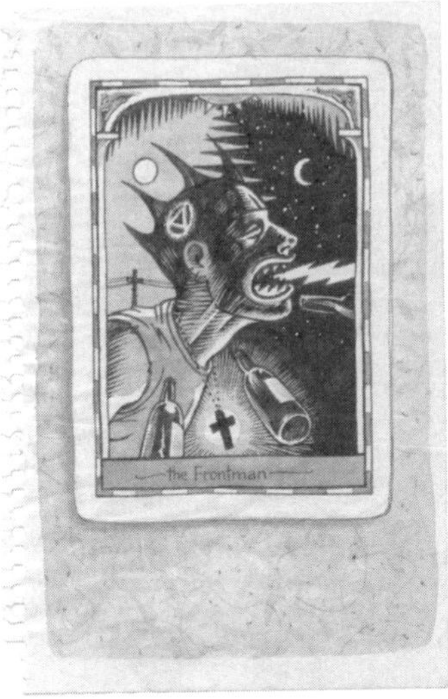
the Frontman

Left: Super Excess Man, as told by my bandmate Sam Cino.

Right: An early study of the punk tarot set piece in the Bucky Haight sequence.

It's worth noting the lineage of the van as an allegory for my own place in the cultural framework of the Bruce McDonald universe. Back in the day, Black Cabbage was starting to gain a strong following in the university party band circuit of Southern Ontario. It was clear that all eight of us could not continue touring in Dave Withers' Ford F150. (In winter, we would take turns riding in the unheated covered cab, among the amps and guitars wrapped in moving blankets and with his carpentry tools flopping about the floor—us a drawer full of meat and cleavers caught in the undertow of the 401.) The addition of Michael Barclay's refrigerator-sized Leslie cabinet made it so we had to start gigging in two vehicles.

Hard Core Logo's home, and also my own, for the summer of 1996.

Somewhere in the middle of our six-year career, we bought this worn out Ford Econoline with an extended body and a sleeper cab from bass player Jason Mercer for four hundred bucks. It was the former touring van of The Bourbon Tabernacle Choir. It had a half million miles on it, no suspension, shitty alignment—and it owed the world nothing. I pictured Chris Brown, Kate Fenner, and Andrew Whiteman driving this monstrous grey whale to festivals on both sides of the border. Their song "Put Your Head On" had been included on the soundtrack of Bruce's 1991 film *Highway 61*.

In retrospect, that van was a death trap, and we were lucky to have survived it. On one occasion we were touring out east on the coldest night of my Canadian experience. Surrounded on three sides by eighteen-wheelers, with visibility limited by snow squalls, we were booking it to a club in New Brunswick, something like this—

INT. TOURING VAN — EVENING

    Mike O'Connell is at the wheel,
    and Dave Withers is the man in the
    passenger seat tasked with keeping
    the driver awake and choosing the
    music.

    Suddenly Mike is panicked. He's lost
    control of the gas pedal. The van
    is gaining speed, and he's afraid
    to break on account of the black
    ice. We're going faster and faster.
    Everyone else in the van wakes up,
    blood running cold, silent.

INT. TOURING VAN DASHBOARD — EVENING

    Somehow Dave rips open the fire
    cover to the engine from inside the

```
cab of this accelerating coffin. The
half-ton of guitars and amps begin
to heave. We fishtail slightly,
but we're still gaining speed,
going 140 km/h now. Dave throws
his arms into the engine. It's so
cold that the throttle has frozen
open, causing the engine to speed up
uncontrollably. With his hands in
the engine block, Dave desperately
unsticks the throttle, and we begin
to recede from the porch light of
death's door, pale, stunned, a
jumbled, jittery mess.
```

CUT TO BLACK

That evening in Sackville, New Brunswick, we played the show of all shows. We had survived. The audience knew it. I had been given a window into the *Hard Core Logo* experience. We were in no way punk, but that night in Sackville, we were pure energy.

So what ever happened to the van? We sold it for four hundred bucks to the next unsuspecting band. The all-woman Corduroy Leda finally drove it into the ground sometime in the late 90s. But inside its walls, for our time on tour, it felt as though we were taking a rock-and-roll sacrament. The van was a vehicle of transference that would smudge its lineage onto us, give us some modicum of rock-star heritage or authenticity by association. In this way, I was doing my best to align myself with Bruce McDonald and his Dionysian endeavors, hoping it might bring the validation that all young creatives seek. Perhaps I could accrue some cultural capital from my distant association with Michael Turner, and further still from W. P. Kinsella and my graphic novel adaptation of Bruce's *Dance Me Outside*.

Hosting the open stage at Guelph's Jimmy Jazz, circa 1994, for $75 a week and a free room above the dance floor (for me and the roaches, that is). Photo credit: Sandy Atanasoff

The transference of cool also presented itself in the form of the archtop acoustic guitar featured on page one of the *Hard Core Logo* graphic novel. It never appeared in the film but featured prominently in my life. When I was on location in Parry Sound during the photography for the *Dance Me Outside* shoot, I discovered an old Sears-catalogue guitar at the local pawnshop, covered in what appeared to be black house paint. In preparation for the work on *Dance Me Outside: The Illustrated Screenplay*, I spent most days reading all things Kinsella to get a handle on the world of Silas Ermineskin. I purchased the beat-up instrument for sixty bucks as a counterpoint to all the sedentary reading. Armed with paint scrapers and methylene chloride, I stripped the paint off to reveal the loveliest blond maple body with a cherry neck. It was an obscure cheap instrument known as a Stewart (coincidentally

Artwork for the Guelph compilation *Guelph Happens*, featuring Black Cabbage, circa 1994.

my father's given name—though his is spelled Stuart). I began to fall in love, imagining all the musicians who played the guitar over its fifty-year life, where it might have come from, only to land here, in Bobby Orr's hometown, all covered in house paint, the mother-of-pearl inlays long-neglected and chipping like delicate miniature vertebrae.

This video of Stephen Fearing's 1998 single "Home," directed by yours truly, features the archtop guitar and touring van (with flames added) in the same project. Photo credit: Tico Poulakakis. Courtesy of True North Records.

Turner's *Hard Core Logo* called for an acoustic reunion, nothing like what we see of the Hugh Dillon/Callum Keith sonic reducers. So I took it upon myself to insert the Stewart as a silent prop in the work. In the 90s I was directing music videos and would include the archtop as the show instrument whenever the performer was agreeable. (See Stephen Fearing, Gil Grand, and our own Black Cabbage.)

The instrument was difficult to play on account of its high action, but I kept it alive for some years, polishing the body with duck oil and using it as a slide guitar. It eventually made its way into the basement of middle age, where its seams disintegrated and the machine heads rusted out. The Stewart found its next life with a stranger at a garage sale.

My son reminds me daily that I am not (nor ever will be) cool, so my hopes of transference have been in vain. Along the way, however, my goal of being in service to the narrative shows significant returns for my effort. The process of adaptation has given me skills in reduction that I bring to my various art practices. These graphic novels have given me the toolset to begin ascent on my current project, entitled *Parchment of Light*.

Thank you, reader, for investing your time in this work. It's such a thrill to see the book leap-frogging into the digital age. Revisiting the artwork has been an indulgent exercise in Photoshop "remastering" and has given me an opportunity to present a more than twenty-year-old work as I had originally intended. Also included (in the deluxe package) is the faux Bucky Haight recording that was always meant to accompany the book but for lack of resources didn't happen back in 1997.

Thanks again, Bruce, for inviting me to the party. Your film set is a dream world, and though you appear to play the rebel, it's clear that you are a powerful artist who defies category. A good friend of mine noted that there are few living, practising Canadian artists whose work he has consumed for more than twenty years. Bruce is here, a great disruptor of expectation, a dream-maker in a world of sleepers.

Nick Craine
January 2017
Guelph, Ontario

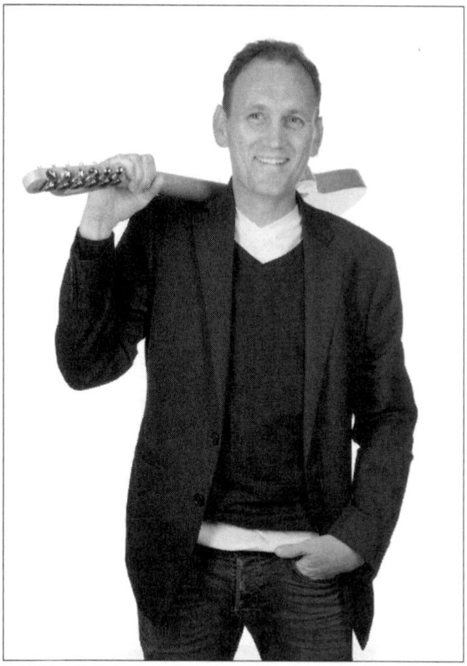

Photo credit: Trina Koster

NICK CRAINE was born in Toronto in 1971 and is a critically acclaimed visual artist whose illustrations have appeared in the *Atlantic*, the *New York Times,* the *Washington Post,* and many more. In 2008 he was chosen as one of six Canadians included in the TASCHEN international anthology *Illustration Now*, a sampling of 150 of the world's best illustrators. He is a much sought-after conceptual illustrator and adapted Bruce McDonald's films *Dance Me Outside* and *Hard Core Logo* into graphic novels; the latter was nominated for an Ignatz Award in the Outstanding Artist category.

In his other life, Craine is the founding member of Black Cabbage and has appeared on over twenty recordings as a vocalist, including on his own solo albums, *November Moon* and *Songs Like Tattoos*. In the 1990s he directed music videos between Guelph and Nashville, including Feist's "It's Cool to Love Your Family."

Craine lives in Guelph with his wife, Sandy, and their son, Michael. He uses STAEDTLER art supplies and Arches papers.

The A List

The Big Why Michael Winter

The Little Girl Who Was Too Fond of Matches Gaetan Soucy

Death Goes Better with Coca-Cola Dave Godfrey

Basic Black with Pearls Helen Weinzweig

Ticknor Sheila Heti

This All Happened Michael Winter

Kamouraska Anne Hebert

The Circle Game Margaret Atwood

De Niro's Game Rawi Hage

Eleven Canadian Novelists Interviewed by Graeme Gibson

Like This Leo McKay Jr.

The Honeyman Festival Marian Engel

La Guerre Trilogy Roch Carrier

Selected Poems Alden Nowlan

No Pain Like This Body Harold Sonny Ladoo

Poems for all the Annettes Al Purdy

Five Legs Graeme Gibson

Selected Short Fiction of Lisa Moore

Survival Margaret Atwood

Queen Rat Lynn Crosbie

Ana Historic Daphne Mariatt

Civil Elegies Dennis Lee

The Outlander Gil Adamson

The Hockey Sweater and Other Stories Roch Carrier